THE BLACK COPTIC CHURCH

RELIGION, RACE, AND ETHNICITY
General Editor: Peter J. Paris

Public Religion and Urban Transformation: Faith in the City
Edited by Lowell W. Livezey

Down by the Riverside: Readings in African American Religion
Edited by Larry G. Murphy

New York Glory: Religions in the City
Edited by Tony Carnes and Anna Karpathakis

Religion and the Creation of Race and Ethnicity: An Introduction
Edited by Craig R. Prentiss

God in Chinatown: Religion and Survival in New York's Evolving Immigrant Community
Kenneth J. Guest

Creole Religions of the Caribbean: An Introduction from Vodou and Santería to Obeah and Espiritismo
Margarite Fernández Olmos and Lizabeth Paravisini-Gebert

The History of the Riverside Church in the City of New York
Peter J. Paris, John Wesley Cook, James Hadnut-Beumler, Lawrence H. Mamiya, Leonora Tubbs Tisdale, and Judith Weisenfeld
Foreword by Martin E. Marty

Asian American Religions: The Making and Remaking of Borders and Boundaries
Edited by Tony Carnes and Fenggang Yang

Righteous Content: Black Women's Perspectives of Church and Faith
Daphne C. Wiggins

Beyond Christianity: African Americans in a New Thought Church
Darnise C. Martin

Deeper Shades of Purple: Womanism in Religion and Society
Edited by Stacey M. Floyd-Thomas

Daddy Grace: A Celebrity Preacher and His House of Prayer
Marie W. Dallam

The Methodist Unification: Christianity and the Politics of Race in the Jim Crow Era
Morris L. Davis

Watch This! The Ethics and Aesthetics of Black Televangelism
Jonathan L. Walton

American Muslim Women: Negotiating Race, Class, and Gender within the Ummah
Jamillah Karim

Embodiment and the New Shape of Black Theological Thought
Anthony B. Pinn

From Africa to America: Religion and Adaptation Among Ghanaian Immigrants in New York
Moses O. Biney

Afro-Pentecostalism: Black Pentecostal and Charismatic Christianity in History and Culture
Edited by Amos Yong and Estrelda Y. Alexander

Creole Religions of the Caribbean: An Introduction from Vodou and Santería to Obeah and Espiritismo, Second Edition
Margarite Fernández Olmos and Lizabeth Paravisini-Gebert

Preaching on Wax: The Phonograph and the Shaping of Modern African American Religion
Lerone A. Martin

The Healing Power of the Santuario de Chimayó: America's Miraculous Church
Brett Hendrickson

The Soul of Judaism: Jews of African Descent in America
Bruce D. Haynes

The Ground Has Shifted: The Future of the Black Church in Post-Racial America
Walter Earl Fluker

The Divided Mind of the Black Church: Theology, Piety, and Public Witness
Raphael G. Warnock

Mental Health Evaluations in Immigration Court: A Guide for Mental Health and Legal Professionals
Edited by Virginia Barber Rioja, Adeyinka M. Akinsulure-Smith, and Sarah Vendzules

Creole Religions of the Caribbean: An Introduction from Vodou and Santería to Obeah and Espiritismo, Third Edition
Margarite Fernández Olmos and Lizabeth Paravisini-Gebert

The Black Coptic Church: Race and Imagination in a New Religion
Leonard Cornell McKinnis II

The Black Coptic Church

Race and Imagination in a New Religion

Leonard Cornell McKinnis II

NEW YORK UNIVERSITY PRESS
New York

NEW YORK UNIVERSITY PRESS
New York
www.nyupress.org

© 2023 by New York University
All rights reserved

Please contact the Library of Congress for Cataloging-in-Publication data.
ISBN: 9781479816453 (hardback)
ISBN: 9781479816460 (paperback)
ISBN: 9781479816484 (library ebook)
ISBN: 9781479816477 (consumer ebook)

This book is printed on acid-free paper, and its binding materials are chosen for strength and durability. We strive to use environmentally responsible suppliers and materials to the greatest extent possible in publishing our books.

Manufactured in the United States of America

10 9 8 7 6 5 4 3 2 1

Also available as an ebook

To the Ancestors

Leonard Cornell McKinnis Sr.

Evelyn Louise Tate

Tamar Coleman

Rev. L. C. Patterson

To the Present

Tamitha Walker McKinnis

Cynthia Tate-Gardner

John D. Gardner

To the Future

Sofia Elisabeth McKinnis

Olivia Maryam McKinnis

Leonard Cornell McKinnis III

Gabriel Jean-Baptiste Augustine McKinnis

If slavery persists as an issue in the political life of Black America, it is not because of an antiquarian obsession with bygone days or the burden of a too-long memory, but because black lives are still imperiled and devalued by a racial calculus and a political arithmetic that were entrenched centuries ago. This is the afterlife of slavery—skewed life chances, limited access to health and education, premature death, incarceration, and impoverishment. I too, am the afterlife of slavery.
—Saidiya Hartman[1]

CONTENTS

List of Figures	xiii
List of Abbreviations	xv
Introduction: Earthquake	1
1. The Origins of a Prophet: Cicero Patterson and the Black Coptic Imagination	35
2. "Ethiopia Shall Soon Stretch Forth Her Hand unto God": Imagination, Ideational Heroism, and the Turn to Blackness	61
3. Rituals of Freedom: Imagining and Performing *Otherwise*	92
4. "Somehow, Someway": Black Coptic Women and the Politics of Gender	125
5. Divine (Primordial) Blackness: Imagination, Hope, and a Word on Afro-Pessimism	152
Conclusion: Imagination and the Future of Black Coptic Religion	185
Acknowledgments	189
Notes	195
Bibliography	217
Index	227
About the Author	239

LIST OF FIGURES

I.1	True Temple of Solomon Black Coptic Church	6
1.1	Ethiopian Flag	36
1.2	Prophet Cicero Patterson	37
1.3	Louis Cicero Patterson's 1942 WWII Military Draft Card	40
1.4	Bishop Booker Lockhart's Ordination Certificate	42
2.1	Standard Bearer	62
2.2	Coptic Heritage Seen in King Solomon's Temple	64
2.3	King Peter Banks on the Throne	71
2.4	Black Coptic Empress and Students	72
2.5	Black Coptic Empress Gathering	88
2.6	Mother Queen Rebekah	89
3.1	Black Women in Hats	101
3.2	Sunday's Best	102
3.3	Women in the Nation of Islam	104
3.4	Royal Empress in True Temple of Solomon	106
3.5	Queen Huldah	107
3.6	Priest Eli	111
3.7	Baptism 2018	122
3.8	Black Coptic Men in Baptism Procession	123
4.1	Black Coptic Queens	126
5.1	Priest Meshach at Podium	153

LIST OF ABBREVIATIONS

AME—African Methodist Episcopal

BCC—Black Coptic Church

CNT—Coptic Nation Temple

COGASOC—Church of God and Saints of Christ

COGIC—Church of God in Christ

NOI—Nation of Islam

MST—Moorish Science Temple of America

TTS—True Temple of Solomon

UHPTS—Universal House of Prayer and Training School

UPHTS—Universal Prayer House and Training School

UNIA—Universal Negro Improvement Association

Introduction

Earthquake

When Prophet Hosea Belcher, a devotee in the Black Coptic Church (BCC), joined the religious movement, he was in search of a religious world that would valorize his Black identity. "The white Jesus on church walls was not a Jesus I could identify with," he explained. "White Jesus was a Jesus who was passed down from slave masters to kidnapped Africans. He was a Jesus who ignored blacks on the slave plantation after our identity was stolen and we were called niggers and negroes." However, Prophet Hosea continued, "when I joined the [Black] Coptic Church I heard about a Black Jesus, and when I say, 'Black Jesus,' He has to stand up; He understands the unique condition we were under here in North America. We are a people who come from ancient kings and queens. Slavery rocked our world. In the [Black] Coptic Church we are in the business of putting lives back together again. That was the mission of Prophet Cicero, to tell us who we are."[1]

* * *

Religious studies scholar Sylvester Johnson has noted that "the globalization of West Africa's gold trade was in and of itself a watershed event that, like an earthquake, quickly transformed the very ground beneath the feet of merchants in Africa and Asia's European cape."[2] Earthquakes, both literal and metaphorical, shatter societies. Whereas the 2010 earthquake in Haiti killed over 300,000 people and brought the country to ruins, the transatlantic slave trade displaced over 12 million Africans and dispersed them across the globe, engendering fractured lives, loss of identity, and their reduction from persons to non-persons. Rebuilding after both such tremors requires imagination and creative genius. Yet earthquakes do not merely cause physical damage and social chaos; they also stimulate a sense of displacement, exclusion, and isolation, as those impacted ponder the state of their being in relation to the broader society. In this sense, rebuilding in the aftermath of an earthquake requires an orientation toward *otherwise*, or the imagination and performance of a new world. This book is about the religious imagination of Black Coptic believers, like Prophet Hosea, as they seek to build in the afterlife of an earthquake.

Historic realities of anti-Black violence, precipitated by colonialism, enslavement, de jure segregation, physical and social displacement, and hyper invisibility stemming from the presumption that Black bodies do not fit into the category of the human, have long defined Black folk's engagement with civil society. The afterlife of Black enslavement, notes literary scholar Saidiya V. Hartman, is a life in which access to necessities such as healthcare and education, and opportunities for human flourishing, are skewed.[3] Such experiences of North American Blacks have given rise to a sense of precarity in which Black life operates in a state of perpetual re-imagination and re-construction; that is, a constant quest to locate oneself. Black religions have been instrumental in this reconstruction effort.

Couched within the archives, both oral and written, of Black religions are stories of imagination and performance.[4] Not performance as an actor on stage "in character," but rather as it reflects the praxis of imagination that moves beyond time and allows for the possibility of transcendence; that is, the potential to experience joy in chaos. Within the diversity of Black religious life, stories of these varied imaginations reveal a shared history of Black folk contending with theological and religious questions such as the relationship of God to human suffering and the place of religion in their quest to locate meaning and personhood. Questions about sinister white religious ideas, such as the elevation of white religious iconography as the symbol of divinity, come alive in Black religious imaginaries. Simply put, as Black religions contend with such theological questions, they aim to debunk narratives of anti-Blackness. Religion thus becomes a foundation for Black hope as well as the means through which questions about Blackness, Black history, and Black futures are addressed. While Black religious imaginations have tended to center on Protestantism, there are, within the undercurrents of Black religious life, a plethora of diasporic religious experiences.

These spawned in the wake of the Great Migration to the urban North, as Black migrants turned to diverse religious worlds and practices in their journey to create and fashion an identity not beholden to Western ideals or conventional forms of Black Protestant religion. These new religious movements afforded Black folk a means by which they made broader claims about Black existence and Black life in North America. They are a critical feature in the study of Black religions, demonstrating the multilayered and diasporic religious sensibilities of Black folk. Indeed, these traditions exhibit various paths toward rebuilding after an earthquake.

* * *

In describing why she joined the Black Coptic Church and her relationship to her spiritual teacher Queen Rebekah (1923–2005), who was known as the mother of the BCC, Black Coptic devotee Brenda Drake noted:

> I am glad, so glad, that I found the Coptic faith and my teacher Queen Rebekah. She brought peace, love, and understanding into my home and life. When my life was filled with misery and hopelessness, she brought sunshine. When I felt no one understood me, and there was no one to belong to, she gave me someplace to go, and showed me how to love, and then I started to receive love.[5]

Likewise, Pamela Miller, a Black Coptic disciple, reported:

> Life for me began anew on Wednesday afternoon, July 7, 1976, when Queen Rebekah laid hands on me and healed my body and my mind. She took me as a newborn babe and nursed me through the summer until classes began in the School of Wisdom in September. At this point in my life, she has helped me to elevate my mind to such an extent that each day is an adventure to look forward to. Queen Rebekah has taught me about my true self, but more importantly, she has taught me about my God who is I Am that I Am. She has taught me about his son Black Jesus, whose image I am created after. Because I have been taught to call upon I Am That I Am Black God, my trials and tribulations have only served to strengthen me. Queen Rebekah taught me to stand still, hold my peace,

and let God do the job for me. Through the Coptic teaching I have gained inner peace, immovable faith, personal strength, and a new awareness of myself as a Black woman.[6]

These stories evoke personal earthquakes related to the search for meaning and belonging, but they also narrate a search for racial identity and pride. Miller, for instance, discovered a way to read and situate her Blackness alongside a belief system that emphasized a "Black Jesus," which contributed to her "new awareness" as a Black woman. Miller was in search of an identity, one that permitted her to integrate her spiritual world with a performance of her racial identity. These are the sorts of possibilities that unfolded with the founding of the Black Coptic Church.

This book argues that Black religions that developed during the Great Migration in response to racism attracted followers seeking alternative religious models outside of mainline Christianity to provide them with the tools they needed to reconstruct their identities after an earthquake. The long history of Black North America has encompassed many such quakes, what sociologist Orlando Patterson describes as social death, resulting from the collision between the enslaver, who performs unchecked power, and the slave, who operates from an extreme position of powerlessness. According to Patterson, the condition of the slave, and the aftermath of enslavement, contributed to a loss of identity, a sense of alienation, and a psychological reality in which slaves' and their progeny's perception of their nature was drastically altered. Such social experiences, compounded by decades of recurring tremors, were intended to damage the souls of Black folks.[7] Black religions have sought to provide refuge, hope, and an identity in the face of moral pandemonium.

Significance

This book is about one group's religious imagination spurred by living in the aftermath of moral and social earthquakes. It describes religious activities of resistance against social constructions that posited Black life as lacking value, meaning, and even being. Of the Black new religious movements that developed during and in the wake of the Great Migration, some, like Father Divine's Peace Mission Movement and the Moorish Science Temple, stood outside of Christianity, while other movements that took shape during this time remained at least somewhat within the Christian tradition. The Black Coptic Church is one of the latter. It combined elements of Black Protestant and Black Hebrew traditions with Ethiopianism, providing a divine racial identity and a royal Egyptian heritage for its African American followers—a heroic identity that was in stark contrast to the racial identity imposed by the white dominant culture.

I argue that a theologically hybrid approach, one that is primarily Christian but that also borrows from other groups, including Black Jews and Black spiritualists, fused with a reclamation of Egyptian and Ethiopian religious and cultural sources, assists the Black Coptic Church in fashioning a Black identity that, for believers, disrupts biases against Black people in North America.[8] Black Coptics embrace the idea that Black people are the "chosen people," and thereby embody a sense of divinity due to their relationship to God. Black Coptics enact religious performances connected to their belief that Black people are part of a royal lineage, and that believers are royalty in a "spiritual kingdom," in which they accept titles such as Queen, Empress, Princess, Prince, and King. I ask, "what does it mean for Black Coptic followers to imagine and perform Blackness *otherwise* through a religious lens?" *The Black Coptic Church* provides a more detailed look at the diverse world of Black religious life in North America, particularly within non-mainstream Christian churches.

The Scene

Sprawling throughout Chicago is an assembly of Black Coptic churches. Prophet Louis Cicero Patterson (1895–1962) originated the BCC there in the early to middle twentieth century, following his movement north to Chicago after experiencing racial and religious tensions in Atlanta. These tensions were related to his spiritualist ministry of faith healing, which encompassed performance—such as laying on of hands to the sick—that was common among African Americans after enslavement. The BCC flourished among other Black new religious movements in the Southside community of Black Bronzeville. The community emerged within the context of the Great Migration, the mass exodus of Blacks

Figure I.1. Black Coptic Church Series, True Temple of Solomon Black Coptic Church, Chicago, IL, January 2021. Credit: Iwona Biedermann Photography.

from the South to the North from 1910 through the 1970s, as Blacks sought to escape racism and lack of economic upward mobility in the South, with the hopes of benefiting from a perceived less vicious racism in the North. BCC temples, as they are called within the religious group, are generally inner-city storefront institutions located in economically depressed communities. This has been the case since the Church's beginning, as many of the early converts were migrants who arrived in the North as members of a lower economic class. The BCC, given its emphasis on identity formation and appropriation of royal titles amongst its membership, offered a sense of social compensation for this generally lower economic class. The roughly thirty Coptic temples in existence today are outgrowths of the second and (for nearly twenty years beginning in 1967) sole BCC in Chicago, the True Temple of Solomon, led by Prophet Peter Banks (1929–1989), successor to the Church's founder.

An intimate cluster of several thousand devotees, composed of practicing and inactive members, the BCC is an insular religious community. Most members are Black women, with men accounting for less than twenty percent of the group. Rarely involved ecumenically with other religious organizations, the BCC is an inward-looking society of believers who can be seen on Sundays in Chicago's South Side and West Side communities (where most Southern migrants had settled), wearing their unique religious regalia of long robes and headpieces called crowns. While the BCC has expanded beyond Chicago, Chicago has long been recognized as the hub of the group.

These churches are mostly headed by charismatic men known as "spiritual leaders" or pastors. These were mostly self-appointed to their position of leadership, typically in response to instability in their religious community due to the lack of a succession plan or blueprint following the death of Prophet Peter. Historically, the BCC has approached theological education with suspicion. For Prophet Jacob, a Black Coptic spiritual leader in his early fifties who became affiliated with the BCC as a teenager, following his mother's conversion,

> It is not so much that Prophet Cicero and Prophet Peter did not want us to have education. The reality is that the theology they were teaching in many of the seminaries was the same theology they used to oppress us. So, Prophet Cicero wanted to train us and teach us in the Black Coptic Church and not rely on white theology schools. So, we have never placed a huge emphasis on getting theology degrees. We believe God has given our prophets divine wisdom which they have in turn given to us.[9]

Thus, many Black Coptic spiritual leaders lack formal education or theological training, but rather rely on "the spirit" and revelation for their instruction. As Priest Meshach asserts, "Like the prophets of old who received visions from God, God still speaks to us today."[10] These leaders wield extraordinary and unchecked authority within the group and may not be removed from office by their local congregation. They represent the vanguard of the BCC.

Priest Meshach helped me to frame the social context within which to understand the religious world of Black Coptic believers. Priest Meshach became affiliated with the BCC when his mother, who had been introduced to the Church by a friend, converted when he was nine years old. Like most converts to the BCC, Priest Meshach's mother accepted the invitation from a friend who was "fishing" for new members, an evangelistic practice in the community whereby members invite potential converts by word of mouth, usually through stories about how Black Coptic teaching had transformed their life. Priest Meshach is now in his late fifties and a spiritual leader in the community. We sat in the backyard of his South Side home as he described at length the BCC's recovery and performance of what he termed "divine Blackness." Analogous to Prophet Hosea's narrative, Priest Meshach maintained that

> Blacks have a history, a lineage, and an identity that supersedes American slavery. We only became descendants of slaves when the old slave master kidnapped us from Africa, made us into niggers, and told us that we were nothing. Prophet Cicero came as a Prophet to teach us back to our identity, a divine identity. He came to heal us from the nigger mind, teach us about our God, and prophesy about our future.

Teaching us back to ourselves, explained Priest Meshach, means "to help Black people reject the idea that we are negroes and for us to reclaim our divine image, which is in the image of God."[11] Crucial within the story of chattel slavery is the invention of the "negro," and the concomitant development and propagation of a negative racial stereotype about Black people, which some Blacks internalized as their identity. Priest Meshach captures the essence of the ontological problem that the BCC strives to overcome: the reduction of Black being and Black humanity from something to nothing. Priest Meshach painstakingly described a situation in which Black life and Black history were harmed by a tragic lie that deemed Black life expendable.

In the wake of Black earthquakes, questions about "being"—or the lack thereof—emerge as Black folk wrestle with the precariousness of their displaced situation. For some, the "negro" symbolizes a catastrophic and enduring loss of identity. Questions about belonging, one's place in the world, life, death, and the meaning of existence, as well as ones that ponder God's relationship to suffering, materialize as individuals and groups aim to "make sense" of the human condition—or lack thereof. The turn toward religion as a means with which to grapple with such questions is captured in conversion narratives of those who become members of religious movements.

In describing why individuals converted to the Nation of Islam, for example, religious studies scholar Edward Curtis notes the following:

Many of these stories were classic American religious conversion narratives whose form will be familiar to many readers, and they evidence how the styles of religious practice and patterns of conversion in the NOI echo those of other American religious groups. These testimonials often described how a convert faced a crisis or lingering problem before they found Elijah Muhammad and the NOI. Converting to Islam provided a way out and a solution to their problems. Some of these narratives, like those of born-again African American Christians, discussed conversion as a sudden and powerful moment in which the believer experienced God's presence.[12]

These stories, many linked to a personal crisis or earthquake, are specific conversion accounts of Black people who were in pursuit of a religious identity beyond mainline Christianity, which many associated with pie-in-the-sky, or escapist, theology. Converts were interested in a religious experience that would save them—as in personal and social soteriology—from a crisis, such as drug abuse or legal problems, or a general sense of social and racial isolation. Such stories are not exclusive to the NOI or the BCC but illuminate a common thread that connects Great Migration new religious movements: they attract adherents who have experienced detachment from the broader culture and a feeling of disenchantment from established forms of religion. In the case of those who converted to the BCC, for example, testimonies, which are usually provided by members during their Sunday service, offer an array of individual accounts of people in search of a new path that would reverse their loss of identity. Yet, while personal crises are part and parcel of explanations concerning why believers converted to the BCC, a dominant testimonial theme among Black Coptic members is that the Church inculcated a sense of pride in being Black. Priest Eli, for instance, a seventy-plus-year-old believer who converted in his thirties after visiting the BCC at the invitation of a friend, reports that, "when I visited True Temple of Solomon [Black Coptic Church] it was like a sea of Black royalty. I wasn't a stranger to religion or the church per se, but this was different. There was no shame in being black in that place. Everyone in the temple walked with their head up. They spoke with authority. They were proud to be black and it showed. I had found my home."[13]

Often, a believer's experience of a personal earthquake is not detached from, but rather tied to, the BCC's general theology and praxis, manifested in a search for identity. Queen Huldah, a seventy-six-year-old spiritual leader at Coptic Temple of Kemet (located in Lansing, Illinois, a suburb of Chicago), reports that her conversion happened in 1973 after she faced legal problems while living in New York. At the urging of a friend, she visited True Temple of Solomon BCC in Chicago in hopes that she might find spiritual assistance as she faced her legal woes, as well as an ethos that would speak to what she described as her "Black consciousness," developed while in conversation with the Garvey movement in New York. Queen Huldah was not in search of a traditional form of religion. Rather, she was in search of a religious community that connected her to a sense of Black pride. She found in the BCC a "religious way of life that was unashamedly black, and black people who were unafraid to say I'm black and proud, and who rejected nigga and negro identities." This was important to her "because traditional forms of black religion were too focused on dying and flying and not about connecting black people to our true identity." It was the religious order's focus on her social location as a Black woman who desired a "deeper connection and celebration of [her] black history, including the black presence in the bible," that she found particularly compelling.[14]

For believers, the BCC provided a theology and way of life that united them to a view of Blackness that contradicted remnants of social, political, and religious orders that were tethered to anti-Blackness.

In Search of Zion: On Ethiopianism and the Black Coptic Church

Several scholarly works offer compelling investigations into Great Migration new religious movements that sought to map and trace their identity back to Africa, toward the establishment of individual and collective identity.[15] Part and parcel of this exploration and longing for identity is the notion of forming an "imaginative birthplace," that is, a homeland in which individuals envision themselves, even though they may be outside its geographical limits. Among Black Coptic believers, their search for identity manifests in the intentional and normative framing of Ethiopia as a source of spiritual and national identity. An enduring theme in this text, therefore, is that of Ethiopianism, which can be succinctly described as the veneration of the African country toward the telos of constructing an elaborate idea of Blackness—Black life, Black culture, Black people.

Centrally present in the BCC is the idea that Black people are of Ethiopian descent, or a performance of Ethiopianism. Within the context of the racialized world of oppression and white supremacy within which the BCC was birthed, looking toward Ethiopia as a homeland was a way to promote and perform racial redemption of Africans worldwide. Prophet Cicero Patterson believed that Ethiopia was the true homeland for Blacks, and that Black people would be redeemed by the "spirit of Ethiopia."[16] Ethiopianism as a political and religious ideology is not represented by a single strand of thought. Indeed, various conceptions of Ethiopianism are held throughout the Caribbean world, on the African continent, in Jamaica among the Rastafarians, and among North American writers of the eighteenth and nineteenth centuries, such as Phillis Wheatley, who used the term "Ethiop" as a way of naming Africans and African Americans.[17] Nonetheless, within the diversity of Ethiopianist thought, there are core ideas that connect the various dots. These include the belief that Ethiopia has special significance for Blacks throughout the diaspora, most notably in light of the biblical reference to the Prince of Ethiopia in Psalm 68, verse 31. Moreover, as seen in the writings of Paul Laurence Dunbar, Ethiopia was cast as a representation of the struggles of African Americans but also as a source of national hope that justice would prevail. In Dunbar's "Ode to Ethiopia," written for and to the "Mother Race," he writes:

> On every hand in this fair land,
> Proud Ethiope's swarthy children stand
> Beside their fairer neighbor;
> The forests flee before their stroke,
> Their hammers ring, their forges smoke,—
> They stir in honest labour.
>
> Go on and up! Our souls and eyes
> Shall follow thy continuous rise;

> Our ears shall list thy story
> From bards who from thy root shall spring
> And proudly tune their lyres to sing
> Of Ethiopia's glory.[18]

Indeed, as anthropologist Charles Reavis Price notes, "In the thoughts and writings of the Ethiopianists of the 1700s and 1800s, Ethiopia and Egypt were significant as emblematic of a golden age and the high civilization of Black life. In true millenarian fashion, some looked to it as the future that awaited them."[19] For proponents of Ethiopianism, Ethiopia was a symbol that pointed toward the redemption of Black people. In the BCC, this idea of redemption is manifested by naming Ethiopia as the ancestral homeland.

Ethiopianism functions as the means to construct transcendental conceptions of the Black person and Black culture that move beyond reading blackness, determinately, in opposition to whiteness—what Victor Anderson neatly describes as ontological Blackness.[20] The notion of Ethiopianism also contributes to a heroic read of Black culture that aims to de-colonize Blackness, and portrays "Ethiopia as an ancestral homeland [that] has played a major role in nourishing racial pride among Blacks of the New World."[21] Indeed, for proponents of Ethiopianism, including Marcus Mosiah Garvey (1887–1940), Ethiopia was a holy land of sorts, one that spoke to the promise of Black autonomy in overcoming colonialism. Ethiopia's victory at the Battle of Adwa in 1896, for example, is not only seen as a military triumph, but as a divine conquest, one in which God was with the Ethiopian people in their struggle to maintain autonomy. In this spirit, Garvey—in his role as president general of the Universal Negro Improvement Association—sent a telegram to Ethiopian Emperor Haile Selassie I (1892–1975) on the emperor's coronation, addressed from "Ethiopians of the Western World."[22] Garvey maintained that

> the Psalmist prophesied that Princes would come out of Egypt and Ethiopia would stretch her hands unto God. We have no doubt that the time is now come. Ethiopia is now really stretching forth her hands. This great kingdom of the East has been hidden for many centuries but gradually

she is rising to take a leading place in the world and it is for us of the Negro race to assist in every way to hold up the hand of Emperor Ras Tafari.[23]

Ethiopianism, for those attracted to the ideology, "transforms the narratives of Ethiopia into metaphors of African magnanimity and correspondingly decodes them as a commentative script to autonomy and assertive sovereignty."[24] Such was the notion of Ethiopianism that Prophet Cicero embraced. For him, Ethiopia indexed a presentation of Black life that disavowed colonial ideas about Blackness. Consequently, conceptions of collective Black history, as well as aims to construct an identity in relation to that history, are at work in the BCC. For Black Coptic believers, Ethiopianism provides a common historical narrative that negates and rejects the supposition of a limited history sprouting from modern tension or existential crisis. Indeed, according to Priest Meshach, for the BCC, "Black history does not begin on slave plantations. Ethiopia is a symbol that gives us our identity and pride. While some were hoping for a return to Ethiopia, Prophet Cicero brought the spirit of Ethiopia to us. [Prophet Cicero] took us back to the beginning of all creation . . . because Ethiopia best represents the nation he wanted us to become."[25]

Prophet Cicero's vision of the BCC was therefore one in which he performed a sort of "going beyond" the spiritual and priestly dimensions of religion via a hermeneutic of retrieval, which was meant to free an "authentic" Black identity from the imprisonment of the white dominant culture. Claiming a Hebrew-Christian theological context, and coupling it with a reclamation of Egyptian and Ethiopian religious and cultural artifacts, the Black Coptic Church reimagines and reconstructs Black identity, and disrupts "normative" assumptions about black persons in North America.[26] To this end, Prophet Cicero rejected even 'modern' 20th century terms like 'colored persons.' This aim to "identity *otherwise*" is further demonstrated in the Black Coptic Church's weekly Sunday ritual recognizing women adherents via the proclamation: "Hail to the Queens of Ethiopia." In other words, the Black Coptic Church, from its genesis, did not seek to jettison racial categories. Rather, as noted earlier, it aimed to devise a racial paradigm that was correlative, corrective, and constructive, on its own terms, through a recovery of a heroic and monumental African [Ethiopian] past that represented, for the Black Coptic community, divine Blackness.

Why Coptic?

It is important to note that the BCC does not have an ecclesial relationship with the Orthodox Coptic church, founded in Egypt by St. Mark around 42 CE. The naming of the BCC as a "Coptic" Church sprang from its founder's goals of theological liberation and identity construction. For Prophet Cicero, "Coptic" resurrects an ancient heritage of Black persons through an imaginative relationship between North American Blacks and that Egyptian Christian community. This framing will be profoundly important as we consider the group's magnanimous and grandiose reading of Black history, especially the Church's lofty and uncritical elevation of Egypt and Ethiopia. Prophet Cicero articulated a radical disconnectedness caused by the transatlantic slave trade and North American chattel slavery. Because followers trace their religious and ancestral heritage to Ethiopia and Egypt, colonialism and slavery are understood as a disruption of their history and future. The BCC becomes instrumental in reconnecting to a glorified and often romanticized past. The designation of this community as Coptic imaginatively connects North American Blacks to African civilizations, which the community uplifts as symbols of Black achievement.[27]

Members of the BCC assert not only "direct lineage" to ancient Egypt, but also that they are Black Jews "out of Israel." Historian Jacob Dorman's analysis of claims made by Black Israelite religions that they are the descendants of Ancient Israelites and that "the ancient Israelites were the ancestors of contemporary West Africans," is helpful here.[28] Dorman contends that "the Israelite faiths of the 1890s arose from ideational rather than ancestral genealogies." And, therefore, "Black Israelites did not descend from ancient Israelites or contemporary Jews in either Africa or the Americas. Rather, like most other 'imagined communities' of the late nineteenth century, [these groups] invented their identities from a host of ideational rhizomes. . . ."[29] The BCC belongs to a category of Black religious traditions that not only constructed imagined communities but asserted what I call assembled heroic identities. By this, I mean that they brought together, or collected into one place, a host of cultures and lineages that contribute to a transcendental read of Blackness, advancing Black life beyond categorical and immediate historical circumstances. In spaces where oppression exists, assembled heroic identities enable Black folk to imagine and perform notions of the self that counter socially constructed notions of Blackness. Moreover, assembled heroic identities are integral to the social salvation programs of those groups that embrace them, like the BCC. Prophet Cicero's declaration of a Black Coptic identity as an umbrella term for a more complex identity is an example of constructing a relationship between social and spiritual salvation.

The Black Coptic Church in Context

The BCC does not exist in isolation. Rather, as we have seen, it is connected to a larger aspect of Black religions during the Great Migration; one that expands our understanding of what constitutes the "religion" of Black religions. The complexity of Black religion(s) lies in the fact that we are not dealing with a neat set of beliefs that point toward a monolithic, shared theology. This is the generative nature of these religious traditions. They exhibit a range of religious activities and theologies steeped in a desire to be free. Without question, in Black religion "evil is accounted for and hope, at least for some, is assured. In short, African American religious life is as rich and complicated as the religious life of other groups in the United States, but African American religion emerges in the encounter between faith, in all its complexity, and white supremacy."[30]

The racial and social circumstances of the early to middle twentieth century urban North provided the conditions necessary for the evolution of independent Black religious movements.[31] The BCC was birthed in a social and cultural milieu that reduced Black people to racialized classifications such as "negro." Therefore, in places like Chicago, new religious movements determined to address both the religious *and* racial identity earthquakes within Black communities emerged. Together with the Black Coptic Church, other smaller religious sects and groups that collapsed spiritual identity and racial formation thrived and flourished. Arthur Fauset asserts:

> With the migration of Negroes from the rural South to urban centers, a transformation in the basic religious life and attitudes also is observable. The church, once a *sine qua non* of institutional life among American Negroes, does not escape the critical inquiry of the newer generations, who implicitly and sometimes very explicitly are requiring definite pragmatic sanctions if they are to be included among churchgoers, or if indeed they are to give any consideration at all to religious practices and beliefs.[32]

Additionally, historian Milton Sernett notes, "Refugees from the South often dreamed of a specific place in the Promised Land. For many of them, [Chicago] was the mecca of the Midwest."[33] Similarly, in his *Canaan Land*, historian Albert Raboteau presents a historical narrative centered on the migration of Black folk from the South to the North during the interwar period. Push factors, such as lack of jobs, problems with crops, and segregation in the South, were influential in the Great Migration. Additionally, pull factors such as the availability of unskilled manufacturing and industrial jobs presented the potential for upward economic and social mobility. Yet, as Raboteau highlights, "The urban situation turned out to be less rosy than the migrants had hoped. As they settled into the poorer sections of the cities, they encountered conflict with white neighbors and white workers, frequently immigrant."[34] Still, this migration north had a major impact on the religious life of African Americans. In many instances, the established Black Church, to which many of the migrants already belonged, was a place of refuge. However, and more significant to this study, "... migration also increased the variety of Black religious life by exposing people to new religious choices."[35] Beyond the Black Baptists, Methodists, Catholics, and other Christian denominations, Northern Blacks were also exposed to a variety of Black religious sects and movements that provided an alternative to mainline Christianity. Sociologist Ira De Augustine Reid summarizes these new religious movements as establishments that were disgruntled with the "prayerful procrastinations" of the more established Black church traditions, particularly concerning race and economic relations.[36] He observed the significant rise of what he identified as "religious cults and sects." Reid notes, "today, Father Divine, Elder Michaux, Daddy Grace, Moslem sects, congregations of Black Jews, and the Coptic Church have been added to the church organizations existing among Negroes."³⁷ This emergence of new religions, therefore, in part, can be attributed to the social, political, and economic crises which Southern migrants faced in the North.

Performative Imagination: Theoretical Considerations

Throughout this book, I employ the term "performative imagination" as a tool for understanding the BCC's religious and theological world. Given that Black identity is not fixed and, within the social context of anti-Blackness, has often been determined by and named in ways that reflect the particular historical moment, performative imagination, within the framework of Black Coptic religion, is the mode through which members of the assembly re-claim and self-fashion their identity. As we have seen, the moniker "negro" presented an enduring problem for the Church's founder. On this issue, I find the argument that Thomas DeFrantz and Anita Gonzalez make in *Black Performance Theory* to be helpful. They conclude:

> To uncover a history of black performance, we begin by considering naming—the mechanisms used to designate black presence. For example: African, Ethiopian, Negro, black, African American. These monikers demonstrate shifts in thinking about black identity and representation. Each label represents a context for packaging ideas about black people in particular places and during particular historical time periods.³⁸

What we encounter, then, in the BCC, is a religious imagination concerned with recovering what, for believers, is their true and authentic identity. I locate this search within the theory and praxis of what I call performative imagination. I turn towards performance studies, particularly Black performance theory, as a foundation for understanding Black Coptic belief. Indeed,

> Black performance theory shows us how the subjects and subjectivities animate Blackness across landscapes that are all spectacularly excessive in the cause and effects of African dislocation, imperialist trade, capital accumulation, human violence, and black abjection, as well as

circum-Atlantic expressions, black labor, Africanist retentions, black diaspora movements, the politics of black is beautiful, and more.[39]

The turn toward the performative, then, is a radical investigation of how some Black folk assemble and partake in their imagination of Blackness to salvage an exalted view of a Black past, transform the present, and create a Black future not limited by previous notions of Blackness. The "performative" is an amalgamation of performance—that is, "forms of cultural staging . . . within a limited time span of action . . ."—and performativity—that "which marks identity through the habitus of repetitive enactments, reiterations of stylized norms, and inherited gestural conventions from the way we sit, stand, speak dress . . . and more, does something to make a material, physical, and situational difference."[40] Black religion(s) is a viable space within which to study and locate performative Blackness, asserting a new identity against contested identities that emerge in the aftermath of earthquakes. Religion, therefore, becomes the vehicle that harnesses a new mode of being and new theologies that depart from those rooted in anti-Blackness.

Within the space of identity construction, which follows a general search for identity, performative imagination asks what constitutes Black identity and Black life. That is, at the foundation of this theoretical approach is an assumption that Black performance, Black performativity, and the performative, are ingrained within the culture of Black folk—a resilience that resists tropes of pessimism and formulates an enduring sense of Blackness. Performative imagination frames a way of being, closed or fluid, about which Black identity subsists in time and space. The "what" of the imagination can therefore be rooted in a sense of historical imagination, Black futurism, or a combination of both. The performative is the staging—or embodiment—of the imagination. It is an act. It is the construction of a stage on which the idea is realized. It seeks to create, as in fashion, space, and place, a world in which Black identity is not merely theoretical. In short, while performative imagination begins with an idea, its culmination is the staging and performance of a new Black identity, which I package as "*otherwise.*"

This book applies performative imagination to the BCC as a way of understanding the community's search for identity. What we discover is a not-so-neat quest to locate itself in a state of homelessness. I use "homelessness" in this setting to highlight the penetrating and lasting impacts of earthquakes and the sense of detachment they cause as people, or more specific to this volume, Black people, journey in search of a home and an identity. This is akin to Emily Raboteau's *Searching for Zion*, in which the author creatively narrates the search for a homeland by those displaced and scattered throughout the African diaspora who are in search of "Zion," or a homeland.[41] This search is not without ambiguities or complexities, and often involves uncritical appropriations of a society—its culture, its religion, etc.—especially one that is revered and identified as the original, and thereby viable, homeland of those seeking an identity. As we will see, for instance, there is a belief among Black Coptic members that Prophet Cicero connected the community, the "tree," back to their "roots." As noted earlier, this sort of performative imagination is a prime example of efforts to trace the ancestral heritage of Black people; it grows out of a deep desire to have a place called home. The concept of African roots provides the stability of "knowing where one came from. [. . .] certainly necessary at a time when heritage was denied and African Americans were deemed to have no past."[42] Nonetheless, the performative imagination at work within the assembly of Black Coptic believers allows members to locate, whether factually or imaginatively, their history in a place that "feels" like home. Thus, in a sense, this imaginative process dislocates the sense of despair brought about by dislocation.

In my desire to deepen the framework of performative imagination, I borrow the notion of "spiderweb" from Nadine George-Graves. She uses the term "spidering" to describe diaspora, metaphorically, closely connected to the action of an internet search engine such as Google, which crawls or "travel[s] the Internet looking for data."[43] For George-Graves, as the search engine scours the internet in search of the most relevant material, it then collapses its finding into a single location. Applying the spidering metaphor to the story of African descendants in search of identity, George-Graves maintains that "Diasporic Spidering allows for many different points of intersection and modes of passage to be woven together around a central core—the individual searcher/journeyer. Rather than describing a fixed moment in time, African diaspora (and black identity) in this sense becomes also a contemporary active process—an act, a performative."[44] Such is the process that unfolds in the BCC as members, rather than focusing on a strict genealogical or biological search, imaginatively assemble an identity, create memories, and thereby lay claim to a sense of Blackness that is performed in ritual, in belief, and in religious practice. In short, spidering is a helpful way to think about the performative because it illustrates the multifarious routes that Black folk have taken to feel at home and lay claim to identity. Moreover, the concept of spidering helps us understand how people "assemble lives, define themselves, are defined by others, and resist simple definitions."[45] What unfolds in this text is one look at performative imagination in light of spidering.

Constructively, Black religious imaginations, especially those grounded in a sense of freedom, envision cosmological, religious, and theological imperatives that, when performed, diminish the impact of competing imaginations (specifically, those not rooted in liberation) on the being of Black people. This sort of liberative, or performative, imagination, manifested in the act of making invisible otherwise possibilities visible, stands as the cornerstone of Black religious life. While it is the case, as Gayraud Wilmore asserts, that "the religious beliefs and rituals of people are inevitably and inseparably bound up with the material and psychological realities of their daily existence,"[46] radical Black religious imaginations do not capitulate to the threat of non-being. Rather, performative imagination reveals a certain transcendence of Black religious life that, in spite of the material evidence, imagines and performs (enfleshes) freedom, not as a counter-hermeneutic, lest Black freedom and Black being are reduced to that which is contingent on anti-human imaginaries and performances,[47] but rather out of divine origin; one that precedes the threat of non-being. In this sense, Black religion, since enslaved Africans first performed a radical religious imagination, has offered a retort to Afro-pessimism. That is, adherents "refused to surrender their humanity under enslavement and never lost sight of the freedom and justice they believed to be God-given."[48]

In Black religions, performative imagination both rejects violent religious tropes rooted in white supremacy and constructs theological and religious claims and practices that advance the dignity of Black people. Such performative imaginations, rituals, and practices that advance Black life as sacred speak to the active religious conception of Black people in North America. Many scholarly texts recognize this element in Black religion. In *Slave Religion: The "Invisible Institution" in the Antebellum South*, for example, historian Albert Raboteau offers a glimpse into the clandestine religious life of enslaved Africans as they imagined a theological and religious world that deemed the given religion of the enslavers inconsistent with the Christian gospel. Chief among Raboteau's arguments is that the religion of the enslaved contested the religious imaginations of the enslavers, while offering a religious praxis that prefaced liberative readings of biblical stories as paramount.[49] For Raboteau, the essence of slave rebellions is not political, but rather theological, making sense of social and theological absurdity which, in the description of philosopher Albert Camus, is the tension between a longing for meaning and a world in which meaning is not offered.[50] In agreement with Raboteau's assessment, Gayraud Wilmore notes that "Nat Turner's revolt heightened the suspicions that religion was a primary factor in slave uprisings."[51] Turner's visions, for instance, reveal that at the core of his religious imagination was freedom. His encounters with the "Spirit," as a source for thinking about revolt, were not merely "alternative" interpretations of the Christian faith.[52] Rather, these imaginaries, religious and theological renderings, and practices that debunked slaveholding religion as heretical, reveal a radical orientation toward the Christian religion that consummated in performance. Indeed, "even though [enslaved Africans] adopted the outward appearance of Christian conversation, they took from it only what proved efficacious for easing the burden of their captivity and gave little attention the rest."[53] The "invisible institution," which can be described as the clandestine and secret religious gatherings of enslaved Blacks on plantations outside the purview of slave owners, then, symbolizes the first real effort of enslaved Africans to execute their radical religious imagination within the context of the absurd.

The Black Christian religious imagination surfaces out of a tension or dialectic that is concerned with the integrity of Christian faith. At the heart of the tension is a question, namely, "What constitutes the essence of Christian faith?" The christianity of the enslavers was one that reconciled human enslavement and religious performance.[54] Enslaved Africans who partook in the invisible institution, however, rebuffed slave-holding christianity, as it ran counter to their deep-seated religious sentiments and the performance of those religious beliefs. The spirit of this rejection is captured in Frederick Douglass' *Narrative*, in which he asserts, "What I have said respecting and against religion, I mean strictly to apply to slaveholding religion of this land, and with no possible reference to Christianity proper; for, between the Christianity of this land, and the Christianity of Christ, I recognize the widest possible difference—so wide, that to receive one as good, pure, and holy, is of necessity to reject the other as bad, corrupt, and wicked. . . ."[55] If slaveholding religion creates a gap between that which is good and that which is absurd, then the performative imagination revealed in Black religion(s), especially as captured in the invisible institution, fills this lacuna.

It should be noted, however, that the radical imagination in Black religions does not merely assist in the development of a liberative theological and liturgical performance. Certainly, liberative motifs that emerge from a divine imagination are important for understanding the religious world of Black Americans, as they seek to build theological visions that repudiate white supremacy couched in theological terms. Likewise, theological imaginations in the traditions of the invisible institution, the Black theology project of the American sixties, and womanist theology, as well as those theologies that attend to matters of gender and sexuality, among others, exhibit the performative nature of the Black religious and theological imagination in that they are not purely theoretical musings, but *already* perform an iconoclastic function while oriented toward the joy of Black life. Meaning, these imaginations contribute to the destruction of systems that threaten Black being. While we have access to a plethora of material that describes performative imaginaries at work in Black religious communities, such as its theology and music, we examine it in order to discover how imaginative communities in Black religion(s) contribute to the broader discourse of radical religious imaginations, especially in non-mainstream Black religious groups.

As we have seen, Black people attracted to religio-racial new religious movements desired religion that offered a spiritual foundation, *and* one that actively combatted the ills of white supremacy. The turn toward new religious movements helped followers to construct a Black identity not indebted to the legacy of North American chattel slavery. Fauset's analysis of the performances of a sample of these movements, as well as their leaders—whom he described as the "Black Gods of the Metropolis"—is a helpful and significant lens through which to survey Black new religious movements. While Fauset left room for many questions about other new religious movements, it is important to emphasize the particular promise of his text and the subsequent literature that explores Black religion beyond the mainstream Protestant denominations that comprise the "Black Church" tradition.[56] That is, Fauset opens an examination of the truly diasporic and creative world of Black religion, demonstrating why Black people were attracted to groups that provided a complex religious world that also engaged their social status in North America. To be sure, as demonstrated in other works, for many participants in these groups, their religious search launched with a search for a homeland. Yet, there is still much to be learned by engaging anew with the emergent new religious movements of the Great Migration.

Methodology: An Ethnographic Study

Fauset's *Black Gods of the Metropolis* offers a textured—as in thick description – ethnographic investigation of smaller religious sects that sprouted in urban cities in early twentieth century North America. Fauset's study is layered and complex, as he considers the inner workings, rituals, and beliefs of the sects he studied. Religious ethnography, however, is not merely about what scholars have said or thought about people in the practice of their religion; it is also about how participants *themselves* understand and make sense of their religious lives. It is an opportunity to expand the discourse whereby religious communities grapple with ways to articulate their faith. This book contributes to a growing body of literature that employs ethnographic methods to interpret and analyze religious worlds.

The BCC: An Ethnographic Blind Spot

There is a scarcity of written sources, whether internal or external to the community, pertaining to the history, theology, and beliefs of the BCC. This is in part because the community has long revolved around a set of charismatic personalities that make up the Church's authoritative arm, composed mostly of the BCC's spiritual leadership and its cadre of "teachers," those responsible for the preservation and dissemination of the oral tradition of the community. There has been a dearth of study among members about their belief system itself. Moreover, the BCC has existed mainly as an insular community with little to no interreligious dialogue, rendering access to written sources limited and, in most cases, nonexistent. I therefore aim to interact with human subjects as depositaries of history.

The BCC has not received much attention in the study of Black religions. Ira De Augustine Reid noted the emergence of the "negro Coptic Church" and added it to his list of emergent religions in the urban North.[57] The same is true of Arthur Fauset.[58] Chicago newspapers such as the *Chicago Defender* and the *Chicago Tribune* also provided journalistic accounts of the tradition.[59] But these sources together only create what might be called a broad outline of the faith. I rely, therefore, not solely on scholarly works that cover the period of the Great Migration broadly, but also on the stories of everyday people of faith.

It is often the case that religious histories and religious studies texts are missing the voices and concrete experiences of the communities examined. In this book, I seek to thicken the theoretical and religious exploration by drawing on qualitative research methods to illuminate the phenomenological and theological world of the BCC. While it is the case that the insufficiency of existing literature makes this approach necessary, my own scholarly interests include hearing and exploring the ordinary; that is, everyday people and everyday faith. In this light, I employ ethnography as way of inviting parishioners into the theological and religious discourse, not merely as subjects of religious investigation, but also as participants and, indeed, interlocutors, in the ongoing quest to better grasp the nature and task of Black religion(s). I compare this ethnographic approach to that of anthropologist Su'ad Abdul Khabeer who, in *Muslim Cool: Race, Religion, and Hip Hop in the United States*, employs the term "teachers" to describe her research participants' relationship to her, "because [she] drew on their generous sharing of knowledge and experiences." Indeed, for Abdul Khabeer, her teachers "are the progenitors of discourse, an epistemology, an aesthetic, and an embodiment. . . ."[60] Over the past ten years, I have observed the Black Coptic community as a researcher, and I have conducted hundreds of hours of ethnographic field work within this religious community. I, then, aim to join in conversation with Black Coptic followers as a way of understanding what is at stake in their beliefs and practices.

The field research for this book was conducted over two major periods. The first occurred between 2007 and 2010. During this phase, I observed religious services, including religious instruction classes and sacred rituals, and completed a series of semi-structured interviews with leadership and lay members of the Black Coptic community, primarily in Chicago. Additionally, I traveled to Atlanta, Georgia, to interview a small group of believers who were among Prophet Cicero's first followers prior to his migration North. The goal of this research phase was to better understand the history and theology of the BCC. The interview questions focused almost exclusively on the historical and theological development of the community from its origins to present times.

The second major phase of my research was conducted in the summer of 2017, with the assistance of a research grant from Saint Louis University. During this period, I explored church archives, which consisted of internal writings on theology and beliefs and audio recordings of church services that spanned from 1950 to the present day; and I completed another 45 hours of semi-structured group and one-on-one interviews with believers. In this second research stage, I expanded my interview questions beyond history and theology to better align with the aims of this book. In addition to a new round of historical and theological questions, I asked my participants about a range of topics including their understanding of race and identity, Ethiopianism, gender, and religious practices in their community (i.e., adoption of spiritual names and the wearing of spiritual garments). Given the gap between the two research phases, I spent some time re-posing previously-asked questions in order to establish consistency of thought.

Throughout this book, I employ theologian Paul Tillich's method of correlation to show how the theology of the Black Coptic Church is in dialogue with and pronounces Christian doctrine. I also rely on a correlative method to illustrate how the BCC provides new theological and religious insights via an engagement with Black life, culture, and social and human sciences, expanding what constitutes a canon of authoritative sources for the construction of theological claims. I demonstrate how the theology of the BCC aims to articulate and perform Black theology by providing new resources for this vital theme, including the Black Coptic Church's retrieval and usage of African-centered themes and worldviews, as well as rituals and practices such as Passover, that celebrate God's active involvement in freedom and emancipation in the North American experience. Yet, the tradition's claim of liberation is suspect on matters of gender.

To fully immerse myself in the contemporary world of the BCC, I spent hundreds of hours in religious services, observing rituals and holy days of the Church's liturgical calendar. Interview participants included twenty-one believers whose membership in the Black Coptic tradition spanned twenty-five to sixty years. These participants included seven men and fourteen women. The educational background of the group included twelve people with at least a high school diploma, six college graduates, three post-college graduates, and two with military service. All participants self-described as middle-class. Within the community, hierarchy matters. Given the paucity of written documents, the oral tradition relies very heavily on those who are deemed to be internal experts in the Church's theology and rituals. Typically, for one to be considered an authority on Church teaching, one must be a spiritual leader in the community (i.e., pastor or a pastor's wife), and recognized as a person of influence by the larger BCC. Outside persons in leadership positions, teachers in the community (such as those responsible for the training of new members), ordained clergy, and those with an extended length of service to the Church are also recognized as authoritative figures. The research participants all fit into the above categories, with most functioning as Black Coptic spiritual leaders.

While questions abound about ethnographic research, especially in relation to insider-outsider positionality, or the extent to which an ethnographer can be detached from her work, ethnographic methods do provide new resources for religious studies scholars. To this end, "religious studies has undergone an ethnographic turn. More and more, scholars attend to the social location and significance of religious practice."[61] Rendered in the form of a question, we can ask, "What are we able to glean from communities of faith as we enter into and observe their performance of religion within the sacredness of their imaginations?" This engagement is no easy task, and it raises several questions about the place of the ethnographer in relation to her work. My own orientation toward ethnography is influenced by anthropologist Marla Frederick, who notes:

> Scholars criticize the notion of the "detached observer," one who merely writes about a particular society without any reference to his or her own emotional or unideological commitments. Such criticism arises largely out of anthropology's history of studying remote and distant societies in order to produce scientific documentation of the societies' functioning. Recent anthropology, largely informed by feminist and post-colonial critiques, has attempted to rewrite this style not only by altering the ethnographic form but also by raising questions about the very nature of anthropology's focus, "remote" societies.[62]

Moreover, Gladys Daniel and Claire Mitchell, in their work on religious ethnography, seek to complicate the insider-outsider fixed notion of ethnographic research. Instead, they make a case for a more dynamic approach toward religious ethnography, one in which the lines are not static and fixed, but rather fluid and contestable. They argue that, in the tradition of Durkheim, "'pre-notions'—our pre-existing ideas and biases—are treated with suspicion." Yes, they further argue, "we must take account of how our own cultural expectations influence the research process. But the notion that we can rise above our own location within the research is problematic." Recently, however, "with the reflexive turn in the social sciences, it is no longer assumed that researchers can remain objective."[63] It should be noted, nonetheless, that the strict so-called "objective" and scientific process in the realm of research is largely a product of modernity and the Enlightenment. The emergence of voices from below has engendered a suspicion toward such categories, which fail to take seriously the subjective experiences of the researcher in the research process. The researcher does not approach her subject as a *tabula rasa*. Quite the contrary, we bring with us everything we have gathered along the way—that is, our standpoint—and are always thinking about thinking and interpreting our observations.

While my own position is closely aligned with a post-modern and post-colonial approach, one that questions notions of objectivity, it is important to note that critics of ethnography "also suggest the notion of ethnographic 'truth' is the greatest of misnomers. If there exists any grain of reliability in the ethnographic text, it must come, they argue, from the author's immediate and upfront acknowledgment of her limitation and of her ability to encapsulate only 'partial truths.'"[64] Indeed, ethnographic approaches already tell a story about power: the power of the author to determine the questions raised and the selection of what observations and voices to include in the ethnographic text. In short, I align with the critics in saying that self-positioning—one that lays bare the biases and the place of the author in the work—is critical to the ethnographic project. Mindful of these tensions relating to the place of the ethnographer and the search for understanding in religions, and the necessity to unveil our own biases, it is essential at this juncture to acknowledge my own position within this volume.

Self-Positioning

I am from Chicago. Chicago is a distinctive place in the study and practice of Black religions. As a child, it was not uncommon for me to come in direct contact with several Black religious groups on any given Sunday. Within my extended family, an array of Black religions was represented, from Black Protestantism such as the Church of God in Christ (COGIC) and Missionary Baptists, to members of the Nation of Islam (NOI), as well as Black Catholics and members who belonged to quasi-Islamic groups such as the El-Rukns. My earliest interaction with the BCC was through the lens of my youth. My aunt converted to the BCC after meeting her future husband, who was already a member. I remember being inquisitive about the unique style of dress—the church regalia—she donned. At the time, my immediate family were members at Chatham-Avalon Church of Christ on Chicago's South Side. We regularly "got dressed up" for church. As with most Black churches during this time, Sunday was the day to sport your best clothing, which included suits and shined shoes for men, and long dresses and elaborate hats for women. However, my aunt's church attire was unlike anything I had ever seen. Instead of dresses and hats, she wore long colorful robes and headpieces. This was especially intriguing in the eyes of a five-year-old boy. I petitioned my mother to permit me to visit my aunt's place of worship, to which she agreed. Such was the beginning of my long engagement with the BCC.

I recall entering True Temple of Solomon Black Coptic Church in Chicago. While the style of worship and musical selections were akin to other Black churches I had attended, two things stood out: The community's dress and the vocal declaration of "Black Jesus." To be sure, I was a theologically curious child who was never quite satisfied with accepting religion or beliefs merely because they were those of my parents. Images of white Jesus in church edifices filled with Black bodies had puzzled my childhood sensibilities. In fact, my mother often recounts a story of our time in the Church of Christ when I asked our pastor about Black people in the bible and church imagery. She recalls my frustration at not receiving what was, for me, an acceptable response to my query. Accordingly, the religious scene at True Temple of Solomon was appealing to my five-year-old sense of religion. I would go on to spend the next several years in the BCC, uncritically accepting its rituals, its customs, and its theology. I approach this investigation with a very different set of lenses; those informed by the academic study of religion and theology.

Mapping *The Black Coptic Church*

Chapter One traces the history of Prophet Louis Cicero Patterson from his birth in Orangeburg, South Carolina, to his death in Chicago, Illinois. Among Black Coptic followers, Prophet Cicero is shrouded in mystery and legend, which contributes to the community's perception of him as an enigmatic character. This chapter seeks to unravel the mystery and the place of Prophet Cicero in historical context, tracing his lineage and familial relations, as well as his route to Black Bronzeville in Chicago. This discussion addresses who Prophet Cicero Patterson was and why he identified his organization as "Coptic." It asserts that the Black Coptic movement was an imaginative community—that is, one that reaches into the past in search of a heroic view of Blackness, with the goal of establishing a religious and cultural tradition that imagines itself as part of a transcendental history not determined by social crisis or existential absurdity. Relying on ethnographic and archival research, Chapter One asserts "Coptic" as the link between adherents of this community and the past within which they locate their identity. Indeed, the ethnographic material reveals that members of the BCC perceive their founder as reconnecting them to the authentic root of their social and spiritual identity. Queen Maryann Martin, for instance, an eighty-plus-year-old member of the BCC who converted under Prophet Cicero, suggested that "during the slave trade, we were not allowed to take our God with us," and therefore, "we had lost our connection to our God, and so Prophet Cicero connected us back to the image of God so that we would not allow ourselves to be cut off from the root again."[65] She further articulated that by "naming us as Copts, Prophet Cicero took the tree back to its roots. Egypt is the beginning of civilization. So, by naming the organization as Coptic, he connected us to the origin of God's creation."[66] Chapter One narrates this story as a way of building a foundation for an examination of the Black Coptic Church as a religious institution in the successive chapters.

The chapter then focuses on the establishment of the Black Coptic Church as a place of religiosity in Chicago. Prophet Cicero's naming of his organization as "Coptic" represented an early paradigm shift in the history of Black religion in North America. It rejected derogatory interpretations of Black life and culture, opting instead for the creation of a "new earth," in which members of the Black Coptic Church reject demeaning racial categories and instead locate their true identity in their Coptic "way of life."

Chapter Two focuses on the Black Coptic community's construction of a heroic identity that seeks to jettison notions of identity and race that are tethered to anti-Blackness. Believers imagine conceptions of the Black person as rooted in the Divine. This chapter grapples with what it means for the Black Coptic Church to exist as an "earthly spiritual kingdom" in search of identity. It explores the function of language as symbol in the community vis-à-vis a weekly ritual in the community that commences with the phrase "Hail to the Queens of Ethiopia." This chapter traces the Black Coptic Church's construction of identity through "retrieval of ancient Egyptian and Ethiopian culture and heritage as symbols that point toward Blackness as [a] possibility of *otherwise*; that is, an idea of Blackness not rooted in what Calvin Warren names "ontological terror,"[67] but rather Blackness as grounded in and interpreted through a longer—read transcendental, indeed divine—history. A notable stanza in the Black Coptic Church's statement of faith reads: "We believe that we are Black Egyptians, Black Hebrews, Royal Black Jews, the Royal Black priesthood who are the descendants of the Hamitic and Shemitic bloodlines, out of Egypt, Ethiopia and Israel, the 'I Am' has made us unto our God kings, queens, and priests, and we shall reign in the kingdom of God on the earth...."[68] Making a decisive break with the majority of Black religious institutions, adherents in the Black Coptic Church are not simply known as "brother" or "sister," but rather in addition to clerical titles (i.e., minister), members are bestowed with royal titles such as Golden or Royal Princess, Prince, or Supreme or Imperial Queen. This chapter probes why and how such constructions of identity are at work in the community, as well as the utility of these titles in the construction of identity, both personally and collectively, and the relationship of these titles to the Church's soteriology.

Chapter Three deliberates the relationship between religious identity and religious practices. Moving beyond historical analysis, this chapter is attentive to how claims toward identity manifest in Black Coptic religious exercises and performances. Within this tradition, identity and culture are woven together and come to fruition, religiously, in the observances and rituals of the group, which speak to a sense of personal and communal identity. This chapter investigates how practices such as the Pentecost (the initiation or "second birth" of adherents into the BCC) and the changing of names of adherents from their given names (what the community identifies as "slave names") to "spiritual names," point to a sense of identity that rejects the notion that African-American religions are *merely* cultural productions that emerge, dialectically, out of slave religion. Instead, through the lens of the Black Coptic Church, we see that these religions appeal to a transcendental imagination of Blackness within the framework of divine origin and a liberative teleology.

Chapter Four sits at the intersection of race and gender in the BCC. The construction of a racial identity rooted in a transcendental view of Blackness, in which the joy of being Black precedes the ontological dilemma of Blackness as a cultural production of North America, is foundational in the BCC. However, a discussion of racial categories alone is insufficient to fully grasp the search for identity in the Black Coptic community. Women have played an extraordinary role in the founding and continued progress of this religious community. Like many religious groups, in fact, the community has survived because of its women. Yet, there is a paradox within this institution that leaves the status of women in the group ambivalent at best and oppressed at worst.

This chapter, drawing from interviews with women in the BCC, articulates how women in the movement understand and build upon the Church's notion of identity formation while establishing a sense of Black womanhood. I place the ethnographic material in conversation with womanist thinking to articulate how women in the Black Coptic group think about the "self" and the community of Black Coptic women in relation to a male-dominated leadership. I explore whether there are distinct ways of being Black and woman in the BCC that help us understand how the intersection of race and gender is filtered through a religious lens. Moreover, Chapter Four unsettles the notion of holistic liberation that runs through the BCC, via a focus on the location of women in the movement—a location that often checkmates the position of women to non-leadership roles. That is, the BCC's male governance renders it difficult for women in the group to achieve a status equal to men. I therefore call into question the claim of liberation theology made by the group, given the disparity of leadership so rampant in the organization.

Chapter Five interrogates the broader theme of divine Blackness. Bringing the text to its climax, this chapter opens with a summary of an interview I conducted. During this interview, a leader in the community, Priest Meshach, explained how the BCC understands "Blackness." In his definition, Priest Meshach relied on a metaphysical and mystical read of Blackness, posturing Blackness as an immaterial essence that is bequeathed to Black bodies, as in a sort of incarnation. He then referred to a scripture from the Hebrew Bible in which God is described as existing in the "thick darkness," which he names a divine Blackness. This chapter scrutinizes the relationship between divine Blackness and identity construction in the Black Coptic religion. That is, how and in what way does the turn toward the mystical (primordial Blackness) impact the understanding of identity, anthropologically and ontologically, among adherents in the Black Coptic Church? This chapter theorizes that incarnational Blackness is a central building block in the Church's understanding of Black identity and Black bodies, and in its performative imagination. In a constructive move, this chapter aims to think with the Black Coptic Church, pondering how such a theoretical and religious notion might provide new resources for thinking about Black being. To this end, I engage with thinkers such as Victor Anderson, Nahum Chandler, and Calvin Warren, and advance the claim that primordial

Blackness occasions a religious studies and theological intervention in the contemporary discussion of Afro-pessimism.

This exploration of the Black Coptic Church comes to three main conclusions. First, given the narrative and the evidence presented, I argue that the Black Coptic Church is a missing link in African-American religious studies—one that merits the attention of scholars as we seek to conceptualize a more vibrant and fuller picture of Black religious traditions in North America, especially regarding religious responses to the problem of race and identity. Second, this work enhances our understanding of Black theology as lived religion, thereby offering new perspectives on Black theology of liberation as embodied practice. The third and final conclusion of the book takes the form of a critical examination of the place of the Black Coptic Church in the modern world. I ponder to what extent the Black Coptic Church takes seriously the social context of its founding and the world in which it currently exists, and question whether a theological renewal is necessary for its longevity and sustainability. Arthur Fauset posited that non-mainstream Black church traditions would be in jeopardy as African Americans assimilated into the dominant culture, and historical progress lessened racial tensions in North America. I conclude that the BCC must respond to other, more recent theological trends that manifest as liberation motifs in order to survive. For example, while the Black Coptic Church undoubtedly embraces a theology of liberation, I argue that there is room for progressive engagement with those voices who challenge Black theology's historical focus on race, such as womanist scholars. Moreover, matters of gender imbalance, class conflict, a male dominated leadership, and a heteronormative posture run rampant in the community, and thereby fail to reflect modern liberation efforts.

At the theological center of the BCC is a spiritual striving to imagine and perform a Black identity that is of divine origin, and connected to a history of African societies, in order to inculcate pride among Black Coptic followers. What we encounter in the BCC is not an entirely new system of religiosity, but rather one that deepens our understanding of all Great Migration movements, especially those that place a significant emphasis on the question of Blackness and identity.

What follows is my attempt to engage one Black religious tradition in order to help us think about Black religions in general, from the vantage point of scholarly inquiry in conversation with people of faith. I do not aim to assess or determine the legitimacy of the Christian heritage or religiosity of the BCC. A study of this sort is often couched in a pejorative or racist read of marginal Black religious traditions. Indeed, a fixation on identifying "legitimate" religion, which is often part of a religious normative gaze that introduces binaries, such as religion and cult, as a means to categorize religions that do not fit within the matrix of dominant religious forms. Such an approach diminishes the epistemological possibilities that become available to us as we engage, in this case, religions that respond to oppressive cultures and push back against them. I seek to illustrate such a fusion of horizons through the lens of the BCC. More profoundly, however, religious movements like the BCC furthers the need for elasticity in how we think about orthodoxy and the ever-unfolding opportunities available to us as we study Black religions.

1

The Origins of a Prophet

Cicero Patterson and the Black Coptic Imagination

Imagination is a Magic carpet
Upon which we may soar
To distant lands and climes
And even go beyond the moon
To any planet in the sky
If we came from
Nowhere here
Why can't we go somewhere there?
—Sun Ra, "Imagination"

Sunday. June 2017. 11:30 a.m. Coptic Nation Temple. Chicago, Illinois. Two ministers are positioned front center of the temple. To the right of the ministers, positioned atop the church's rostrum, is a large imperial Ethiopian flag with the Lion of Judah in the center, bearing a cross and scepter, and wearing a crown upon its head.[1] The ministers, wearing black vestments, begin service with prayers for the community, followed by a responsive litany of liberation and identity. The first stanza of the litany is a recitation of the Gospel of Mathew 2:15, but with an addition of "Ethiopia" at the end of the text. The minister proclaims loudly: "Out of Egypt *and Ethiopia* have I called my son."[2] The community repeats the phrase.

The Beginnings

I traveled to Atlanta, Georgia, several times between 2013 and 2017 in search of the religious roots of the Black Coptic Church. My goal was to construct a biography of Prophet Cicero Patterson (1895–1962), who had migrated in 1948 from Atlanta to Chicago, where he organized the

Figure 1.1. Imperial Ethiopian Flag. The bars on the flag are red, green, and gold, from top to bottom.

BCC. The narratives surrounding Prophet Cicero are mostly captured in oral tradition. For most of its history, the BCC has relied heavily on oral stories related to its history, theology, beliefs, and practices. The inward-looking nature of the group allowed the Church to preserve its beliefs and performances independent of outside influence. "Prophet Cicero designed the Church as a private organization," insisted one of my informants, Empress Hatshepsut, a thirty-something-year-old woman whose parents are spiritual leaders in the Black Coptic community.[3] Like the wider Black Church in North America, the Black Coptic Church originated as a sort of invisible institution, worshiping outside the gaze of white society—yet it abandoned mainline forms of Black religion. Many Black Coptic followers appreciated a religious group that existed as a type of "brush harbor" or clandestine community.[4] Given the principally oral nature of the community's history, there is an absence of written material, internally or externally, about the internal workings and belief structure that guide Church teaching and practices. This situation has not weakened the unity of thought in the Black Coptic community. Indeed, there is a profound sense of cohesiveness among its members.

Figure 1.2. Prophet Cicero Patterson, Founder, Black Coptic Church, c. 1955.
Credit: Photo courtesy of Coptic Nation Temple Black Coptic Church.

Still, my purpose in traveling to Atlanta was to investigate the genesis of the BCC by uncovering the religious and social life of its Prophet, Louis Cicero Patterson, through engagement with outside sources.

Prophet Cicero's backstory is shrouded in mystery and legend among Black Coptic believers, which contributes to the community's perception of him as an enigmatic character. Yet there are a few known details about his past that offer insight into the founding of the community. One such detail is the historical context, in which we situate Prophet Cicero alongside other emergent Black religious leaders such as Nation of Islam (NOI) founder Elijah Muhammad (1897–1975), and founder of the Moorish Science Temple of America (MST) Noble Drew Ali (1886–1929). These men were grappling with similar questions related to race, religion, and the construction of identity as a response to the rejection of "negro." We see that Prophet Cicero was indeed a man of his times, a religio-race-man, who organized a religious community which, in his Black radical imagination, offered a path toward the destruction of the negro and the construction of a new Black being postured toward the divine. Placing him and the movement he created in this context allows for an examination of the Black Coptic Church as an imaginative religious institution.

Among Black Coptic believers, Prophet Cicero is also recognized by his spiritual name, "Melchizedek." His spiritual name relates to an important narrative that is upheld within the Black Coptic community. Melchizedek, who appears in both the Hebrew Bible and the New Testament, is variously considered as an earthly messiah and a priestly messiah in Second Temple literature. In the New Testament book of Hebrews, the author writes, "Without father, without mother, without genealogy, having neither beginning of days nor end of life, but resembling the Son of God, he remains a priest forever."[5] Black Coptic believers imagine a spiritual relationship between their Prophet, as Melchizedek, and this biblically important figure. This imaginative relationship is deeply significant among believers. Queen Maryann, an early disciple and student of Prophet Cicero, said that

> to us, Prophet Cicero was the Melchizedek king in the flesh. He came to us without mother or father, no one knows where he came from or who his parents were. He came to us as our prophet, and like Melchizedek in

scripture, he is a christ for us. That's why, after he performed so many miracles, we called him Melchizedek and Black Jesus.⁶

Queen Maryann's description reflects the fact that, for Black Coptic believers, Prophet Cicero was deeply enigmatic. Indeed, the oral tradition of the community portrays him as a mysterious character who unassumingly "appeared" on the scene. Beyond anecdotal stories, Black Coptic followers are largely unaware of Prophet Cicero's biography. The lack of genealogical information available to the Black Coptic community, however, is not distressing for members, but rather deepens their reverence for Prophet Cicero as a divinely appointed agent. What matters, for the community, is that Prophet Cicero was a representation of Christ who accomplished a salvific work in their individual and collective lives. This grand narrative about Prophet Cicero—as Melchizedek—links Black Coptic believers to similar groups such as the Rastafari of Jamaica, who treated Melchizedek as the root of a divine lineage that includes Jesus and Emperor Haile Selassie. Indeed, said Queen Huldah, "Prophet Melchizedek for us was a representation of Christ. When we speak about Black Jesus we are not just talking about the historical Jesus. We are talking about the Prophet who came our way as a savior. He represented the highest ideal of the Christ mind that we should all strive for."⁷ Until this writing, many details of Prophet Cicero's past were unknown among the Black Coptic community.

Louis Cicero Patterson was the sixth child born to Primus and Claudia Patterson in Orangeburg, South Carolina, in 1895.⁸ His father was a farm laborer and his mother a homemaker. In 1917, during World War I, while working as a barber in Orangeburg, he registered for and served a short stint in the military, serving as an assistant to the quartermaster in the 436th Reserve Labor Unit, a Black soldiers' unit.⁹ In the same year, Patterson married Maggie Franklin and together they had one child, Helen Patterson (1917–1973).¹⁰ By 1920, shortly after the war, Louis and Maggie had settled in Cincinnati, Ohio, where they dwelled for the next two decades. It is during this period that Patterson, who in 1941 identified as a "traveling evangelist," likely encountered Black Spiritualists and developed a religious and theological imagination that focused on faith healing, prophesy, and combatting racism. Indeed, Black Spiritualists had a robust operation throughout Ohio during this period. By the mid

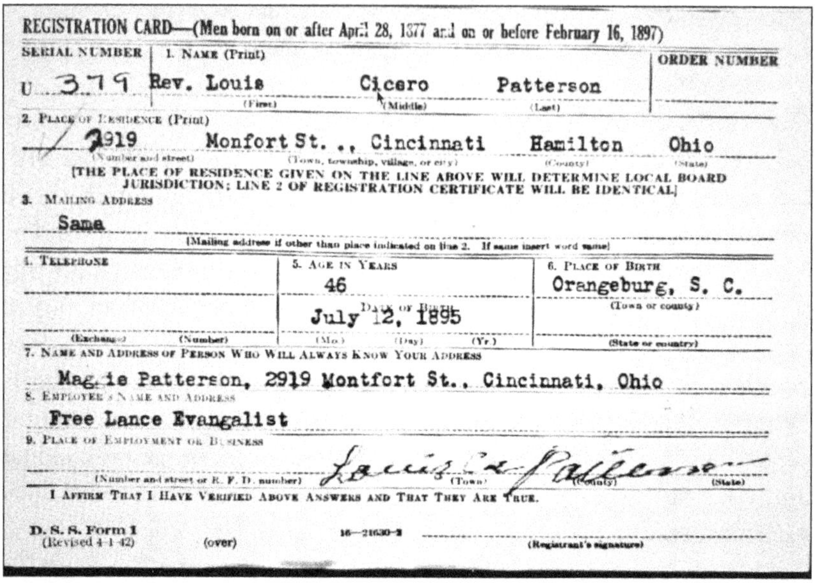

Figure 1.3. Louis Cicero Patterson's World War II Military Draft Card, 1942. Credit: United States Census, National Archives and Records Administration.

1940's, Patterson had settled in Atlanta, Georgia, where he organized his first religious group as a "spiritualist" community that practiced at the Universal House of Prayer and Training School (UHPTS). It is also during this period that he adopted the title of "Prophet." While there is little information about Prophet Cicero's time in Atlanta, there are still several active members of the BCC who were part of Prophet Cicero's early ministry, and who help maintain that primitive religious society's oral history.

The scarcity of written sources within the BCC is touted as a way of keeping the Church as a "spiritual tradition." For believers, the notion of a "spiritual tradition" signals that "God is not found in a book," [and] "everything that was given to [the Black Coptic Church] was given directly by God."[11] The oral tradition is not merely part of the Church's mystical dimension, but it is also a part of the spiritual allure of the group. Followers have relied on an oral tradition for the re-telling of histories and stories, not only about theology and rituals, but also about Prophet Cicero.

As the story goes, Prophet Cicero "was a missionary in Atlanta. While there, he had people who joined his bible class, but he had not yet established a church."[12] For decades, the oral history of the BCC has maintained, without written evidence, that Prophet Cicero's missionary efforts in Atlanta were not long-lived due to a confrontation with law enforcement. The Church maintains that Prophet Cicero's teachings, specifically his theology of Black Jesus—like the theology of figures such as African Methodist Episcopal (AME) Bishop Henry McNeil Turner (1834–1915), who declared "God is a Negro"[13]—were, in the words of Queen Maryann, "not well accepted by white law officials." Queen Maryann further contends that "Prophet Cicero was targeted because they said he was practicing medicine without a license."[14] Indeed, the BCC, like other religious communities with a Spiritualist past, accepted conventional medical intervention while also sustaining a deep reverence for faith healing as accomplished through the laying on of hands by their prophets and queens. Moreover, surveillance of Black religious and civil rights leaders was not uncommon, but rather part and parcel of American history. FBI surveillance of Martin Luther King, Elijah Muhammad, and Malcolm X, among others, was part of a larger reconnaissance operation against leaders of so-called subversive and fringe groups. Queen Maryann relates that Prophet Cicero, following his legal complications, left Atlanta without a proper departure from the Universal House of Prayer and Training School, leaving the community he founded in a fledgling state. In 1948, he relocated his ministry to Chicago. He established the first Black Coptic Church, called the Universal Prayer House and Training School (UPHTS, not to be confused with Atlanta's Universal House of Prayer and Training School), at 4724 South Cottage Grove Avenue[15]—the new site where he would perform his religious imagination.

"He Healed Me"

I arrived at the Universal House of Prayer and Training School (UHPTS) on Rankin Street in Northeast Atlanta for an 11:30 a.m. service on a hot summer day in August 2017. I knew from prior conversations with Black Coptic followers that Prophet Cicero's religious and spiritual strivings first took form as an organization in Atlanta. Given that sixty years had elapsed, I had little hope there would be anyone left in the Atlanta congregation who had had direct interaction with Prophet Cicero.

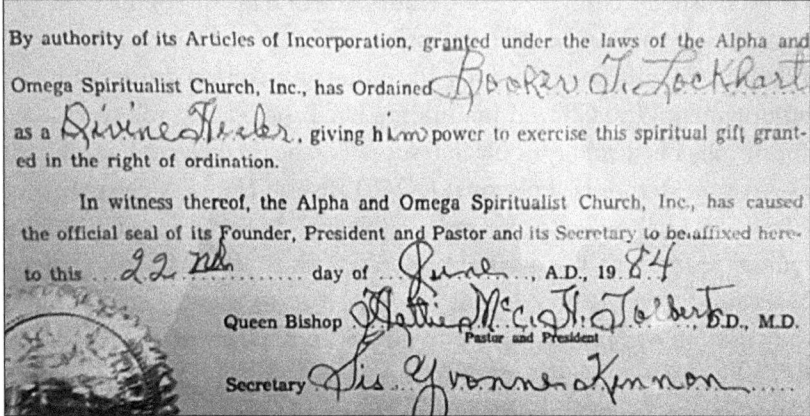

Figure 1.4. Ordination certificate of Bishop Booker Lockhart, Pastor of Universal House of Prayer and Training School, Atlanta, GA, 2001–2020. Credit: Author's picture, Booker T. Lockhart, Universal House of Prayer and Training School.

At the UHPTS, I encountered a small community of roughly forty-five believers who identified as a "spiritualist" community, although their religious ancestry is traceable to Prophet Cicero and they maintained many of his teachings. I obtained two documents at the UHPTS that shed significant light on the religious heritage of the BCC. One of these documents, a small pamphlet on the church's history, indicated that "Rev. L.C. Patterson founded the Universal House of Prayer and Training School spiritualist church in 1948."[16] The other was an ordination certificate of the current pastor, which strengthened the "spiritualist" connection to the UHPTS, stating that he was consecrated at the "Alpha and Omega Spiritualist Church, Inc.," under the authority of "Queen Bishop Hattie Tolbert" (1919–2001), whose death notice in the *Atlanta Constitution* noted that, when "Queen Bishop Hattie Tolbert held your hand, she was not only greeting you, she was looking into your soul."[17] Both the title of "Queen" and the suggestion that when Queen Tolbert held your hand she was looking into your soul are reminiscent of the religious ethos of the BCC. This is significant. These details help to illuminate the religious past of Prophet Cicero and provide key context for his eventual theology and the practices of the BCC. Through these documents, the roots of the BCC are traceable to the Black spiritualist movement.

This designation of "spiritualist" offers significant clues into the origins of Prophet Cicero's religious views, as well as the ecclesiastical structure and religious practices of the BCC, including the assumption of royal titles by members, belief in faith healing, and the embrace of Ethiopianism. Indeed, as anthropologist Hans Baer has documented, some spiritualist churches regularly employed royal titles among their members, a practice which, in turn, became the bedrock of the alternative religious movement founded by Prophet Cicero. To be sure, states Baer, ". . . since Spiritual churches are generally regarded as being among the lowest echelons of Black religious organizations, it is interesting to note that some of them attempt to compensate for their marginal status by creating quasi-royal positions, such as King, Queen, Prince, and Princess. The leader of one of these groups is no longer an ordinary person but a 'Royal Elect Ruler' . . . or perhaps even a god or goddess of a new age."[18] The royal court of the Spiritualist movement would eventually inform the ecclesial structure of the BCC.

I entered the UPHTS that Sunday morning in August and immediately took note of a picture on a wall in the center of the church. The person in the photo, whom I later learned to be Queen Bishop Veronia Walton (d. 2012), was an early follower of and successor to Prophet Cicero. The photo struck me as significant because Walton's religious garb, although not an exact replica, was reminiscent of that worn by Black Coptic members in Chicago. In other words, the connection was evident. After the service, I asked the pastor if I could talk to him about the church's history, to which he agreed. When I asked about Prophet Cicero Patterson, an elderly woman seated nearby glanced up and shouted, "He healed me!" Her response supported the oral history of the BCC relating to Prophet Cicero's departure from Atlanta, which narrates that it was related to his performance of faith healing—a common, and very significant, practice among Spiritualist churches. For believers, this narrative surrounding Prophet Cicero's departure from Atlanta cements their belief that he was a divinely ordained Prophet. While I had known about Prophet Cicero's Atlanta experience and his departure only from the oral narratives of the BCC, those narratives align remarkably well with the written sources, most notably information gathered from *The Atlanta Constitution*, internal documents available at the UHPTS, and census records. And now they had aligned with an oral account from an elderly UHPTS member.

"Prophet Charged with Swindle"

When detectives arrived at the "spiritualist hall" of Prophet L. C. Patterson, located at 173 Pine Street St., N.E., in Atlanta, "they found Dr. Cicero, a Negro, examining a woman...."[19] Police, suspicious of Rev. Dr. Cicero's practices, reported to have found "an impressive array of patent medicines, herb preparations, jugs of apple cider, sherry wine, household ammonia, sarsaparilla and the like."[20] Allegedly, several of Prophet Cicero's "patients" complained of abdominal pains. Following a perusal of Prophet Cicero's ledger of clients, police contended that he was collecting as much as $1,000 weekly from Negro patients by soaking off the labels from medicine bottles and giving them out as prescriptions. In some instances, detectives said, "he mixed medicines together."[21] This practice of using things of nature, including roots and herbs, as medicine was a form of medical intervention among enslaved Blacks and also Blacks in a post-slavery world. To be sure, suspicions about medical doctors—combined with the lack of resources to obtain medical assistance—led to various healing practices. Prophet Cicero was therefore not unique in his usage of herbs and roots; on the contrary, as religious studies scholar Yvonne Chireau writes, "sources from the late nineteenth and early twentieth centuries show a convergence of spiritual beliefs, supernatural traditions, and practices techniques in black healing practices."[22] Moreover, white fear of those who practiced faith healing or conjuring was not uncommon, as whites feared the ability of these "doctors" to use their conjuring powers against them.

At his hearing, Prophet Cicero wore a black frock coat with tails. He was charged with swindle—for "practicing medicine without a license and cheating ... ,"[23] a statement that supports the Church's oral history surrounding his initial time in Atlanta and misfortune with law enforcement. Cicero responded that he was a "faith healer" who had been trained as a minister for 27 years, and in his statement to the court "quoted passages from the Bible to show power was given to the Disciples of Christ to cast out evil spirits." He posted his $500 bond immediately.[24] The archives confirm other narratives regarding Prophet

Cicero as one who accepted "clients" on whom to perform his faith healing practice. In fact, one of my informants, Mother Queen Rebekah who converted to the BCC after an alleged long illness and hospitalization, reports to have been visited by a man in a dream. When she awoke, she was led to the UHPTS, where she encountered Prophet Cicero, whom she recognized as the man from her dream. Mother Rebekah reports that he told her, "I am Moses and I have been waiting for you."[25] Her characterization of this encounter as part of her conversion is common among early BCC devotees.

Although Black Coptic devotees do not have access to their history via written sources, their stories' alignment with archival evidence is striking. Documents confirm the travails of their prophet in his religious quest. But more than this, Prophet Cicero's arrest—and what Black Copts would later identify as his religious persecution—supports the notion among Black Coptic believers that Prophet Cicero was not simply a religious leader among other religious leaders. Indeed, they perceived him as a messianic figure whose mission was to employ religion as the conduit through which Black Copts would come to understand their salvation and recover their true divine identity, which could only be revealed by a prophet.

Messianic typology is not foreign to the Spiritualist world. It is an important motif that contributes to the framing of several religious groups, including the BCC. As with other messianic sects, Prophet Cicero's group developed nationalistic features, and harnessed an idea of Black life as rooted in a superior past, a past that needed to be recovered. Indeed, such groups represent a "religious counterhegemonic tradition that rejects the label Negro as a white invention and seeks to replace it with a more satisfying self-definition based on a belief in the unparalleled spiritual and historical significance of African Americans."[26] In the world of Black Copts, Prophet Cicero's function was to save Black people from the invented construction of the negro. As a savior-type prophet, Prophet Cicero was revered as a representation of Christ who possessed the ability to perform supernaturally. For believer Priest Gehazi, who joined the BCC as a child following the conversion of his mother, "there is a definitely a commonality between the thoughts and life and works of the Christ in the New Testament and the life and works of [Prophet Cicero]. When I think of Jesus, I think of him as a teacher and one who is able to demonstrate divine works. I see the commonalities with Prophet Cicero."[27] Similarly, Queen Magdalene, a woman in her early fifties who is a spiritual teacher in the BCC, and who became a member as a child after her mother moved the family from California to Chicago and was introduced to the community by a neighbor, relates:

> The lives parallel for me. You may not be able to find a relationship with Jesus in the [Bible] because it's not personal, you do not have a direct connection. But with the teachings of Prophet Cicero, I can see myself, I can be a part of this story, I can participate, I can explore, and I can live. So, Prophet [Cicero] was the manifestation of the Christ consciousness.[28]

For Black Coptic disciples, however, the central focus in his messianic function was to deliver and liberate Black folk in America. Like other Black Spiritualist leaders who occupied a space in the messianic-savior typology, Prophet Cicero is deemed by Black Coptic followers to have been "sent by God on a divine mission to save [Black people]. He was God's mouthpiece."[29] Envisioning their Prophet as one cloaked in a cryptic and lavish history, chosen by God, and without a known ancestry, contributes to an unstated imagination and performance in the BCC: Prophet Cicero is another "Black God of the Metropolis."[30] Significantly, it was in the Black metropolis of Chicago that Prophet Cicero's function as a messianic figure would come to fruition and where he initiated his new religious movement; a religious movement that saw Ethiopia as a homeland.

Out of Egypt and Ethiopia: A Homeland Imagined

The opening vignette of this chapter, one in which prayers are followed by a scriptural recitation that grounds the BCC in Egyptian and Ethiopian heritages, is a ritualistic performance in which Black Coptic believers imaginatively place themselves within a biblical arc of history, in which Ethiopia is their homeland. Such performance forms the foundation of their religious life, part of a more general quest to uncover their identity. To be sure, since their first arrival and enslavement, Black people have wrestled with their identity and their place in a world that denied their being. W.E.B. DuBois' postulation of a double-consciousness captures the paradoxical nature of Black folk's nonexistence in America: the transition from involuntary displacement [slave] to a citizen outsider.[31] For DuBois:

> It is a peculiar sensation, this double-consciousness, this sense of always looking at one's self though the eyes of others, of measuring one's soul by the tape of a world that looks on in amused contempt and pity. One ever feels his two-ness,—an American, a Negro; two souls, two thoughts, two unreconciled strivings; two warring ideals in one dark body, whose dogged strength alone keeps it from being torn asunder.
>
> The history of the America Negro is the history of this strife—this longing to attain self-conscious manhood, to merge his double self into a better and truer self. In this merging, he wishes neither of the older selves to be lost. He does not wish to Africanize America, for America has too much to teach the world and Africa. He wouldn't bleach his Negro soul in a flood of white Americanisms, for he knows that Negro blood has a message for the world. He simply wishes to make it possible for a man to be both a Negro and an American, without being cursed and spit upon by his fellows, without having the doors of opportunity closed roughly in his face.[32]

This peculiar condition of locating and building identity within the context of an exilic experience—that is, away from one's home—lends itself to an understanding of what Cornel West describes as African Americans in conflict, especially in an America seeking to define herself in the shadow of European culture.[33] Such struggle presents itself in the process of negotiating space and place in an oppositional culture that deems Black bodies as the theological and ontological other. The early Black struggle for identity, then, was exaggerated on three fronts: (1) European and American culture were not necessarily secure in and of themselves as they traversed *modernity, colonial provinciality, and localism*; (2) the situation for American Africans was made worse by the fact that, in both locations, their identity was not forged within the culture, on the one hand, and, not accepted on the other; and (3) on the European front, the Cartesian turn toward the self as a thinking and rational subject was not applied to Africans, as their reason was not understood as equal or even modern. The worth of Black people, therefore, was not attached to intellectual achievement, but rather to labor and toil.[34]

What might it mean, in this context, to search for Black identity and employ religion as the vehicle by which to do so? In his religious imagination, one rooted in Ethiopianism and a geographical turn away from the West, Prophet Cicero implemented religious practices and observances that provide one approach to the question. His answer is not without its complexities, and it is certainly not my intention to make an essentialist claim about the nature of Black religions. Rather, I argue, given the proximity of Black people to various oppressions and a historic loss of identity resultant from chattel slavery and its aftermath, Black religions are indebted to the religious movements of resistance that manifested among enslaved Africans as they dreamt of other worlds, while also wrestling with their status as non-humans who lacked souls and whose bodies were not redeemable. In this, the religious imaginations that developed on North American slave plantations are as much about constructing and reconstructing identity as they are about cultivating a sense of the divine. Indeed, in the world of enslaved Africans, the so-called sacred and profane collided such that both became a focus of their theological and spiritual undertakings. The search for identity, then, has persistently been part and parcel of Black religious imaginations.

What we glean from this history is a tragic reality for Black life in America, or what historian and philosopher Eddie Glaude describes as "a preoccupation with identity formation among African Americans . . . amid the absurdity of a nation committed, at once, to freedom and unfreedom."[35] This dichotomy has complicated the search by Black folk in America for the meaning of their being and their disposition in the world. From the period of enslavement through the rise of the Great Migration's new religious movements, the process of re-constructing identity was an ongoing endeavor. And still, "questions of Black identity remain. How should African Americans understand themselves as individuals and as a group in relation to a nation that historically denied them recognition?"[36] Great Migration new religious movements—including the Black Coptic Church—utilized various methods and approaches toward the re-construction of Black identity, including cultural syncretism and religious imaginations. Black new religious movements, then, illustrate a deep desire of Black folk to wrestle with the existential absurdity, loss of identity, and religious isolationism experienced in white Christianity and mainstream forms of Black religion.

The Religio-Racial World of Prophet Cicero Patterson: Religions in the Black Metropolis

The Great Migration was a momentous era in Black religions and the construction/re-construction of Black identity. Not only do we see the growing religious commitments of Blacks who migrate, but also the sundry ways in which the search for identity emerges, as Black people, in their desire to claim a space within urban centers, are confronted with racial challenges that signal the need for organic Black centers. The movement North opened great possibilities for religious ingenuity. Judith Weisenfeld notes that, "no longer bound by the traditions of small community life and often feeling that Protestant churches had failed to address their material needs and spiritual longings, many migrants set aside long-standing ways of thinking about black identity, claiming different histories and imagining new futures."[37]

Chicago was well-established as a religious "mecca for African Americans ... before World War I." As Milton Sernett observes, "The Great Migration afforded [the established churches] a challenge and an opportunity," as more Blacks flooded the city, particularly the South Side, in search of community and social engagement. Sernett nonetheless seems suspicious of an over-emphasis on religious movements like the BCC, arguing,

> The diversification of religious institutions among African Americans was a significant feature of the northern urbanization process. This fact alone suggests that African American religious history must be read differently because of the Great Migration. No implication is suggested that established denominations were displaced by so-called cults and sects that appeared in northern cities between the two world wars, though scholarly fascination with the religious exotic might make it appear so. The essential story in Chicago is not the multiplication of religious groups on the margins of Christian orthodoxy, but the growth and transformation of the mainline Protestant traditions.[38]

Sernett's summary reads as paternalistic. His classification of new religious movements as "exotic" and on "the margins of Christian orthodoxy" seems to minimize the value of a serious investigation into these religious movements and how they might provoke necessary questions and a critique of purported religious orthodoxy. Further, Sernett's contemptuous approach to Great Migration new religious movements assumes an orthodoxy largely indebted to the West and fails to take seriously the critique these groups advance concerning assumed orthodoxies. Stated differently, for many believers in new religious movements, mainline Christian faith failed to viably address the social dilemma of Blacks in the urban north. Religion, for these converts, was the vehicle through which they had access to a higher sense of self and the collective, in ways they apprehended established religion unable to provide. While the broader cultural *geist* of this period seemed to flourish within the Black arts movement—the Harlem Renaissance—a similar cultural revival and construction bourgeoned within Black religions, such that "the racial and ethnic pride demonstrated in the literature and arts of the period was matched by the proliferation of creative expressions within black NRM's."[39] Chicago was the epicenter of such inventions.

By the time Prophet Cicero arrived in Chicago in 1948, he identified religiously as "Coptic," and would proceed to build his new religious movement as a Black Coptic organization with Spiritualist as well as more complex syncretistic roots that became evident in both style of worship and, more important to our consideration, vernacular employed in the process of constructing Black identity. At 47th Street and Cottage Grove Avenue in Black Bronzeville, in the middle of the Black Metropolis, there co-existed an array of Black religions among which Prophet Cicero organized the BCC. It is befitting that Prophet Cicero would choose Bronzeville as the site for his experiment in Black religion. To be sure, Chicago is a unique space in the study of Black religious life and culture. From gospel music to a unique style of Black soulful preaching, to an array of Black religious imaginations, Chicago has been home to a broad and diverse geography of Black religions.[40] Bronzeville, that cultural hub and beehive of Black imaginations, was the focal point of Black culture, Black arts, and Black religions. There, on the South Side of Chicago, it existed as a cultural womb for the Black radical imagination; an imagination that dreamed and performed *otherwise* possibilities of Blackness. Indeed, as prominent sociologists of Black life and culture Sinclair Drake and Horace Clayton note, "one of the most striking features of the area is the prevalence of churches, numbering some

500. Many of these edifies still bear the marks of previous ownership—six-pointed Stars of David, Hebrew and Swedish inscriptions, or names chiseled on old cornerstones that do not tally with those on new bulletin boards."[41] A Black spirit of innovation and curiosity was as commonplace in Chicago as it was in Harlem Renaissance New York. Religion, in summation, was not untouched by this cultural reclamation, but rather was a vital aspect of the performance of the Black radical imagination.

The assortment of mostly storefront churches and diverse religious communities in Bronzeville during the Great Migration were not merely places of spiritual instruction, but rather also institutions of social change and racial uplift. Leaders in Bronzeville, including its ministers, were "constantly urging the community to raise its sights above 'survival,' enjoying life, and 'praising the Lord.' They presented getting ahead as a *racial* duty as well as a personal gain."[42] In other words, the spirit of Bronzeville was manifested in a performance of advancing the race via a multiplicity of vehicles, including education, business, social groups, and religion. Religion, then, "should be understood only by relating it to the economic and social status of the groups in Bronzeville."[43] It is here, in Black Bronzeville, where the radical Black imagination came to fruition in the religious thought of Prophet Cicero Patterson.

Situating the Black Coptic Church in African American Religions

Prophet Cicero's designation of his movement as "Coptic" typified a paradigmatic shift that manifested among new Black religions within this period. Indeed, as Arthur Fauset maintains,

> The desire for freer self-expression than was possible in the prevailing white churches, plus an insistence on the part of certain Negroes, especially in the North, that the Christian philosophy of the universal brotherhood of man [sic] must include Negroes, did much to foster the separation which began to develop between white and Negro worshipers.[44]

Moreover, in "northern centers, Negroes fought vigorously against segregation in church edifices and against other forms of racial discrimination."[45] Consequently, Black religious institutions seeking to make a correlation between religious identity and the longing for Black emancipation was a familiar occurrence in 1940's Chicago. In naming his organization as Coptic, Prophet Cicero recovered a religious philosophy that he likely gleaned from his Black Spiritualist past, which held that Coptic is the oldest religion of Black people. Queen Maryann stated that Prophet Cicero's decision to identify his organization as Coptic was not intended to isolate this community from the larger black church community, per se. On the contrary, Prophet Cicero's pronouncement of a Coptic community was precisely to inculcate an identity in a people whose heritage and culture had been stripped from them by a world that deemed them inferior.[46]

As we have seen, among Black Coptic believers, "Coptic" communicates the radical imagination of a movement that sought to resurrect a perceived ancient heritage of Black persons through the construction of a "relationship between North American Blacks and the oldest Christian community," which the community understands, "diasporically, as a Black community."[47] It also illustrates the persistent struggle of Black people in this period to negotiate notions of citizenship and allegiance to a society in which their identity was tied to a history of anti-Black violence. For Prophet Jacob, a spiritual leader in the BCC, the Church reconnected Black people with "their true identity and homeland."[48] Prophet Jacob's emphasis on identity and homeland offers both a critique of North American culture and a construction of *otherwise* possibilities that extend outside the invisible barriers of Black life within the context of the absurd. Imagination, in this sense of "returning home" to Ethiopia, compels a fugitive discourse of crossing boundaries, imagining beyond "what is" toward "what is possible." Moreover, given the BCC's focus on disconnectedness—from their original homeland, resultant from the slave trade, and in its legacy in North America—the posture toward Ethiopia (home) signals an act of retrieval. For Queen Huldah, "bringing Ethiopia to us shows the attempt of our founder to reconnect us to an ancient heritage of ancient Egypt, in which black life, black culture, and black religion flourished and were celebrated."[49] "Coptic", then, within the religious imagination of believers, generates a cultural, psychological, and religious yoke between the progeny of North American enslaved Africans and ancient Egyptian kings and queens, and Ethiopians.[50]

An imagination of Blackness *otherwise* is at the heart of the BCC. More broadly, however, a radical performative imagination in African

American religious traditions expands what we understand about religious imagination. While religious imagination relates to the phenomenology of religion or how individuals and groups construct an idea of an unseen world occupied by divine and other disembodied beings, in African American religions we encounter a sense of the imagination that moves beyond contemplations of non-corporeal beings and the immaterial world. Their radical performative imagination encompasses the totality of the Black sacred cosmos; that is, it does not disregard the material world via privileging reflections on that which is immaterial. A radical Black performative imagination operates at the intersection of the *kairos* and *kronos*. The material world is as revered as that which is unseen, thereby adjudicating Black life and Black bodies as sacred and divine. At its core, "the black sacred cosmos permeated all of the social institutions and cultural traditions of black people. . . . The black sacred cosmos also reflects the deepest values of African Americans, giving primal consideration to the necessity of freedom as an expression of complete belonging and allegiance to God."[51] In this sense, the notion of freedom was anti-gnostic and therefore not divorced from bodily freedom and bodily reclamation. The radical imagination in Black religions, then, commences with the posture—Black life is sacred—and performs this imagination theologically, ritually, and communally. At its core, the function of imagination in Black religions is to envision and perform *otherwise* possibilities that disprove the absurd. We see this within the Black Coptic setting as believers look toward Ethiopia for their salvation.

The Black Coptic Church's religious imagination, steeped in Ethiopianism, accentuates but one effort of Black religions in Black Bronzeville to abandon philosophies of race that were destructive to Black people, and appeal to an *otherwise* possibility. As we have seen, the rejection of negro in the BCC was similar to that of peer groups, who refuted the negro identity because they understood "Negro identity as an oppressive white creation and the substitution of a new ethnic identity predicated on the belief in the unique spiritual importance of Black people."[52] Members of this religious group perform the intersection of race, religion, and identity in their unbashful elevation of Ethiopia as God's chosen land and the geography within which one can locate God's chosen people. The beginning of a BCC religious service is replete with Ethiopian symbolism and a vocal declaration of the Psalm's edification of the Princes of Ethiopia. From the Ethiopian flag to the to the verbal declaration of the African country, the radical religious imagination at work within the BCC comes alive as representative of the portal to an *otherwise* reality.

Ethiopia, our Home: The Black Coptic Church, a Geographical Turn, and the Recovery of Identity

For members of the Black Coptic Church the quest for identity and heritage began with an inverted normative gaze toward Africa; one that centered Blackness as the epitome of that which is true and that which is beautiful. Certainly, "as the hostile racial and political climate of post-reconstruction America questioned the ability of the race to survive outside the bonds of slavery, African Americans countered this dominant ideology by embracing identities that they found empowering and instilled hope. For some, this inspiration came from within mainstream religions such as Christianity or Islam. For others, new religious movements spoke most clearly to their present situation."[53]

As the search for identity gained traction among Black religious communities, Ethiopianism also increased in prominence within the religious imagination of Black folk, including that of some Black Spiritualists. Indeed, more than any other Biblical country, Ethiopia stands tall in the imagination of Black religions. "Ideologies of Ethiopianism," notes literary scholar Nadia Nurhussein, "were cultivated around Psalm 68:31 . . . , based on the premise that a time would come when the black race would rise up as prophesied in Africa."[54] Ethiopia symbolizes the possibility of *otherwise*; that is, performing freedom within the absurdity of various forms of oppressions. Moreover, Ethiopia, for religious and non-religious groups that oriented themselves toward that African country, inculcated a sense of the Black self that was free and able to withstand the horrors of white supremacy and colonialism. In short, Ethiopia represented the shining city on the hill. As historian Robin G. Kelley notes in his *Freedom Dreams*:

> Most black people believed there was an order higher than the Constitution. Psalm 68, verse 31 of the Bible had promised redemption for the black world: "Princes come out of Egypt. Ethiopia stretches forth her hands unto God." This passage was as important to Pan Africanist and

emigration sentiments as the book of Exodus, and became the theological basis for what became known in the nineteenth century as Ethiopianism. Ethiopianism spread though the black world, from the Americas to Africa, calling for the redemption of Africa by any means necessary.[55]

Ethiopia, therefore, allowed Black folk to dream and imagine other worlds, other futures, and a transformed present. Still, it is important to bear in mind that Ethiopianism in the nineteenth century was not only about making a transatlantic migration back to Africa, although this was certainly the sentiment of some actors in this period. As impractical and unrealistic as a mass movement back to Africa may appear, there is an important point to be gleaned: "the desire to leave Babylon, if you will, and search for new lands tells us a great deal about what people dream about, what they want, how they might want to reconstruct their lives."[56] The turn toward Ethiopia lays bare the radical and often gut-wrenching tension of Black folk hoping and dreaming of a world where "we would all be free." The opening vignette showcases a performance of Black religious folk dreaming about freedom and performing *otherwise*.

The Ethiopian turn in the BCC did not become manifest in a vacuum, apart from a broader cultural turn. Rather, for many of the new religions within this period, identity construction was grounded on an imagined homeland. The embrace of an imagined homeland in the process of identity formation introduces the performance of *otherwise* identities, insofar as imagination makes a radical break with temporal limitation. Indeed, imagination engages with the infinite, the boundaryless horizon of human and divine endeavor. Performative imagination, in this sense, renders the conditions of possibility for identities *otherwise* to emerge. As such, *otherwise* identities are the organic productions of radical imaginations that refuse to yield their being and humanity to oppressive structures, be they religious or *otherwise*, that envision and perform the non-being of Black life.

Ethiopia became a cornerstone of the Church's theology and religious performances, but we don't know where Prophet Cicero first encountered Ethiopianism. The evidence, however, especially his involvement with Black Spiritualists as well as his adoption of Coptic as the religious identification of his new religious movement, suggests that he was impacted by a brand of Spiritualism propagated by Prophet George Hurley

(1884–1843). Hurley, founder of the Universal Hagar's Spiritual Church and a proponent of Ethiopianism, opened at least eight Spiritualist churches throughout Ohio during the time that Prophet Cicero was there and claimed to have been trained as a minister.[57] Father Hurley also asserted that he had founded the largest "School of Wisdom" in the world, which became the name of the teaching arm of the BCC. As Prophet Cicero settled in Chicago, he founded his second religious community, the Universal Prayer House and Training School, which claimed Coptic as its religious and spiritual tradition, while emphasizing Ethiopia as significant to his brand of religious performance.

Prophet Cicero's performance of Ethiopianism was an approach that comprised both a longing to retrieve an august view of Blackness, and to salvage what was, in his religious imagination, the original and oldest religion of the Ethiopian (Black) people. As stated, Cicero was likely inspired by Prophet Hurley, whose teachings, in part, were strikingly similar to those of Marcus Garvey; he taught that Ethiopians were the oldest people in the world and were thereby God's chosen people. For Hurley, not only was Ethiopia the cradle of civilization, but "the first religion was the Coptic Ethiopian religion." Hurley further argued, although misnaming patriarchs, that "all the Old Testament patriarchs—including Adam, Abraham, Moses, Solomon, and Daniel . . . were Ethiopians."[58] He concluded that "White people organized their church, the Catholic Church, upon what they mistakenly believed were the principles of the 'old Coptic spiritual church.'"[59] Prophet Cicero, posturing toward Ethiopia and equipped with his Spiritualist past, cemented his search for identity and a homeland in the rituals and performances of his new religious movement.

The prevalence of Ethiopian symbols within the BCC conveys the radical imagination at work within the institution that is aimed toward the construction of Black identity. As articulated earlier, this radical imagination is evident in the BCC's Statement of the Faith, which says that followers are members of a royal Ethiopian community. Akin to similar religious movements, especially those examined by Judith Weisenfeld which, as she notes, "participated in a shared discourse with many black Christians that linked racial identity and spiritual destiny to their homeland," Black Coptic followers' turn to Ethiopia was a way of building a bridge to an imagined past in part to construct a salvation narrative. Accordingly, Ethiopian narratives "provided different answers than those black Christians offered to the question of Africa's place in individual and collective identity, rejecting the focus on Christian redemption."[60] Therefore, "like most other 'imagined communities' . . . [these groups] invented their identities from a host of ideational rhizomes. . . ."[61] The BCC, subsequently, belongs to a category of Black religious traditions that not only formed imagined communities, but perform what I referred to earlier as assembled heroic identities. For the BCC, radical imagination is best seen in the Church's identification as "Coptic," with Ethiopia as the imagined homeland.

Queen Huldah, for instance, who relocated to Chicago from New York after having been exposed to and active in the UNIA under Marcus Garvey, joined the BCC because she "witnessed black people who were unashamedly black while claiming, 'we are Ethiopians!'"[62] For Queen Huldah, the connection to Ethiopia was a repudiation of the treatment of Black people in North America. When she declared her Ethiopian heritage, it afforded her a "sense of pride and a national heritage older than the American experiment in human exploitation and bondage."[63] Blackness *otherwise* is grounded in a national heritage that, for Priest Gehazi, allowed members of the BCC "to sing the Lord's song in a strange land."[64]

Ethiopianism as Fugitive

Prophet Cicero's identification as a Black Coptic and Ethiopian performs a fugitive function in the process of identity retrieval and reconstruction. I employ "fugitive" here in the tradition of cultural theorist and Black study scholar Fred Moten. For Moten, "Fugitivity . . . is desire for and a spirit of escape and transgression of the proper and the proposed. It's a desire for the outside, for a playing or being outside, an outlaw edge proper to the now always already improper voice or instrument."[65] As fugitive, the formation of an imagined homeland in the BCC seeks to de-stabilize notions of citizenship and national (State) allegiance. For members of the BCC, "to the dominant religious and cultural forms in North America, black people have always been, in the words of Ralph Ellison, invisible people. We are here but are not granted full citizenship because of America's racial understanding."[66] In other words, as we have seen, parishioners in the BCC understand themselves, and Black people in North America more broadly, as existing on the boundaries of North American society. To be Black is to be valued merely for one's contribution of labor to the State. Yet, members of the commune do not acquiesce to this production of Blackness. Rather, the radical imagination at work in the BCC is a fugitive one, whereby followers of the group see themselves as citizens of an invented nation within North America. Empress Hatshepsut, who was born into the BCC by virtue of her parents' affiliation, recalls that

> [Prophet Cicero] was trying to give us an identity within this nation. And his movement was about building a spiritual identity. It was not one or the other. It was both. During the period in question, the cultural and mental condition of black people was low. Many of us had accepted negro as our identity. [What Prophet Cicero] was dealing with was a matter of deprograming to reprogram us from the brainwashing we had gone through in slavery, Jim Crow, and beyond. [. . .] Prophet Cicero had his initial plan and blueprint in mind, and that was that we would become a sovereign nation within the nation. Especially since the nation didn't recognize us as people anyway.[67]

In the BCC, while adherents do not renounce their status as Americans, they are aware of their marginal citizenship and therefore perform *otherwise* in their search for identity. The fugitive imagination toward Ethiopia de-centers North America as "home," fostering a collective sense of identity with Ethiopia as the center. This aligns with a 1921 prospectus cited by the Chicago Commission on Race Relations, in its sociological study which examined race relations in Chicago following the race riots of 1919. The report, published as *The Negro in Chicago: A Study of Race Relations and a Race Riot,* cited the prospectus offered by "The Ancient Order of Ethiopian Princes" in an opinion section on race consciousness. The Commission quotes the prospectus in this way:

> Ancient history knows no "Negro," but ancient history does know Ethiopia and Ethiopians. Change a family's name and in a generation you cannot tell whether its foreparents were rogues or saints. It is the same with a race. . . . take away our birthright, our ancient honorable name "Ethiopian," and you have stopped the very foundation of our inspiration. If we are "Negroes" we are, by the same dictionary also, "Niggers." The moment we realize, however, that we are "Ethiopians," we can see the beams from the lamp of Ethiopian culture lighting a pathway down the shadowy ages,

and the fires of ambition are rekindled in our hearts because we know that we came from the builders of temples and founders of civilization.[68]

The fugitive imagination guiding the turn to Ethiopia in the BCC, then, was as much about the recovery of a civilization as it was about the recovery of divine and biblical history.

The placement of the Ethiopian flag in Black Coptic churches and not an American flag is not a matter of happenstance. On the one hand, flags are symbols; they point to something larger than the object itself. But more than this, flags also make a statement. Empress Hatshepsut's conclusion that, for Prophet Cicero, the implementation of Ethiopian symbols such as the flag was to build a nation within the nation speaks to a teleological and eschatological dimension of such symbols in the BCC. For Empress Hatshepsut, the "both and" element of Ethiopian symbols, spiritual *and* nation building, is an important feature of the performative imagination that we see unfolding among Black Coptic believers. Indeed, what is a nation without a flag? The centering of the Ethiopian standard as the official flag of the BCC is a radical assertion of an *otherwise* identity in which members of the BCC locate their heritage, culture, and religious orientation outside the restrictions of the Western imagination. Such a posture accentuates Priest Meshach's claim that, in the BCC, the genealogy of Blackness does not commence with the North American institution of enslavement, but rather, begins in the cradle of civilization, which the Church identifies as Ethiopia. Notes Nurhussein: "Because most civilizationist arguments assumed the view that black cultures were uncivilized, the antiquity to Ethiopian culture provided African Americans with a well-documented example of originary blackness that exploded the logic of racist accounts of civilization."[69] In this sense, the turn toward Ethiopia is a teleological turn in that Ethiopia "represents the nation Prophet Cicero wanted us to become. The goal was to create an Ethiopian heritage in Chicago."[70]

Theologically, the utilization of the Ethiopian flag illuminates a radical fugitive eschatology grounded in imagination of other Black futures. Ethiopia in this sense is not merely the proposition of an imagined geographical homeland, but rather Ethiopia and its flag symbolize a future that is possible; one that breaks with the absurdity of Black death in North America. Priest Meshach's interpretation of Ethiopian symbols in the BCC as "representative of the nation Prophet Cicero wanted us to become" serves as the catalyst for understanding the BCC's eschatological treatment. Indeed, believers envision Ethiopia as what is possible for the community and the self. Queen Huldah, in an assessment of the church's eschatology recounts the following:

> The Ethiopian flag at the center of our tradition is a constant reminder that our future is not bound to the American future or how North America seeks to direct and create our future. Ethiopia and the Ethiopian flag is about what is possible here in this earth as black people search for dignity. Prophet Peter would often tell us "you don't have to die and fly to get to heaven in order to wear your crown." The Kingdom is here and now. Ethiopia means that our past, present, and future is not *because of* North America, but *in spite* of North America. Ethiopia is home. The flag is a reminder of that hope.[71]

Queen Huldah's interpretation of the Ethiopian flag, and her description of Black hope as a present hope, are reminiscent of the performative imagination present in spirituals of the enslaved. Like those eschatological tunes that postured toward hope in the face of absurdity, members of the BCC assert the possibility of *otherwise* futures via an imagined homeland that lends itself toward an idea of Blackness that breaks with the normative gaze of the West, and rejects the ontological description of Blackness as nothingness.[72] Rather, what we glean from the BCC is a proposition of Black identity retrieved from a logic of Blackness grounded in what Queen Rebekah described as the "root of civilization." Indeed, for Queen Rebekah, "if you want to talk about Black history. You have to go back to Ethiopia. You need to dig up the ancient queens and kings. You need to talk about Black Jesus."[73] The Ethiopian flag, then, not only points to Ethiopia; it is a statement about imagined possibilities.

At the core of Black religions is imagination. Imagination proposes an interruption of presumed borders and offers a radical movement toward limitless possibilities. In all their diversity of theologies, of practices, and rituals, what connects these Black religions are their various imaginaries that seek to perform Blackness as a joy, not as a reaction to whiteness or white supremacy. Imagination then, as seen in the BCC, is a performance of Blackness *otherwise*.

2

"Ethiopia Shall Soon Stretch Forth Her Hand unto God"

Imagination, Ideational Heroism, and the Turn to Blackness

Observance

July 2018. Sunday afternoon. 12:00 p.m. Worship service at Coptic Nation Temple in Chicago. Believers are seated after a ritual has concluded. The ceremony included a procession of women in the community known as queens, empresses, and princesses, outfitted in "royal garments" and headpieces known as a "crowns." The temple is quiet and still. A young man clad in a black military-style uniform trimmed in gold, with an insignia of the Ethiopian flag over his left chest, walks up the middle aisle carrying the Ethiopian flag with the lion of Judah at its center. He stops in the center of the temple facing the women. He raises the flag, stomps three times, and asserts in a confident voice: "Hail to the Queens of Ethiopia!" The women stand.[1]

* * *

In a March 10th, 1973 *Chicago Defender* newspaper article titled, "Coptic Heritage Seen in King Solomon's Temple," religion editor Rev. R. C. Keller incorporated photographs taken inside True Temple of Solomon Black Coptic Church, located at 7138 S. Halsted Street in Chicago.[2] The pictures were taken during an "elevation" ceremony, in which the community's longest-serving spiritual leader, Prophet Peter Banks, "crowned" a number of women in the community as "heaven born" and "heavenly" queens.[3] The 1973 newspaper article and its accompanying photographs revealed three significant facts: (1) ecclesial titles in the Church assert what Rev. Keller calls the "spiritual hierarchy" of the group (i.e., "Queens," "Prophets," "Prince," and "Princess"); (2) members of the denomination adorn "holy garments" representative of their particular title or position in the congregation (e.g., queen

Figure 2.1. Standard Bearer, New Heaven Coptic Temple, 2015. Credit: Photo courtesy Coptic Nation Temple Black Coptic Church.

or princess); and (3) adherents adopt a spiritual name, typically biblical (e.g., Peter, Capernaum, John), or that of an Egyptian ruler (e.g., Nefertiti). Such spiritual performances within the BCC are ways in which religion is employed in the search for identity and personhood grounded in retrieval, remembrance, and imagination. These exercises both reject the hyper-racialized categories in the North American context and re-construct/remember an identity rooted in a reclamation of a heroic African past, yet substantiated in the image of God. Identity, then, in the Black Coptic Church, is not viewed or performed as a cultural production, but rather locates its meaning and essence in a transcendent reality mediated through [Ethiopian] cultural and heritage symbols.

This chapter probes the use of royal titles among Black Coptic devotees as performative imagination of identity, salvation, and a future for Black life in North America. In the BCC, believers become members of a royal society in which they obtain the aforementioned titles, which they call "degrees." The degrees, Queen Huldah explained, are obtained either as a result of one's age or one's spiritual development. "The leaders of individual churches," she continued, "in conjunction with the Holy Spirit, typically are the ones with the authority to elevate members in their churches."[4] In this chapter, I argue that the deployment of an ideational view of Black royalty, and its accompanying symbols, contribute to the process of mediating identity among Black Coptic members. The ideational view permits the group to wrestle with DuBois' "twoness" while promoting a sense of the self outside the social circumstances that relegate Black life to the margins. To achieve this performance of Blackness, I further argue that the BCC intentionally recovers an identity grounded in a "hero" narrative, and that the implementation of regal nomenclature participates in the Church's notion that salvation is accessible in the material world. Royal titles offer a heroic assessment of the Black past and frame a discourse of social salvation. Yet, the Church's male-dominated hierarchy suggests that social salvation is provided to different degrees for women and for men.

Performing *Otherwise*

The vignette that opens this chapter displays efforts of BCC adherents to not merely imagine, which itself is *already* a certain presentation and protest, but rather to perform such imaginations to assert their newfound identity. Their performative imagination moves them from thought to act in re-claiming and reconstructing Black identity. *Otherwise* captures the theological, spiritual, and intellectual labor of Great Migration new religious movements such as the BCC, which vehemently

Figure 2.2. "Coptic Heritage Seen in King Solomon's Temple," Rev. R. C. Keller, *Chicago Defender*, March 10, 1973. Credit: Reprinted courtesy of Real Times Media.

reject identities that emerge from anti-black imaginations. *Otherwise* is a rejection of social and spiritual designations, like "negro," that fail to recognize the sacredness of Black life. In Black Coptic congregations, *otherwise* commences with a verbal declaration, "Hail to the Queens of Ethiopia." In this announcement, multiple performances happen at once that help to re-construct Black identity for believers. Candace Queen Rachel synopsizes the procession in this way:

> When the standard-bearer (young man who carries the flag) announces "Hail to the Queens of Ethiopia," he is not only talking to the women in the church; he is talking to everyone. The phrase, "Hail to the Queens of Ethiopia," is a symbol of who we are because of who God created us to be. When I hear the phrase, it brings me to attention; I know he is talking about me and my children. We are not negroes or niggers, we are a royal people. I am a queen. My daughter is a princess. My son is a prince. We declare "we are somebody." We are a royal people of Ethiopia, a land greater than this land. This [Black Coptic Church and Ethiopia] is our nation; a divine nation.[5]

Candace Queen Rachel's interpretation extends our understanding of how members negotiate the intersection of race, religion, and resistance, with an orientation toward *otherwise*, and rejection of the absurdity of the present social order in the process of identity formation. That is, in the BCC, *otherwise* is not merely a theoretical turn, but also a metanoia performance—a theological reclamation of Black identity that does not recapitulate the absurd, and a refutation of identities that compete with their divine identities. Other Black new religious movements of the same period, such as the Nation of Islam and the Moorish Science Temple, "did not repudiate blackness or dark skin but, rather, endowed it with meaning derived from histories other than those of enslavement and oppression,"[6] and the BCC operates from a similar posture. Such positionality frames the core of the BCC's search for identity—Blackness despite performances of anti-Blackness.

Candace Queen Rachel's description of the imaginative performance captured in "Hail to the Queens of Ethiopia" provides clues about the semiotic relationship between the announcement of the phrase and what it communicates to the hearer at the emotive and psyche levels. In her assessment, although the phrase is gendered via the usage of "queen," the expression bears importance for her son as well, as it situates her family as members of a royal household. She notes: "If I am a Queen, then my son is a Prince. He is not whatever the world says he is. He is a Prince."[7] Correspondingly, "Hail to the Queens of Ethiopia" as symbol participates in a sense of meaning-making for the community and illuminates the function of symbol in the cultural and religious world of the group, which is not dissimilar from other religious groups. That is, symbols and imagery assist religions in conveying a relationship to the divine, to the world, and to other humans.

Grounding the phrase "Hail to the Queens of Ethiopia" within the context of symbol is important in that it allows for considerable treatment and interrogation of symbol in the religious life of Black Coptic believers. The function of symbol is to represent and reveal a reality. In the life of Black Coptic followers, as narrated above, the phrase "Hail to the Queens of Ethiopia" transmits knowledge of self and the broader community. That is, as we saw earlier, given the prominence of Ethiopia in the community as a spiritual homeland and biblically important country, the phraseology situates the hearer of the expression within a space that allows for the possibility to move beyond manufactured borders, in this case borders that regulate Blackness, and conceptualize radical difference as it relates to an anthropological disposition, and an ontology of Blackness. The phrase, as symbol, opens "otherwise inaccessible aspects of reality," and inculcates somebodiness and thereby a denial of Black non-being.

Candace Queen Rachel's testimony that hearing the phrase "Hail to the Queens of Ethiopia" brings her "to attention" sheds light on the emotive feature of symbols, namely, that "symbols grasp individuals in especially powerful emotional ways."[8] I do not mean that an emotional appeal or response to symbol is the absence of intellect or a thoughtful response. Rather, in addition to the emotive function, symbols provide a context within which—or the conditions of possibility—to think about and frame a narrative about the self, or in the case of the BCC, the space within which identity is imagined and performed. The framing of a discourse around identity recovery among Black Coptic adherents commences, then, with a ritualistic announcement that, without a doubt, impacts the emotive, yet bears significant consideration at the intellectual level. The announcement begins a process of individuals in the community "making sense" of the symbol in their personal and communal lives. For Candace Queen Rachel, her interpretive process permits her to apply the symbol of the phrase toward her son and thereby grapple with both her and his identity, precisely because for believers, "Ethiopia" and "queen" are signals that direct their attention to *otherwise*, or the otherness of Black culture, Black life, and Black existence.

Theologian Paul Tillich's nuanced interpretation of symbol, that both connects it to and differentiates it from a sign, is helpful in understanding how symbols function within the Black Coptic community. Whereas both signs and symbols point to a reality beyond themselves,

> [d]ecisive is the fact that signs do not participate in the reality of that to which they point, while symbols do. Therefore, signs can be replaced for reasons of expediency or convention, while symbols cannot. This leads to the second characteristic of the symbol: It participates in that to which it points: the flag participates in the power and dignity of the nation for which it stands.⁹

Tillich's definition of symbol, one that elevates symbol beyond mere descriptors or "standing-in-the-place-of," as in representation, to that which reveals and participates in a supernatural reality, is a suitable method for thinking about the utility of the Black monarchy as performed in the BCC and announced in the ceremonial procession "Hail to queens of Ethiopia." The emphasis rests upon the inculcation and performance of royalty among adherents. Within the community, the announcement, "queens of Ethiopia," expresses and participates in a divine relationship which, for believers, cements an ontological claim—namely, that to be Black (Ethiopian) is to partake in a royal kingdom in which Blackness is in close proximity to the divine. While chapter five will interrogate the ontological claim, this chapter proceeds with the structure of identity as related to the Black monarchy as symbol. Indeed, religious symbols communicate a correlation between humans and the divine and, as we have seen, "Hail to the Queens of Ethiopia" communicates a distinctive relationship between adherents and God. To be sure, for Tillich, "when these powerful symbols, often having a transcendent reference, take hold in a culture, their use allows for humans to participate in fully embodied ways in what is most meaningful in that culture."[10] What one encounters in the weekly ritual of "Hail to the Queens of Ethiopia" is an imagination and performance of an embodied experience of the human and of divinity.

A Royal Black Monarchy

The turn to Blackness, or *otherwise*, in the Black Coptic community is the performative imagination of other worlds. For believers, turning to Blackness includes a retrieval of an idea of Black life that presents a dialectical opposition between damaging imaginations of Blackness, and an imagination of Blackness as a performance of Blackness as *free*. In the Black Coptic community, performative Blackness as free, as explored in the preceding chapter, includes the destruction of social, cultural, and spiritual borders that aim to relegate the movement of Black bodies, or to ghettoize Blackness. Considering this existential condition, members of the Black Coptic community employ and perform cultural and spiritual fugitivity toward the process of claiming a way of life that is the antitheses of modes of Blackness invented by a cosmological imagination rooted in whiteness.

"Fugitive" is a helpful category toward the delineation of ritual and performance in the Black Coptic community in that, as referenced earlier, it points to a deliberate act of breaking away from and overcoming powers that monitor, control, apprehend, or surveil. Like enslaved persons who intentionally broke through the borders and social constructions meant to destroy Black life and maintain a slavocracy, Black religion as fugitive imagines other worlds in which Black freedom is an expression and a practice. Imagining other Black worlds is part of the fugitivity performed among Black Coptic parishioners as they seek to execute a sense of freedom, agency, and a departure from Black life as marginal. Such performance of fugitivity in the quest to assert Black life is neatly captured in the community's performance of a Black nation of individuals who boast royal titles as part and parcel of their sacred identity. Yet the assertion of royal titles within the community is not a counter-cultural political statement, but rather points to the prospect of *otherwise* in which a perceived stolen identity is recovered.

Central to the theology and religious life of the BCC is a liberative imagination that seeks to dispel myths of Black people. For Queen Huldah, the "negro is a myth created by white people to substantiate their acts of dominations in the world. But we are not negroes. And Prophet Cicero knew the first step in the process toward liberation was to wake us up and rid negro language from our vocabulary. He had to teach us back to ourselves."[11] When asked what she meant by "teach us back to ourselves," Queen Huldah explained:

> Our identity was stripped from us. The goal of the slave master to create a docile slave who lacked any dignity, any worth, any value, or humanity. Nigger and negro were not simply titles. They were how they saw us. They did not see us as people with souls, people with divine origins, or people worth value. They simply saw us as niggers. And over the years many black people internalized nigger and negro as their identity. But Prophet Cicero knew that's not who God created us to be. God made us in God's image and then made us to be kings and queens on the earth.[12]

Queen Huldah's articulation of the myth of the American negro is a vital part of the Church's performed religious resistance aimed at not simply performing *otherwise*, but rejecting nomenclature, like negro, that does not align with the community's sense of self or asserted identities. Queen Huldah's reference to the myth of the created negro echoes sentiments shared by James Baldwin. In 1963 in San Francisco, Baldwin noted the following:

> ... what you say about somebody else ... reveals you. What I think of you as being is dictated by my own necessity, my own psychology, my own fears and desires. I'm not describing you when I talk about you. I'm describing me. Now here in this country we have something called the nigger. [. . . .] We invented the nigger. I didn't invent him. White people invented him. [. . . .] I had to know by the time I was 17 years old, what you were describing was not me and what you were afraid of was not me. It had to be something else. You invented it. [. . . .] I have always known that I'm not a nigger. But if I am not the nigger, and if it's true that your invention reveals you, then who is the nigger?[13]

For Baldwin, "negro" was not an authentic descriptor of Black people, because the degrading myth behind it was constructed by a white supremacist ideology to manipulate and control Black folk. Indeed, in their attempts to dominate, Europeans developed a variety of pseudoscientific and biblical justifications, masquerading as objective reasons, for why they were superior, and other races inferior. Like Baldwin, Queen Huldah maintains that a constitutive element in the Church's doctrine is to rid from the minds of believers that they are bound by the imagination of others who seek to define Black life. This element is captured in the formation of a spiritual royal hierarchy, one in which Black Coptic believers understand themselves to belong to a heavenly kingdom on earth.

This performance of a royal hierarchy is not a political statement, nor is it the declaration of a separate state. This is important because members do not renounce their American citizenship, nor are they hostile toward the U.S. Prophet Peter Banks enjoyed a cordial relationship with local politicians and, under his leadership, True Temple of Solomon Coptic Church (TTS) was frequented by politicians who sought the support of his congregation. Edward R. Vrdolyak, for instance, who ran for mayor of Chicago in 1987 under the Illinois Solidarity Party, "took his campaign into the black community in a visit to True Temple of Solomon, 7138 South Halsted. There, he was welcomed by a standing ovation and endorsed by Prophet Peter Banks, who called Vrdolyak a great man and a friend. 'He is the best,' Banks said."[14] Prophet Peter's connection to the political sphere extended beyond political endorsements and included affiliations with politicians, including Cook County Executive Maria Papas, who was a frequent visitor at TTS.

In his 1973 article, Rev. Keller employed the phrase "heavenly hierarchy" to describe the structure of the Black Coptic community. Such framing allows us to examine this religious community as an earthly spiritual kingdom, in which followers no longer ascribe to an identity as defined by anti-Black cultures, but rather as Black Copts, accepting a belief that they are "Royal Black Jews."[15] Part of this endeavor is the rejection of mainstream religious ecclesial structures and the inculcation of an ecclesial arrangement that recovers Black identity while uniting devotees to their sense of the religious life. It is a "both and" approach toward a religious imaginary.

Figure 2.3. King Peter Banks on the Throne, c. 1983. Photo courtesy of Coptic Nation Temple.

Figure 2.4. Black Coptic Empress and Students, Black Coptic Church Series, Chicago, IL, January 2021. Credit: Iwona Biedermann Photography.

For Prophet Cicero and members of the Black Coptic community, the turn "back to ourselves"—a phrase often used among Black Copts to describe the transformative process that takes place in the teaching apparatus of the BCC, the "School of Wisdom"—is a turn away from racial imaginaries, such as negro, that perform anti-Black theological violence and social death. In turning to Blackness, members orient themselves toward divine darkness, which will be explored in later chapters, and toward a heroic read of black history that includes a "royal identity that was interrupted by the invention of slavery."[16]

The idea of Blackness asserted among Black Coptic believers helps to shed light on the performative imagination that materializes in the Church's ecclesial structure. Jacob Dorman's theory of the ideational attractiveness of "Hebrew" and "Israelite" in African societies helps us understand the notions of Blackness and history in the BCC. As noted earlier, it is unlikely that members of the BCC literally had ancestors in Ethiopia or Egypt. For members of the community, tracing a biological or genetic line to Ethiopia and Egypt is not the objective, nor do such issues affect the ways that imagining *otherwise* functions in the community. Attempting to understand the BCC's lineage claims from a literal standpoint will lead one to misunderstand the community. For members of this imaginative community, a gaze toward Egyptian and Ethiopian cultures provides ways of understanding, indeed epistemologies, that assist in identity formation. The rejection of negro, for Prophet Cicero Patterson, was a denunciation of racial imaginations of white supremacy as cultural productions of modernity. What was required, then, for Prophet Cicero, was a way of seeing and reading Blackness that did not have its origins in the innovations of white society. "In ancient Egypt, Prophet Cicero located identities that were capable of instilling dignity in Black people and undoing many years of indoctrination that relegated us to nothing. For Prophet Cicero, ancient Egypt provided the best moment in time where Black people thrived as people of dignity of and value."[17] Egypt's appeal in building a narrative of Black people, therefore, rests upon a lofty idea of Egyptian and Ethiopian life that disproved the invention of racialized identities in North America.

* * *

"Hail to the Queens of Ethiopia" publicizes a royal Black identity. The Church's statement of faith details: "we believe . . . [God] has made us unto our God kings, queens, and priests, and we shall reign in the kingdom of God on the earth. The kingdom of God is within you and at hand, to order and establish the new heaven and the new earth."[18] In the same way that nations are composed of people who assert their heritage, cultural sensibilities, and identities, the BCC is composed of Black people whose read of Black history offers personal and communal salvation. Prophet Cicero organized the BCC such that its theological character and assertions would lend themselves toward the performance of the same.

Prophet Cicero's arrangement of the BCC as a royal Black monarchy, and the ensuing organization, reflects the liberation theology that grounds the Church. He sought to unite race and religion such that they would inform each other. This effort was partly achieved by religious performance that connected Black Copts to an idea of a Black God, while also imparting dignity resultant from the imagination and performance of the Black monarchy. Prophet Jacob Washington, a leader in the BCC, states that

> Prophet Cicero knew we needed more than traditional black religion. Most of the early converts came from other black churches. Some were Baptist, Methodists, and even Catholics. But those churches were not providing what we needed. We were lost and in need of a savior. Some people chose the Nation of Islam. But those who joined with Prophet Cicero did not want to leave the Christian Faith. They loved Jesus. So, in the Coptic Church we found a way to be Christian while also addressing the fact the white people called us niggers. Coming into the Coptic Church was like coming to a world of fantasy. There were royal people who had a higher opinion of themselves.[19]

Prophet Jacob's account offers insight into the appeal the BCC had for some of its early converts. The royal monarchy that Prophet Cicero established was, in fact, the introduction of a new way of being and performing "black church." Its royal titles were part of a religion that was not merely theologically distinct from white churches, but also aesthetically different, and presented an imagination of Black life that compensated for the social location of Black folk in North America. For Empress Selah, a forty-something-year-old paralegal and graduate of Syracuse University who became affiliated with the BCC as a young child when her mother converted, the titles that African American churchgoers were accustomed to, were a "mere carbon copy of the Methodist and Baptist church titles from which their founders sought to make a distinction. Commonplace titles such as brother, sister, elder, and deacon, while biblical, did not help to transform our situation. White Christians called us brother and sister, but their actions did not align with their words. Prophet Cicero, therefore, gave us religious titles that also gave us a social identity."[20] Prophet Cicero created a prophetic Black church experience that did not simply focus on religiosity, but also instilled a sense of dignity and pride in Blackness. He created a sort of clandestine religious world in which the adoption of royal titles performed an act of fugitivity.

As previously noted, the BCC emerged within a context in which Black identity was relegated to subaltern status, most notably tied to the invention of the negro. Prophet Cicero's teaching about the classification of "negro" was similar to that of "Black messianic-nationalist sects, such as some of the Black Jewish groups and the Nation of Islam under the leadership of Wallace D. Fard and Elijah Muhammad."[21] We see the denunciation of this term from other leaders of Hebrew Israelite traditions such as Josiah Ford (Congregation of Beth B'nai Abraham) and Rabbi Arthur Matthew (Commandment Keepers). For Ford, "All I recognize by 'Negro' is an African or person of African descent whose mind is a by-product of European civilization but has not traditions of its own. Hebrews are not Negroes."[22] Like his contemporaries in other movements (as summarized in the work of Hans Baer), Prophet Cicero taught that "the white race all over the world styles the name Nigger, Negress, Negritos, Negro as inferior. Therefore, the term Negro must be eliminated from the dictionaries, eradicated by law, and replaced by "Black" or "Ethiopian."[23] Further, in the BCC, rejection of "negro" as a legitimate racial category was not limited to its social implications as marginalized people. Rather, for the Black Coptic believers, negro "distorted the image of God in black people. The name itself sought to remove our divinity and deny us our humanity."[24] Moreover, "Negro and nigger are slave classifications. These names keep us in slavery and limit our history to that of slaves. But we are not slaves. We are not negroes. We are God's chosen, holy, and anointed people. We are Black Ethiopians with a royal ancestry. Negro denies us of that, says Priest Meshach."[25] In Black Coptic theology, the rejection of negro was a necessity. The BCC aims to fill both a spiritual and a social chasm—to interpret and perform Black life in a way that is capable of bearing salvation.

In one of my interview sessions, it became clear that the BCC's ecclesial structure is tied to the Church's understanding of the need for social salvation. Prophet Judah (1967–2021), who was a spiritual leader in the BCC, noted that

> when one thinks of a negro or colored person, this is a person without a future except a future in the world to come. Meanwhile, black people are catching hell in this earth while white people prosper. A negro is a person who is made to suffer in ghettos without resources to get out. Prophet Cicero taught us that as a royal black nation, God made us to be free and to prosper like everyone else. So, we don't accept terms like negro or colored because they are conditions created by white people. As God's chosen people we can now proclaim our ability to live without the conditions set by white people, especially white Christians.[26]

Prophet Judah's connection between a given racial identity and social conditions in which black people "catch hell" lends insight into the function of the ecclesial structure in the BCC as performative imagination. That is, the performance of Black people as a "royal nation" seeks to repudiate negro classifications as well as debunk theologies that perpetuate the view of Black people as subalterns. The establishment of a "royal black priesthood" inculcates a new identity among adherents and envisions *otherwise* futures in which the body and the earth are recipients of a social salvation.

An important feature of Black new religious movements, and prophetic Black religion more generally—those with a political and social vision interconnected with their theology—is a suspicion of eschatologies that include spiritual salvation while neglecting the temporal realm. In many instances, this has been the story of white theology in North America. However, the Black religious imagination has questioned such theologies since the gathering of enslaved Africans in the New World. Spirituals, for example, were often used as coded messages objecting to a material world in which Black bodies suffered now and received a "crown of glory" only in the afterlife. Theologians such as James Cone describe Black theology as a protest against such an eschatology:

> The most corrupting influence among the black churches was their adoption of the white lie that Christianity is primarily concerned with an otherworldly reality. White missionaries persuaded most black religious people that life on earth was insignificant because obedient servants of God could expect a "reward" in heaven after death. [. . . .] This otherworldly ethos is still very much a part of the black churches. This is not merely a problem of education among the black clergy; it mainly shows that white power is so overwhelming in its domination of black people that many blacks have given up hope for change in this world. By reaching for heaven they are saying the odds are against them now; God must have something better in store for black people later.[27]

Similarly, in a rejection of this theological model, Rev. Dr. Calvin O. Butts of the Abyssinian Baptist Church in New York offered the following in a sermon:

There was a religion of compensation, which said that, if you didn't get your reward down here, and we were suffering down here, that you would get your reward by and by. But it was my labor, it was my work, it was my brain power, it was my nursing of the children, it was my tilling of the soil. [. . . .] It was my creativity . . . that gave America all that it had. [. . . .] So, uh, why did I have to wait to get my reward? What was it about this mythology, this theology, that said I had to wait 'til I get to heaven before I could enjoy? So, we embraced it. 'I got you shoes. You got shoes. All God's children got shoes.' when we get to heaven. Everybody else wearing shoes down here. [. . . .] Why do I have to wait? It was a religion of compensation because we were catching nothing but hell down here. And once our minds were set free . . . once we could think for ourselves. . . . We were able to . . . define a culture, and we were able to move forward primarily through our faith in God. It wasn't the same faith that the white man was talking about in their churches. It couldn't be. You brought me here on a ship named Jesus. [. . . .] You don't think I can see and understand for myself and see the chicanery and the trickery you put on me?[28]

New religious movements, such as the Nation of Islam and the BCC, constructed theological programs in like fashion; one that impacted the present as a sort of right-now-but-not-yet theology. In the BCC, the introduction of a royal ecclesiology is not only meant to shape their identity, but also serves to function as a repudiation of disembodied theology. Priest Meshach understands the degrees in the church as replicating the kingdom of God. Prophet Cicero, he notes, "told us to drop the negro degree. We adopt royal titles and proclaim we are black and beautiful and shall reign in the kingdom of God on earth. We are not waiting until we die to experience the kingdom. The kingdom is right before us. And as the chosen people of God, we can walk in the kingdom now."[29] The BCC, therefore, aligns with a prophetic imagination of Black religion that was common among new religious movements in this period.

In his work on the Black spiritual movement, Hans Baer provides evidence of a prophetic posture in Black religious life—a posture that questioned the motives of white religionists. For instance, Baer writes:

> It was Farther Hurley's contention that whites forced the Ethiopian people to join their churches during slavery times and held up before us a white

God, a white Jesus, white prophets, and white prophetesses. He views the traditional Christian concepts of the afterlife as a means of oppressing Blacks with a pie-in-the-sky philosophy, and argues that "Christianity has caused segregation, Jim-Crowism, hatred, and jealousy, covetousness and selfishness to exist throughout the world."[30]

Edward Curtis, in *Black Muslim Religion in the Nation of Islam, 1960–1975*, reports a similar message:

> After his conversion to Islam, Omar said, he rejected such "pie-in-the-sky stories," and decided to work in this life for "justice, freedom, and equality." Similarly, for Brother Hiram X, a former Black Student Union volunteer who converted during his student years at one of the California State University branches, Islam was a religion that spoke to his need for a faith that addressed the practical problems of black life.[31]

Similarly, in the BCC, Prophet Cicero admonished members to see heaven "as a state of mind and hell as a condition created by white people for the so-called negro."[32] Identity formation in the BCC is therefore as much about a social eschatological vision and performance, as it is about rejecting negro and adopting a royal history with royal titles as demonstrative of such a history. The materialization of a royal identity frames the BCC's theology of what I identified earlier as an assembled heroic identity, or an identity construction that brings together various salvaged identities to aide in personal and social salvation.

Identity and Salvation

At the center of the BCC's religious platform is a sense of "liberation" connected to the performance of assembled heroic identities. This connection assumes that the adoption of Ethiopian and Ancient Egyptian cultural artifacts, as well as the taking on of royal titles, perform the Church's understanding of salvation as a "right now" experience. Though the BCC does not say that it is grounded in "liberation theology," I suspect this has more to do with a lack of awareness of liberation theology among members than it does with any theological disagreement. Indeed, my informants admitted they had not heard this term prior to our conversations. However, after their own investigation of the phrase "Black Liberation Theology," there was a general consensus that the church "emphasizes liberation Theology" and "in a very practical sense this is what [the church has] been doing—dispelling the idea that God created lesser people based on race."[33] As one participant contended, "When we look at the nature of the teaching ... it does liberate the mind, the conscience, and the spirit of the people from past or previous errors and bondage."[34] The assertion of a liberative theological character in the Church gestures toward a "freeing" theology, grounded in a hermeneutic of counter-indoctrination and conscientization.[35] Philosopher William Jones describes the first step toward this theological orientation:

> At the base of oppression lies a complex of beliefs that define the role and status of the oppressor and the oppressed, and this same complex of beliefs legitimates both. The oppressed, in part, are oppressed precisely because they buy, or are indoctrinated to accept, a set of beliefs that negate those attitudes and actions necessary for liberation. Accordingly, the purpose and first step of a theology of liberation is to effect a radical conversion of the mind of the oppressed, to free his [sic] mind from those destructive and enslaving beliefs that stifle the movement toward liberation.[36]

In a similar fashion, given the interrelationship between identity and theology that grounds the Church's beliefs, the BCC teaches that the consciousness of Blacks in North America needs to be redeemed or set free "from what [they] have been exposed to previously."[37] This process is reminiscent of Paulo Freire's conscientization.[38] Conscientization, notes Empress Selah, is rooted in a "doctrine of science ... that is aimed at reversing or changing social, political, [and] economic structures [that were] birthed in the American experience as Africans in this country had to deal with those constructs that were created to explain small brains ... [and] to explain inferiority."[39] This brand of liberation theology "deals with all the manifestations of very negative ideology [blacks] have been indoctrinated with, introduced to, taught, [and] promoted through blood lines [and] social teaching...."[40] Consequently, the BCC asserts what I call a transformative theology of liberation deliberately aimed at consciousness raising and spiritual development.

As a theology of liberation rooted in a hermeneutic of counter-indoctrination, the theological program of the Black Coptic Church advances an element of contradiction, which has as its goal the overturning of false images and ideologies that safeguard the social and theological foundations of North America as they relate to Black life, Black culture, and Black religion. The transformative characteristic of this program is rooted in the Church's materialization of religion, particularly white Christianity, as a negative influence in the history of Blacks in North America, but is consummated in the church's construction of a *new person* who affirms his or her creation in the image of God and as a royal person.

Swiss theologian Karl Barth's articulation of time and the function of theology is helpful in further probing the BCC's theology as intrinsic to its notion of identity. Barth argued that modern theology is a theology of the "time between the times."[41] In this declaration, Barth argues that theology must address the situation of the human being. It cannot be a theology of paradise, because we are not there anymore. Nor can it be a theology of the future, because we are not there yet. Theology, then, for Barth, is the science that addresses the human being in this existential reality. Or, as Tillich posits, theology is that subject which concerns itself with one's "ultimate concern," which is a matter of being and non-being.[42] So it is with the BCC, grounded in a theology that seeks to radically shift how believers think about Black existence and Black identity as a whole, but also how followers perform their personal sense of identity. In addressing these matters, the theology and rituals of the Church are directed toward a refutation against "false" characterizations of Black people. Herein lies the "contradiction" element inherent in the BCC's teaching.

Contradiction has its roots in the Latin *contradicere*, meaning to speak against or to assert the contrary. Among Black Coptic believers, "contradiction" arises from the Church's proclamation that to be Black is to be created in God's image. This radical assertion of Black humanity intrinsically linked to creation was pronounced by Prophet Cicero Patterson, who utilized the Bible to contradict social, political, economic, and most notably, theological constructions that denied full valuation to Blacks in North America. Hence, the Church rejects "disembodied" theology that fails to relate the Christian gospel to existential experiences of Blacks in North America. Indeed, the social gospel tradition has been foundational in the Black religious experience ever since enslaved persons, practicing fugitive religion in the invisible institution, imagined and performed a religion and theology of freedom. As one former enslaved person recounted:

> Our preachers were usually plantation folk just like the rest of us. Some men who had little education and had been taught something about the Bible would be our preacher. The colored folks had their code of religion, not nearly so complicated as the white man's religion, but more closely observed.... When we had our meetings of this kind, we held them in our own way and were not interfered with by the white folks.[43]

This theological positioning also echoes theologian Jürgen Moltmann, who maintained that any theology that advocates that "this earth is not our home,"[44] as in Augustine, runs the risk of neglecting not only care for the earth, but also care and attention to the human being, both soul *and* body.[45] As one respondent indicated, the BCC denounces any "pie in the sky" theology that creates a radical distinction between lived experiences and the life to come.[46] In the final analysis, to be created in the image of God encompasses both body and soul. Hence, the Church's attention to both earthly and spiritual salvation.

The Black Monarchy as Social Salvation

For Black Coptic followers, "Hail to the Queens of Ethiopia" is an instance of Black futurism. It is a collapsing of time, namely the bridging of history, the future, and the present, as a performance of the Church's idea of freedom; one in which Black life is redeemed from both the margins of society and from the captivity of anti-Black imaginaries. In many respects this performance is an interruption of an interruption. Earlier in this chapter, Queen Maryann claimed that North American Black enslavement was an interruption in the royal ancestry of Black folk. In the Black Coptic community, the performance of a Black monarchy is both a recovery of a royal imagination and an interruption in cosmological performances that seek to regulate and defeat Black life. The BCC's concept of liberation, as partially observed in a performance of a Black monarchy, is thus connected to the Church's understanding of salvation. To be liberated cannot be separated from the process of salvation, which results from the adherents' encounter with the Black Messiah. This relationship between liberation and salvation is a Christological framing couched within a liberative reading of the Lukan narrative of the New Testament. "When we think of Jesus," noted Priest Stephen (1948–2015), who served as the spiritual leader of Coptic Temple of Kemet in Chicago, Illinois until his death, "we think of the Black Jesus who said in Luke that he came to set the captives free. That is liberation."[47] Priest Stephen's emphasis on the social salvific reading of Luke's gospel is a critical component of the Church's turn toward Ethiopia as a means of imagining salvation as a "right now" event. It should be noted, however, that this association between liberation and salvation is not unique to the BCC. In his *A Theology of Liberation: History, Politics, and Salvation*, liberation theologian Gustavo Gutierrez theorizes this interrelationship as realized in the church's eschatological hope. For Gutierrez, the eschatological promise is "already but not yet."[48] To be sure, in dogmatic theology, eschatology has classically been regarded as the "theology of the last things." In political theology (such as in the works of Metz[49] and Moltmann[50]), eschatology has been reworked to the extent that it is related to the prophetic tradition, in which the prophets "have 'eschatologized' Israel's conceptions of time and history. However, for Gutierrez, what is characteristic of the prophets is, "on the one hand, their orientation toward the *future* and, on the other, their concern with the *present*."[51] Such a tri-dimensional paradigm of liberation, salvation, and eschatology is reflected in the BCC's interpretation of liberation.

Salvation as liberation offers an occasion for a nuanced elucidation of the Black Coptic Church's eschatological vision. It is my contention that the BCC's eschatology repudiates any that refuse to acknowledge the act of creation itself (*imago dei*) as the ground of hope, expressed in one of the final promises of God, "Behold, I make all things new."[52] Queen Huldah Morgan described liberation as "the blessing in this world, not flying and dying to the next."[53] This construction of salvation as liberation embedded in an eschatological posture, interprets hope as having temporal ramifications. This theological bearing is not to obscure the "not yet" of Christian eschatology, but rather seeks to make the case that salvation for humanity includes a restoration of the world *and* human beings. To be sure, the BCC upholds that in salvation, "There is a redeeming of the earth. [. . . .] There is a new heaven and a new earth,"[54] which represents the end of systemic injustice. Further, "Because of the nature of the Black man [sic] and his [sic] experience under Euro-centric dominance . . . [The Black Coptic Church] wanted us to refocus from the afterlife to now. This is where we will experience the new creation."[55]

As we have seen, Prophet Cicero rejected salvation narratives that created a radical distinction between the soul and the body. Thus, in some sense, Black Coptic teaching is always oriented toward both the state of the soul and the state of the body. In fact, a preoccupation with immaterialism is shunned in the BCC. The afterlife, maintains Prophet Jacob, "is already taken care of. Our job is to assist God's people with living."[56] Accordingly, their teaching on salvation is in opposition to Black social death in a society that maintains anti-Blackness as a priority, indeed a necessity, for its existence. When queried whether the performance of a Black monarchy was in response to anti-Blackness, and thereby a conditional performance that would not find resonance beyond the cultural milieu in which the Church was founded, Queen Huldah argued "not so much." She continued, "We are not only responding to oppression. We are re-claiming that which was ours prior to white domination. We are simply rejecting what they say about us and lifting up God who made us to be free."[57] Queen Huldah's refutation of a conditional read of the Church's ecclesial performance rests on a belief that Prophet Cicero salvaged a royal ancestry not *because of*, but rather *in spite of*, the conditions in which the BCC emerged. For believers, the performance of a royal birthright is a reclamation of a bodily presentation that disavows disembodied theology.

The Black monarchy is a gesture toward afro-futurism in that the performance of the Black monarchy encompasses a cultural, aesthetic, and art-form imagination of a future, a Black future unhindered by the present.[58] This curating of a salvation narrative in conversation with identity formation is a critical component of the BCC. The imagination as performed in the construction of the Black monarchy, accordingly, comprises a salvific goal in that the orientation toward Ethiopia and the acceptance of a royal title are intended to personally and communally transform members. This assembled heroic identity reaches into the past toward the declaration of Black autonomy. For Priest Meshach:

> In the BCC we construct and destruct. We destruct the identity and perceptions of black people that were given to us. The building of our religious monarchy was Prophet Cicero's way of offering an answer to the question: "Who are we?" But the real question is, why is this even a concern? One assumes that because we are in North America then we must be Americans. But America has never loved us. We reach back historically to an ancient time and period where we as God's divine people were given a certain remnant of God's divine identity on earth. We look toward royal Ethiopia because there you will find the garden of Eden, the Mother of civilization, the land that has never been colonized, the royal monarchy of Solomon and Sheba, and even the Candace Queen who holds the keys to the treasures. Prophet Cicero did this because there were many ideas to describe us. He removed all of those and gave us Ethiopia and royalty.[59]

The assemblage of Ethiopia and royalty in the process of identity formation illuminates how Black Coptic members connect imagination to salvation. Indeed, the congregants are not direct descendants of a royal lineage, yet the hermeneutics employed in the community help believers assert autonomy of thought as they re-construct Black identity. As we have seen, both the Ethiopian and the royal identity participate in the Church's soteriology. Priest Eli narrates his first encounter with the BCC:

> When I first entered the doors of the True Temple of Solomon, I was amazed. Like most people who came to the Church I had belonged to other churches. I always felt like something was missing in those churches. When I came the Coptic Church, I remember seeing King Peter march in the temple. I heard black people saying, "we have a higher opinion of ourselves." And then I saw the flag come in the temple, and the prince shouted, "Hail to the Queens of Ethiopia." It was like I had finally found my salvation. I was saved from the negro and colored person degree. I could walk with my head up and not be ashamed. I could say with enthusiasm, "I am black and I am proud."[60]

Priest Eli's account illustrates both a social and a personal salvation story; that is, a deliverance that impacts the materiality of Black life. In the BCC, these assembled identities provide adherents with personal dignity in being Black and liberate Black people from given identities such as negro. To be Ethiopian and a member of a royal heritage, for Candace Queen Rachel, means that the members of the BCC "strip the ideas of white people and claim something different as to who we are. We now know that who we are is not given to us or determined by what the world says. We have been freed from allowing others to define us."[61] For Empress Selah, "When I hear 'Hail to the Queens of Ethiopia,' I hear my freedom. I celebrate the joy of blackness knowing as an Empress of God I am already saved from the evil of white theology."[62]

One might think of the salvific work of the BCC as an affirmation of "somebodiness." Somebodiness is a rejection of the casual construction of "nobodiness," which is intended to diminish the dignity and humanity of groups who exist in society as subalterns. In the tradition of Martin Luther King, Jr., somebodiness is a radical affirmation of human dignity in the face absurdity. In a 1967 speech entitled "What is your Life's Blueprint?" King said, "Number one in your life's blueprint should be a deep belief in your own dignity, your own worth, and your own somebodiness. Don't allow anybody to make you feel that you are nobody. Always feel that you count. Always feel that you have worth. And always feel that your life has ultimate significance."[63] King's description of somebodiness captures one aspect of performing Blackness in the BCC and other Black religious groups. As with many who were attracted to the burgeoning Black new religious movements of the Great Migration, many of the early converts to the BCC belonged to a socially constructed underclass. Queen Maryann recounts that when she joined the Church, "many people who joined were nobody to the world. They wouldn't educate us. We were left to think of ourselves as nothing."[64] However, for Queen Huldah, in the Black Coptic Church, "the same people who were the janitors, the factory workers, the domestic workers, and the nobodies throughout the week, were known as queens, prophets, and princes, and princesses on Sunday mornings." Queen Huldah suggests that this transformation of identity that took place in the church-house resonated in the daily lives of the churchgoers.[65] The taking on of a royal title fostered a sense of agency among the churchgoers, such that "they were psychologically able to transcend all that the world had said about them."[66] The "genius, then, of Prophet Cicero," maintained Empress Selah, "is that while some groups, such as the Marcus Garvey movement, were calling for a migration back to Africa, Prophet Cicero, in naming his organization as Coptic, brought an ancient African culture to North America."[67] Queen Huldah's articulation of the way identity formation in the BCC was not limited to Sunday mornings, but rather had impact on the congregants' daily lives, helps us understand how collective identity and social salvation brought into conversation the material and immaterial. That is, when members of the BCC perceive identity, there is a holistic deportment assumed by members, whereby "who I am on Sunday is not disconnected from who I am on Monday."[68]

Between Sundays

An important feature of imaginative communities, especially those that construct an identity in which *otherwise* is performed, is that they contest general assumptions of space and place as fixed realties. Claiming Ethiopia as "home" allows for a degree of cultural fluidity whereby geographies become intentionally blurred. Queen Huldah's contention that "we have to move beyond the notion of permanent geographies," speaks to this construction.[69] To be a member of the BCC, says Queen Bethel, whose mother converted when Bethel was a child, "is not to be a queen *only* on Sunday. Everywhere I go, even on my job, I am a queen." Queen Bethel was adamant during our conversation that the BCC helped her to claim her dignity and "make other people respect me as well, even those that, in their mind, would want to reduce me to what the world says I am." To be a member of the BCC, says Queen Bethel, is not to belong to a religion per se; it's an adoption of "a way of life."[70]

Queen Bethel's description of religion as a lived reality, rather than merely a ritual within a religious space, sheds light on the manner in which Black religion bridges the sacred and secular, reclaiming a cosmology that does not operate in dualities. During my interview sessions, it was clear to me that believers in the BCC do not separate their spiritual identity from what happens between Sundays. On the contrary, they perform their religious imaginaries in various publics, disregarding boundaries between church space and other space. Queen Shiphrah (1948–2022), a Candace Queen (a title reserved for wives of leaders in the community), noted:

> As a black queen, I walk in this degree every day of the week. Everywhere I go I walk with my head up. I speak with authority. I demand to be respected. We were taught that in church or not, in our holy garments or not, in our crowns or not. It matters not. I am a queen every day of the week. So, it doesn't matter what other may say, think, or feel about me. I walk with dignity. The world didn't give this to me and the world can't take it away.[71]

Her spiritual identity as a "black queen" has a profound impact on her understanding of human dignity. "The world," as in the imagined and performed world of anti-Blackness, does not have control over her imagined identity, and therefore cannot strip her of human dignity. The bridging of the imagined religious identity and the public identity, then, is part and parcel of the turn to Blackness in the BCC.

In one interview session during the first phase of this project, I pondered with my participants whether the gap between the Church's founding and the present day required such an ecclesial formation to continue. My question was really about the contextual nature of the turn toward a royal imagination. The categorization of "negro" as a descriptor for Black people was commonplace when Prophet Cicero organized the BCC, but is less so now. I asked whether the continuation of the imagined and assembled heroic identities was still required. Priest Meshach responded quickly:

> Black boys and girls are still seen as less than white children. Their schools are in poor condition. Everywhere we turn, we see black children and adults who have lost hope because of the way the world treats them. There is still an identity crisis with black people not knowing who they are because of what they see and hear on television. So, what we do in the BCC is first instill hope and pride. We remind them that God made them to be a special people. A divine people. A royal people. But this is not limited to a time where black people are called negro or nigger. We are not responding; we are pulling out of them what God put in them.[72]

This was the second time during the second phase of my interview sessions that a member of the community rejected the notion that the BCC

Figure 2.5. Black Coptic Empress Gathering in True Temple of Solomon Black Coptic Church, c.1978. Photo courtesy of Coptic Nation Temple.

exists merely as a "responsive" religious organization whose longevity is contingent on a particular set of social circumstances. Like other religious traditions, members of the Black Coptic community believe there is a transcendental reality within their tradition, one that supersedes and is not limited by context or history. The community therefore seeks to locate its *raison d'etre* in both a material and an immaterial read of history. As we saw earlier, Black Copts do not deny that the existential crisis with which Black Americans were confronted at the time the community's founding played a pivotal role in their faith tradition being "revealed" to their Prophet, but they emphasize the revelatory aspect; that is, God revealed their *true* identity and religion to Prophet Cicero. The pronouncement of a royal identity couched in Ethiopian heritage is really, for the BCC, an anthropological claim about the "somebodiness" of Black people. Priest Meshach's claim that "God made them" to be royal, collapses notions of creation and identity to a single claim of Black royalty that is tied to their understanding of the "isness" of the

Figure 2.6. Mother Queen Rebekah, Mother Queen of the BCC until her death in 2005. Credit: Photo courtesy of Coptic Nation Temple Black Coptic Church.

Black person. "Hail to the Queens of Ethiopia," therefore, is Black Copts' assertion—or reclamation—of their true identity. "We are merely claiming our birthright," noted Priest Eli. "Slavery, Jim Crow, and segregation, all tried to take this away from us. Prophet Cicero and the Queens reminded us that our birthright is God's Holy people. So, when we say, this is a way of life, we are saying that even without the interruption of slavery, this is who God made us to be."[73]

Identity and Hope

As we have seen, identity construction in the BCC is the performance of imagined *otherwise* ideas of Blackness. This performance, practically speaking, is an assertion of hope in a space in which Blackness is read, determinatively, as the property of the imagination of whiteness. While chapter four will take up the issue of ontology and afro-pessimism, for now it is sufficient to pronounce how the royal identity in the BCC contributes to the Church's understanding of black hope. In his response to the question of the utility of royal titles for believers, Priest Meshach grounded his response in a double hermeneutic. He said that the retrieval of royal titles and the turn to Blackness is, primarily, a recovery of the "isness" of Blackness and the image of God. Moreover, within a context of absurdity, noted Priest Meshach, the retrieval of such an identity is an assertion of hope and pride.

Hail to the Queens of Ethiopia and the Problem of Gender

"Hail to the Queens of Ethiopia" is more than a ritualistic declaration. While the statement is part of the weekly ceremony, it also connects royal titles to the spiritual hierarchy of the community. To be sure, the emphasis in the statement rests on "Queens" as a symbol for the larger Black Coptic congregation of "a royal people." That is, the declaration of "Queens" is an actual performance of *otherwise*. *Otherwise*, in this sense, is the act of asserting and performing Blackness as both a recovery *of* and protest *within*. It is a recovery of Blackness that is mystical and transcendent—not beholden to the material order or organization of the West. And, it performs protest—that is, it declares something (somebodiness) *within* a milieu that declares nothingness. However, in its declaration of a world in which women are adored as queens, the BCC has failed to take seriously the plight of Black women alongside its desire to imagine the free Black. That is, as we shall see, the spiritual hierarchy of the BCC is also a patriarchal world, in which women have been relegated to the periphery.

3

Rituals of Freedom

Imagining and Performing Otherwise

Ritual

Sunday afternoon. 4:30 PM. Chicago. Coptic Nation Temple. Priest Meshach approaches the pulpit. He expounds on how he has enjoyed the testimonies offered by members of the community. He continues, "The time has come for a change. A change must be made." He asks Princess Debra, a twenty-something-year-old woman in a gold robe and crown, to approach the pulpit. The entire assembly, in anticipation of an event, stands and faces the podium. Princess Debra is also now facing Priest Meshach, who informs her, "I have been watching you. The spirit has been watching. You have been 'on trial.'[1] The time has come for your name to come back." The community exclaims, "Amen," "Praise God," and, "Thank you, Black Jesus!" Priest Meshach continues, "when I change your name, the world won't know you. Friends and family may turn their backs on you, but if I change your name, everything will be alright." He says, "The time has come to let go of that ol' slave name. There is a name written in heaven, a divine name." He asks one of the members to remove Princess Debra's crown from her head. He proceeds, "From this day forward, the world will no longer know you as Debra. . . . But from today onward, you shall be known as Mariyah." Priest Meshach lays his hand upon her head. The community expresses praise and jubilation for what they have witnessed.[2]

* * *

The turn to Blackness is not merely a theological posture in the Black Coptic Church. It is, rather, the goal, indeed the *telos*, of the liberative theology as thought and performed by members of the group. The rejection of white constructions of Blackness and an acceptance of a new life in which Blackness is revered is at the center of the Church's theology and rituals. Queen Huldah attests, "As Black Copts, we are in the business of transformation. [. . . .] [This includes] Black men and women who know who they are. It is a complete denial of the negro and the adaptation of a new identity. A divine identity. An identity found in Black Jesus."[3] It is, in other words, Blackness as a mystical reality.

This chapter considers how rituals and practices in the BCC assist their imagination and performance of Black identity—specifically, what I identify as rituals of liberation. I argue that the construction of identity in the BCC does not conclude with a glance toward Ethiopia or with the erection of an earthly heavenly kingdom, as explored earlier. Rather, those aspects of the Black Coptic sect, while important for an understanding of the intersection of race, religion, and identity among believers, must be read in conjunction with Black Coptic rituals and practices, which contribute to a comprehensive epistemic about performance and imagination of Black identity inside and beyond the BCC. This chapter therefore grapples with how the BCC performs *otherwise* as ritualism, and how the examined rituals provide a sense of liberation among believers. I employ "liberation" here as an act of breaking away from negative modes of identity, toward the possibility of a new Black being.

Otherwise

Embodying *otherwise* in the BCC is performed in ritual that aims to make a radical break with the absurd and point to Black life as joy, including the acceptance of a salvaged identity, and of Black people as "chosen" and "holy."[4] This chosen-ness is demonstrated in the changing of names, the wearing of "holy royal garments," the observation of Passover, and the practice of baptism. Each of these elements treats Black life as sacred. *Otherwise*, in the BCC, can be summarized as the radical assertion of righteous indignation via divine recovery.

Such indignation in the BCC is a part of the very way that they imagine things. For Empress Selah, "everything we do in the [Black Coptic Church] is because we read the scriptures in such a way where we see ourselves in the text. We see ourselves as God's holy people. Despite what the world might say, we see ourselves as royal people."[5] Priest

Stephen maintained, "Prophet Cicero saw something in us that we did not see. Like John on the Isle of Patmos, Prophet Cicero was able to look beyond the social conditions of the world and see us as God sees us. Only God could reveal this to Prophet Cicero."[6] Empress Selah's and Priest Stephen's emphases on seeing and revelation are critical in that they stress the act of imagination in the process of identity formation and ritual performance. While it is true, then, as we have seen, that the BCC is attracted to an idealized conception of Blackness, imagination is the point of departure for such an idea. Priest Stephen's reference to the opening of the Book of Revelation suggests that the BCC's idea of Blackness comes through divine authority. This imaginative approach allows for the act and ritual of Blackness despite the absurd. We see *otherwise* in various religious observances in the community that remind the membership of their recovered identity and their election as God's chosen people.

"I Told Jesus It Would Be Alright If He Changed My Name"

As with other Great Migration new religions (or what Weisenfeld describes as religio-racial movements), such as the Nation of Islam and the Moorish Science Temple, members of the BCC adopt "spiritual names." Weisenfeld notes that, "for members, adoption of new names derived from particular religio-racial commitments changed the individual, and just as the group names renewed spiritual connections severed by slavery, shaming, and false history, new personal 'spiritual cognomens' fostered powerful connection with the divine."[7] In the BCC, spiritual names replace birth-given names. In many respects, the assumption of a spiritual name is the final turn in the rejection of Black identity as tethered to Western notions of Black inferiority, especially as they relate to the term "negro." Such a turn is consummated in a name-change ritual. Indeed, the transformation from one's birth—or given—name is a significant moment in the life of believers; it is a completion of one's spiritual journey steeped in Blackness.

For many believers, the acceptance a spiritual name solidified the BCC as a "way of life," and not merely a religious affiliation. It is the realization of the BCC's ambition to create a liberated Black person oriented toward the divine. For Priest Gehazi, who was born Steven Willis, receiving his spiritual name cemented the idea that he "had been fully separated from a past social condition that limited [his] existence." For him, accepting Gehazi in place of Steven "was a point of great jubilation inside and outside of the church."[8] To be sure, "for members of some other groups taking a new name was an essential part of transforming themselves into something other than Negroes and of the daily experience of that transformed religio-racial identity."[9] In this sense, "[spiritual] names are more than individual identifiers; they are keys and symbols that represent how God's is active in our lives every day of the week,"[10] and so they help followers navigate the world. Queen Huldah emphasized that spiritual names are revered because they represent a new birth. "No longer are we haunted by names of slavery, names with no meaning and or purpose," she said. Rather, "when we receive a spiritual name, it is the awakening of a spirit in us that makes permanent our identity, our new identity, that the world didn't give to us, and the world can't take away. It is our way of saying Black identity is not the property of racism. Leaving negro behind, our spiritual names foster the power and agency of personal and communal change." Therefore, maintains Queen Huldah, "when a name is released from heaven, the congregation shouts with praise, because God has revealed who we really are as a divine people."[11]

As with the assumption of royal titles in the BCC, spiritual names point to the possibility of *otherwise* via performative imagination. Spiritual names are derived from the Christian Bible, and Egyptian culture. They are borrowed from both people and cities—the latter seen in the case of Prophet Peter's wife, Queen Capernaum (1928–1986). Spiritual names are not selected by those receiving them. Rather, leaders of individual temples, "in conjunction with the Holy Spirit, receive the names when [God] is ready to release these spirits or names back into the atmosphere. This could happen in a dream, a vision, or come through one of the higher queens in the church. But the names are not revealed until it is time."[12] At their core, however, spiritual names in the BCC perform *otherwise*, as members "leave behind their past and fully become the person or spirit that was handed down to them."[13] Religious imagination, then, in the process of assuming a spiritual name, provides the conditions of possibility for members to assert (perform) a radically different religio-racial identity. Moreover, spiritual names point to and participate in the otherness of Black existence and afford believers an occasion to self-fashion their performance of Blackness apart from and not bound by oppressive imaginations.

When Candace Queen Rachel was born, her mother named her Yolanda. She was reared in a Black Baptist community. At age 20, she was introduced to the BCC by Roderick Gardiner (Priest Meshach), whom she would later marry. She recounts:

> Growing up in the Baptist Church, I always felt something was missing. I remember growing up and often thinking, "Where is the black presence in the Bible?" All of the pictures of Jesus, angels, and God where white. I would often wonder if there was anything in the Bible that applied to me. The church I attended as a kid didn't talk a lot about the racial troubles in Chicago. We talked a lot about getting to heaven and wearing a long white robe, singing in the heavenly choir, and walking around with Jesus all day. But, I heard people around me being called niggers, colored people, and negroes. So, I always felt that something was missing from that church. When I joined True Temple of Solomon [Coptic Church] it was like heaven on earth. I was told I was somebody, I was a Princess. Black was not lesser than white, but to be Black was to be beautiful. My history was bigger than slavery. [. . . .] And when I was called before the Prophet [Andrew] to receive my name, I remember the instant joy. I cried as I walked to the rostrum because I was finally about to know who I was. My birth name was limiting. It was a Western name. I knew there was a divine spirit in me. So, when Prophet Andrew released Rachel as my name, I shouted with praise. I shouted because, um, I finally knew my true identity. Not only was I princess, but I was Rachel. And that spirit has blessed me ever since.[14]

In a similar reflection, Empress Hatshepsut, who was born Shaloma Lee, narrates a story of name conversion as a moment of receiving the resources to fulfill her destiny.

> When I received the name Hatshepsut, it was a new beginning for me. Although I knew I was a royal Ethiopian, and that my Black is beautiful, I did not know *who* I was. The name Hatshepsut provided me with the information I needed to understand my purpose. Shaloma was a name that

did not do it for me. Hatshepsut was the first female pharaoh of Egypt; a strong Black woman warrior. So, when I was given the key of Hatshepsut, I was given a blueprint for excellence. I knew nothing could conquer me without my permission. This name is more than just a name; it's an identity of freedom and liberation from the limitations of the world.[15]

In the accounts above, the efficacy of spiritual names is located in their ability to contribute to the development of personal agency. Both Candace Queen Rachel and Empress Hatshepsut's testimonies highlight a relationship between knowledge of self and agency. In other words, the taking on of new names is not uniquely about identity re-construction. Spiritual names also operate as vehicles for instilling a sense of purpose in the life of the believer. When Candace Queen Rachel received her name, she gained a better sense of her life's purpose and the path she should take. Gaining the courage to assert her Blackness as powerful, Empress Hatshepsut found the freedom and liberation within to chart a path for her life that differed from the one to which she had been accustomed. Such narratives of race, religion, and identity speak to the ambitiousness of Prophet Cicero's aims in the liberative imaginative re-construction of Black identity. For him, "a name is the key to information great and small. Once you unveil the name you have access to the purpose and destiny of mankind [sic]. A name is a like a clue to uncovering the meaning of that which it signifies."[16] So in a sense, the revelation and bestowing of spiritual names in the BCC is the process of uncovering the true meaning and destiny of the recipient of the name.

The hermeneutical key to spiritual names in the BCC is their potential to assist believers in the creation and recovery of a heroic identity linked to a divine history. As is also the case with royal titles in the BCC, spiritual names possess a salvific function or, rather, are part of the salvific process. It is not by chance that spiritual names in the BCC are mostly of biblical origin. Unlike peer movements such as the Moorish Science Temple, which drew largely upon names that were Moorish in character, Prophet Cicero's Church taught that "biblical names had the power to completely transform the individual because they were sacred names."[17] In Father Divine's Peace Movement, in which, similarly, a spiritual name "did more than disrupt connection to PM members' past, Divine preached that spiritual names remade his followers."[18] Prophet

Cicero taught his followers that their spiritual names connected them to a "divine genealogy," and so they were not "adopted into the family of God," a reference to Paul's theology of the gentiles.[19] Rather, spiritual names represent a re-birth or self-fashioning of an identity. In this sense, one might read the changing of names in the BCC as a return to a divine history that accomplishes the comprehensive fashioning of an identity that participates in the individual salvation of a believer.

In the opening vignette, before he laid hands on Princess Debra and changed her name to Mariyah, Priest Meshach informed her, "When I change your name, everything will be alright." No doubt, the language employed in this ritual is taken from the spiritual, "Changed Mah Name," which asserts the following:

> I tol' Jesus it would be all right
> If He changed mah name
> Jesus tol' me I would have to live humble
> If He changed mah name
> Jesus tol' me that the world would be 'gainst me
> If He changed mah name
> But I tol' Jesus it would be all right
> If He changed mah name

The changing of names in the BCC is an intensely spiritual practice in which followers understand the process as a movement toward freedom and salvation. It is a baptism into a new life, one directed by God and not imprisoned in an idea of a stolen life traceable to chattel slavery. Queen Huldah attests that this act of religio-performance in the BCC is analogous to "newly freed enslaved or kidnapped Africans who desired to disconnect from the names that were used in slavery. In the BCC, we see our birth names as identifiers of a life of bondage. Black Jesus reveals our spiritual names to the leaders, making everything alright."[20] The new name bestowed on believers is a name "written in God's book of life. God knows this name. It is a spiritual name because it represents our complete submission to the Holy Spirit. Unlike our natural names, spiritual names have the ability to save us from the troubles of the world."[21]

Priest Meshach's description of the salvific function of spiritual names is particularly significant, as it further clarifies the mystical nature of *otherwise* in the process of salvation, given the emphasis in the BCC on spiritual names as revealed by God to individual leaders in the community. The postulate in this construction is that spiritual names originate in an unseen realm and are made manifest in the material order for the purpose of completing the salvation process for adherents. Believers interpret the ritual mystically, believing that the Coptic spiritual leader, in dialogue with "the spirit," receives names and bestows them on believers whose body, in essence, becomes a host for the name. Indeed, Queen Bethel maintained, "when my name was changed, I was no longer who I was before my name. Bethel, and all that Bethel represents, now lives in me."[22] In this sense, "everything will be alright" because believers make a transcendent—mystical—turn toward the Holy Spirit who, in conjunction with their new names, guides their very being. Such a metanoia experience is foundational in the life of the Black Copt as they make an ascent toward a "new being." Embracing a new name, then, is an intentional and spiritual performance of *otherwise*, or, as we have seen, a way of performing identity as that which is derived from an immaterial, indeed mystical, source.

Spiritual names in the Black Coptic community are symbols that point toward a freedom that disrupts remnants of North America's enslavement of Black people and the invention of the negro. Most notably, spiritual names disrupt pejorative notions related to birth—or given—names that insinuate and identify a connection to anti-Black imaginaries as performed in social and religious structures. Spiritual names permit believers to participate in what they believe is a higher, or divine, sense of the self, imagined and performed as Black autonomy. Disciples' belief that their names are disclosed to leaders of their community shows how the BCC intentionally implements fugitive performances that are meant to assert a distinctive relationship with the divine. Spiritual names display an intersection of race, religion, identity, and resistance that converge at the level of mysticism. Yet, while the bestowing of a spiritual name is a high point in the life of the believer, not every parishioner will receive a spiritual name, and for those who do, there is not a specific time when this event happens. They are given at the discretion of spiritual leaders. However, one element that is standard within the BCC is the self-fashioning ritual of dress among adherents, which contributes to the notion of identity within this institution.

"All God's Children Got a Robe"

An immediate observation upon entering a Black Coptic temple is a sea of people dressed in robes, which the group classifies as royal or holy garments, and headpieces, which the Church calls "crowns." From community leaders to children, an assortment of holy garments of various colors, determined by the Sunday of the month, are worn. Such holy garments, which differ among churchgoers according to their position in the Church, are a distinctive mark of the BCC. Indeed, it is not uncommon to drive by a BCC temple on a Sunday and see followers in the streets wearing their garments and crowns. This act of performative imagination seeks to materialize—within the visible culture—a view of Blackness that is heroic, royal, and rejects derogatory depictions of Black life. It asserts, outwardly, Blackness as *otherwise*.

The theory behind the wearing of holy garments in the BCC is similar to what historian Stephen Greenblatt calls self-fashioning. For Greenblatt, self-fashioning refers to the process by which groups or individuals construct an identity in light of socially acceptable norms.[23] However, groups and individuals also have the capacity to self-fashion *against* a set of cultural norms, or what I like to call fugitive self-fashioning: imagining, re-creating, and performing an identity that seeks to disrupt and de-stabilize pejorative constructed notions of the self, invented by imaginaries immersed within a normative gaze predicated upon superiority. Fugitive self-fashioning is a reclamation of personal and communal agency aimed at rejecting the absurd and uncovering the scandal of the human project—a project that objectified the other. Self-fashioning, in short, recovers and performs an idea of the self and community in vocabularies defined by oneself.

Black churchgoers have often negotiated identity via the churchhouse. In fact, the notion of "Sunday's Best"—one's nicest clothes, which one wears to church—speaks to this re-imagining and self-fashioning of identity. The "nobodies" during the week—the despised, the ghettoized, and the socially rejected persons—would present themselves in church wearing their best suits, shined shoes, long dresses, and big hats as a way of asserting dignity. Insofar as the church was the institution where many Black folks embraced a sense of dignity, it made sense that those participating in the service would turn to their best as a kind of self and communal affirmation. As noted sociologists of the "Black Church" C. Eric Lincoln and Lawrence H. Mamiya point out:

> The Black Church has no challenger as the cultural womb of the black community. Not only did it give birth to new institutions such as schools, banks, insurance companies, and low-income housing, it also provided an academy and an arena for political activities, and it nurtured young talent for musical, dramatic, and artistic development. [...] Much of black culture is heavily indebted to the black religious tradition, including most forms of black music, drama, literature, storytelling, and even humor.[24]

The Black Church as cultural womb of the community was a place of refuge where Black dignity was recognized. It fulfilled both a spiritual and a cultural need of the community. It provided an aesthetic of Blackness as resistance, and apparel was one form of that resistance. Sunday's Best, then, offers insight into modes of Black resistance mediated through

Figure 3.1. Black Women in Hats. Credit: Jack Delano, "Church Service," Woodville, Greene County, Georgia, U.S. Farm Security Administration, October 1941.

Figure 3.2. Sunday's Best, 1941. Credit: Russell Lee, "Negro boys on Easter Morning, Southside Chicago," Farm Security Administration/Office of War Information collection at the Library of Congress, 1941.

bodily form. Such self-fashioning is an act of religious resistance; it is an approval of the Black body.

Clothing as protest illustrates an important motif in Black religious life and practices. Employing the body as a vehicle for protest and indignation is a performative move of Black affirmation. Sunday's Best highlights not only the beauty of the Black body, but the worthiness of Black culture against the backdrop of human misery. In the above 1941 photograph, for instance, titled, "Negro boys on Easter Morning, Southside Chicago," often referred to simply as "Sunday's Best," photographer Russell Lee captures the audacity of Black folk to perform Black imagination within a context of social and economic depression. Although the Black community was largely a working-class community buried in poverty and economic isolation, the suits worn by the five young men illustrate a high degree of self-confidence. The Black body, as shown here, transmits a negation of the absurd.

Sunday's Best also speaks to the degree to which Black churchgoers view the church-house as a sacred space in which joy and jubilation are expressed. When Blacks point to "Sunday's Best" as the attire for church, they express their respect for that sacred space. The Black church has styled itself as a beacon of hope, and offered adherents a space in which to "steal away" from the world. Accordingly, Black worshipers sported their finest clothes to look their best in what was, for many, the climax of their weekly activities. Church was the space in which Black joy was most uninhibited. So, the long dresses, suits, and elaborate "church hats" pointed to the expressive freedom that, unlike any other institution, the Black Church was able to evoke in the imagination of its worshipers.

It was not Black Christians alone, however, who performed Blackness and imagination while also negotiating identity in their "Sunday's Best." Other Black religious communities, particularly during the Great Migration, also integrated a characteristic dress for its members. In the Nation of Islam, "becoming Muslim also meant changing the way one dressed and adorned oneself."[25] To this end, "[w]omen were to dress modestly and avoid makeup. Believers were also supposed to fix their hair in an Islamic fashion,"[26] and avoid perms or other means of processing one's hair. In the NOI, negotiating racial identity meant adopting a modest dress that separated them from white people, whom they "associated with immodest dress." They argued "that Black women must dress differently in order to be true to their racial identity."[27] Muslim women in the NOI therefore avoided European dress, but also did not wear clothing from African countries deemed to be uncivilized, such as "tribal dress," and Americanized appropriations of such garb, such as kente cloth.[28] Instead, in an attempt to display purity, Muslim women donned white dresses and *hijabs*. For members of the NOI,

> Clothes and other forms of adornment played an important role in the making of the Black Muslim body. A clear form of public identification, Muslim styles of dress and adornment became a form of resistance against potential harassment by men and what many female members saw as the temptation to imitate white fashions. NOI members, both male and female, also testified that adherence to these codes of ethical behavior made them feel proud, dignified, civilized, and respectable.[29]

Figure 3.3. Women in the Nation of Islam, 1963. Credit: Everett Collection Inc., African American women dressed in white at a Nation of Islam meeting in New York City. Behind the women a sign reads, "We Must Protect Our Most Valuable Property, Our Women." July 26, 1963.

This religious movement thus aims to instill a sense of pride and dignity in its followers and concurrently reject white culture. For the NOI, the body is the temple of God, and by adhering to the dress customs of its founder, Elijah Muhammad, "they were . . . expressing their true identity as God's chosen people." In fact, "Muslim dress and adornment was a sign of their salvation. . . ."[30]

What we see in these examples are ways that Black religions have constructed an identity in the context of Black marginalization, and their followers' experience as peripheral citizens. From big hats and long dresses, to Islamic dress and minimalist approaches to hair style, "Sunday's Best" has often expressed how dress enters the broader discourse of race relations and the search for identity. That religion became a vehicle through which such attempts would be advanced is not surprising. Dating back to the invisible institution, the Black religious imagination has a long and storied history of engaging the social, the political, and the religious via various imaginaries that perform both a constructive and critical function. The BCC is a part of this dialogue. Given the active religious imagination at work in the BCC, from an imagined homeland to the acceptance of royal titles, the transformation of dress by its members "fits" its general salvific program, insofar as Prophet Cicero imagined the BCC as a royal nation (kingdom) within the nation. To this end, the dress and customs of the BCC reflect its announcement as a royal people.

The Moorish Science Temple and Ethiopian Hebrew sect "shared an approach to religio-racial self-making through dress aimed at connecting individuals to the sacred geography so important to their narratives of identity."[31] The same is true of the BCC, whose racial imaginary of Blackness is married to a heroic reading of Ethiopian and Ancient Egyptian culture. This geographic turn is part of the turn to Blackness, and includes religious attire that suggests Ethiopian and Egyptian heritages. To this end, pictures of the late Ethiopian Emperor Haile Selassie I, and his wife, Empress Menen Asfaw, often grace the walls of Black Coptic temples as representations of the "Black monarchy" and the dress required of royalty. Empress Selah noted, "When we look toward Ethiopia and Ancient Egypt, and we see beautiful darker people in royal attire asserting their royal ancestry, we see ourselves as those people, a royal people. When we wear our holy garments, it's like we are transformed, everything about us, to a higher sense of self and pride in who we are."[32] During one of my site visits to a Chicago temple, I stood by a picture of Emperor Haile Selassie and asked one of the parishioners what she imagined when she observed the photo. She responded, "I imagine myself as an Ethiopian Queen. That's why I am wearing this robe, because I am a queen of Ethiopia and queens wear robes."[33] The geography—the crossings of borders—is a critical aspect of the BCC's adoption of holy garments and crowns; that is, the self-fashioning of the Black Coptic man and woman includes garb that connects followers to their divine geography.

Holy garments in the BCC manifest an understanding of Blackness, or the Black person, as transcendent and therefore not bound by colonial interpretations of Black life and Black culture. "While most people think of Sunday's Best as beautiful Western clothes, such as a nice suit and hat," said Priest Meshach, "for us, Sunday's Best is a

Figure 3.4. Royal Empress in True Temple of Solomon Black Coptic Church, 1978. Credit: Picture courtesy of Coptic Nation Temple.

display of Ethiopian robes and crowns as we claim our identity as a royal people. When I look around the temple and see Black people in beautiful holy garments addressing each other as queen, empress, and princess, I see a Black nation that refuses to let anyone define us."[34] Such self-fashioning speaks to the Church's desire for Black autonomy, via ritualistic performance, cementing the church's assent toward divine Blackness.

When Queen Huldah joined the BCC in the mid-1970s, she had arrived from New York, where she regularly interacted with various religious movements that she described as "socially conscious and woke."[35] She recalled:

Figure 3.5. Queen Huldah, Black Coptic Church Series, Chicago, IL, January 2021. Credit: Iwona Biedermann Photography.

> As a young child and teenager, I would often see organizations like Noble Drew Ali, the Nation of Islam, and some more afro-centric religious groups, and was often struck by their attire. In a good way, that is. I grew up in a pretty pro-black household and was introduced to people like Marcus Garvey and Elijah Muhammad at a young age. In fact, my father would often say things to me like, "You think you're pretty classy like Haile Selassie." So, I was shaped in a world where black religion was in fact radical. When I joined True Temple of Solomon [Black] Coptic Church, and saw the women in their royal garments, I knew what was going on. I knew then, this is the place for me.[36]

For Queen Huldah, holy garments were critical in the identity formation of the church's followers: "When members of our temples are in their robes, it's as if we enter into a majestic palace, such that all of the labels of the world, like negro and colored person, are wiped away; they have no meaning."[37]

Queen Huldah's correlation of holy garments and identity illuminates the performative aspect of holy garments, not merely as part of an overall performance, but also the ways that the garments themselves *already* perform. That is, in the BCC, holy garments effect the possibility of identity *otherwise*. There is an association between observation—as seen above in the statement of Priest Meshach—and performance. For many in the BCC, performative imagination as an observable sensory experience is at work prior to their officially becoming members. They are able to contemplate *otherwise* as the symbol of holy garments participates in the not-yet within the already. This possibility is captured in the testimony of Candace Queen Rachel, who claims that holy garments "tell a story about our past. But they also tell a story about where we are and where we are going."[38] Holy garments, accordingly, mediate a sense of self and identity in both the racial and religious imaginaries, such that there is translation at work via an observational—sensory—experience. They also mediate and bridge history with the future.

While holy garments narrate a story about what *is* possible, it is also true that, for believers, holy garments build and maintain their collective identity. For Queen Huldah, our robes are a sort of a neutralizing invention. Prophet Cicero seemed to be as concerned with uniformity among members, as he was with the robes providing individual identity. Prophet Peter, also, wanted to build the self-confidence of his followers. When one enters our temple, you have no way of knowing who is on public aid and who works a white-collar job. We were taught that God is not a respecter of persons, and so our robes assist with this message. The janitor and factory workers were dressed the same as the MD and the PhD. Prophet taught that the world tried to separate us enough, so when one enters the temple, we are all the same in the eyesight of God.[39]

Queen Huldah's emphasis on uniformity and self-confidence among members underscores an important feature of the Church's spiritual practice of wearing holy garments—the aspiration to inculcate a communal sense of Black pride among the followers. Nonetheless, Queen Huldah's claim of an egalitarian church and royal imagination within which a collective identity flourishes among believers begs several questions as they are related to class and economic status within the group.

Black Coptic followers believe that Prophet Cicero organized a religious institution in which followers, without regard to their economic and professional status, were made equal upon entry. Indeed, the institution of holy garments in place of traditional western wear was intended to eradicate the appearance of class and economic differences. "When we are in our [holy garments]," maintained believer Queen Bethel, "we are all equal. There are no 'big I's and little you's." It does not matter how much money you have or don't have. Our robes are a symbol of equality."[40] Equality among believers is a lofty idea. While such a claim allows the BCC to assert or imagine a liberation that privileges the uniformity of the group over class distinctions, the claim is problematized in the actual performance. That is, class and wealth gaps are evident in ways that are not reflected in the Church's liberatory claims.

The promise of an egalitarian community was an appealing feature to those who converted to the BCC. For people who belonged to what was described earlier as a socially constructed underclass, their conversion to the BCC made possible the wearing of holy garments that were a symbol of their royalty. In practice, however, the poorest members couldn't afford the robes. Such is the case of Queen Sarah, a middle-aged woman who is a member of a Black Coptic temple in Chicago.[41] During one of my visits to the temple she attends in Chicago, I asked why she was wearing a black robe and not a gold one similar to others'. She told me that she "could not afford the other robes," and "typically you would wear a plain black robe until you can purchase the others."[42] "The robes," maintained Queen Sarah, "are not cheap. If I purchased all the robes I need, a purple one, gold, and cranberry, that would cost me well over a thousand dollars. I am not working and am a single mother so all I can afford is the black robe."[43] Another woman, Empress Lisa, a member at the same temple, echoed those sentiments:[44]

> We are supposed to buy a bunch of robes, crowns, matching shoes, matching earrings, and matching jewelry. That's too much money. So, I have been an Empress for a couple of years and all I have is a black robe. Even if I had the money I don't know if I would buy the robes. I have a child and can't be spending all my money on church robes. So, I just wear this robe. Do I wish I could afford them? Yeah. I am an oddball compared to the other Empresses, but this is the best I can do.[45]

The testimonies of these women are revealing, and shed light on the ways in which the royal imagination, one predicated upon a notion of equality, unintentionally reinscribes class and economic divisions among believers, and how these divisions are specific to women in the group, as men are not required to acquire as many robes.[46] Indeed, Queen Huldah's claim that the economically depressed and working-class converts are spiritually and socially transformed upon their entry into the BCC does not account for those members for whom conversion did not alter their social standing within or outside their membership. Given that the Church's conception of "royalty" includes significant attentiveness to material culture, such as the acquisition of royal garments, women within the group who are unable to procure the various robes, crowns, and accompanying items experience a sense of inequality. Empress Lisa's self-identification as an "oddball" points to a sense of economic exclusivity within the community; her financial status precludes her from participating fully in the royal imagination of the group. "Everyone knows," she says, "that those of us in black robes can't afford

Figure 3.6. Priest Eli, Black Coptic Church Series, Chicago, IL, January 2021. Credit: Iwona Biedermann Photography.

the garments, and no one has ever asked me if I need help purchasing my robes."[47] Members who are unable to afford their spiritual regalia are thus noticed among other believers, and often carry a sense of shame or guilt connected to their economic standing. Yet believers, those with and without the economic resources to purchase their spiritual regalia, connect their royal garments to a lofty recovery of an African past that contributes to their Black Coptic experience.

As I observed a Sunday service, it became clearer that members in the community understand their wearing of garments as connecting the Church to a momentous view of Black history that they psychologically translate as efficacious in the present. At a memorial service honoring a deceased member of the congregation (Mother Queen Rebekah), for example, a member had the following to say:

> Queen Rebekah taught me that I have always been a queen. When I entered the church, I didn't have anything. I barely had clothes on my back. I thought, "I can't go to the church as a queen wearing run-down clothing. Queens don't live like this." But I thank God for Mother Rebekah. She told me to "robe up" and follow Black Jesus. I came to church the next week and they had a robe ready for me. Instantly I felt a change take place. I didn't need a long dress. God provided me with a holy robe. I knew then that I belonged to God's royal family.[48]

The parishioner's testimony offers insight into a significant performative characteristic and function of holy garments and crowns in the BCC—the possibility of holy garments to transform time; that is, the joining of the *kairos* and *kronos*.

A weekly processional in the BCC includes the women in the congregation marching to their respective seats, wearing their holy garments and crowns. As they do so, a remake of a familiar song in the Black church is sung. The original lyrics of "I Shall Wear a Crown" proclaim the following:

> I shall wear a crown
> I shall wear a crown
> When the trumpet sounds
> When the trumpet sounds
> Oh I shall wear a crown

> I shall wear a crown
> Soon as my feet strike Zion
> Lay down my heavy burden
> Put on my robe in glory
> Shout and tell Him my story.
> Soon as I can see Jesus
> Tell Him all about my trouble
> Put on my robe in glory
> Shout and tell Him my story

During the BCC's processional, however, the community sings "I Shall Wear a Crown" with the following lyrics:

> I'll wear crown
> I'll wear crown
> I shall wear a crown today . . .

There is a certain joyfulness among the community as the song is sung. The lyrics not only fit with, but emphasize, the Church's soteriology; that is, a theological supposition that does not divorce the salvation of the world to come from the present reality. Such presentation, the wearing of holy garments and a crown, serves as a material reminder of the imagination at the heart of the BCC; an imagination that defies the radical "otherness" of salvation. Queen Magdalene, a teacher in the Black Coptic community's School of Wisdom, maintained that

> in our tradition, we don't celebrate teachings that inform us we have to wait and die to get to heaven to wear a long white robe. We don't accept teachings that say when we get to heaven, then we will get a crown. No, we have our robe and crown right here in this earth. And that's a black robe. When we put on our robes and crown, we are making a statement. God has delivered us in the here and now, and we can walk into our divine reality here on this earth. We have been tricked to believe we must suffer like hell, die, and then someone gives us a robe. When I put on my robe and my crown, I am saying God has delivered me now! This is what salvation looks like. God has delivered from being a nigga, or a negro, or a colored person. In my robe, I want the whole word to know that white

racism has not won because God has delivered me. So, I shall wear a crown today *and* tomorrow.[49]

Queen Magdalene's association between the wearing of holy garments and earthly freedom, or the time between times, finds particular expression in the most sacred observance of the BCC, the Passover. For members of this community, each religious performance and ritual, from holy garments to the changing of names, is in some way related to the highest point of the Church's liturgical calendar, the season in which the community acknowledges God's redemptive power as demonstrated in the liberation from chattel slavery, otherwise known as the "400 Years Passover." In this season, members of the BCC read the story of Black folk in America in relation to, or as an extension of, the story of Exodus. Prophet Jacob reports, "Our observance of the Passover is also a remembrance that our true identity is God's chosen people. We celebrate the Passover as a way of reminding the younger generation that God has not and will not abandon us in the face of persecution."[50] Theologically, the Passover ritual in the BCC is the performance of social and lived salvation facilitated by divine intervention.

400 Years Passover

On Sunday, July 27, 1986, Prophet David, a member of True Temple of Solomon Black Coptic Church, mounted the pulpit to offer remarks on the celebration in which the church was engaged. Queen Rebekah, the "head queen" of the church, was leading the worship service. She asked Prophet David to consider the meaning of Passover. Prophet David, dressed in a black holy garment and a black crown, offered the following:

> Today is the 400-year Passover. It doesn't matter what year may come, it will always be the 400-year Passover, for this is the remembrance of God, a Black God, reaching down into the world of slavery and delivering us. Like the children of Israel, that's who we are, when God had mercy and rescued them, our 400 years Passover shall always be a remembrance of the God choosing to liberate us from slavery and Jim Crow. This is a celebration of black freedom. Only a Black God could do what God did for us. So, this 400-year Passover is a moment to remember the God who

brought us out of Egypt, and the God who brought us out of slavery in North America. That's the same God. We are the same people. This is the 400 years Passover.[51]

Prophet David's observations capture the religious and theological beliefs that unify the Church's teaching and telos, a new Black identity and a new Black being who is liberated. Standing at the core of their theology and accompanying rituals, the Passover is the apex of their worship and the most important event in the life of every believer. Whereas most believers will receive a spiritual name, *every* member will experience the Passover, as it is necessary in order to be considered a full convert into the BCC. In fact, Priest Meshach stated that "everything we do during the year is directed toward the Passover. There is no day in our calendar that is more sacred. Not Christmas nor Easter. The Passover is about God and us. It tells a divine story."[52] It is the story of a historical arc, a unified view of history that connects Black people in North America to the children of Israel, such that institutions like the BCC assert their community as "God's chosen people." At a secondary level, the divine story at work is reflected in Prophet David's commentary, in which every Passover in the BCC is the 400-year Passover. For Prophet David, like Priest Meshach, there is a unity of thought, a divine imagination, that bridges the Israelite story with the story of Blacks in North America.

The story of Exodus, the biblical account of God's special relationship with Israel as the chosen people who are liberated from slavery under a harsh pharaoh, has been a staple in the Black religious imagination since the invention of the invisible institution. To be sure, as James Cone offers, its "theme of survival and liberation is found in sermon, prayer, and song...."[53] Undeniably, its theological emphasis that God will liberate the weak from the injustice of the strong is found in many hymns, including this one:

> When Israel was in Egypt's land,
> Let my people go;
> Oppressed so hard they could not stand,
> Let my people go;
> Go down, Moses, 'way down in Egypt's land,
> Let my people go.[54]

In other words, the social context of Black religion, together with Black exilic experience in North America, provides an epistemological framing for how Black folk read and understand the biblical narrative. The biblical witness, for Black Christians, has never been an abstract reality limited to otherworldliness. Rather, Black folk have employed a correlative hermeneutic whereby they imagine themselves in the text, and thus, aim to close the distance between the biblical world and their own experiences. An appeal to experience in interpreting the Exodus narrative in Black culture is not an essentialist argument narrowly focused on Black Christian life. While it is the case that Black Christians have elevated this story in their religious life,

> there is, however, a shared, transcendent cultural reality experienced by Black Christians and non-Christians alike: black suffering. Black suffering bears and has borne a voluble burden. On the one hand, Black suffering shares the suffering that is common to all human beings, sickness, broken homes, tragedies of detachment, accidents, wars, etc. On the other hand, that suffering has been compounded by slavery, discrimination, and racism. This sociological grid of blacks provides a solidarity that transcends even membership in the Christian religion.[55]

In this sense, the religious imagination of Black folk has been concomitant to their imagination of justice and freedom.

The turn to experience in the Black theological imagination enabled Black people to conceive of theological assertions that not only questioned the white religious imagination but cemented the claim that God desires for people to be free. It included a turn to Exodus, in which imagination allowed for their interpretation of the storyline. Biblical scholar Cain Hope Felder stresses that "vivid images are crucial for comprehension and transmission of stories. [. . .] Although in the past some scholars have stressed imagination, many in the rationalist tradition thought this was inappropriate and beneath a true educated person. Emphasis was on the intellect."[56] In talking about religious ideas, then, and invoking biblical narratives in their freedom stories, Black people have long relied on their experience to read, to interpret, and to perform stories of redemption. To be sure, "there is no truth for and about Black people that does not emerge out of the context of their experience. Truth in this sense is Black truth, a truth disclosed in the history and culture of Black people."[57] Biblical stories like Exodus illuminate a view of God that assists in the construction and performance of a Black religious imagination; one in which the Black sacred cosmos, inclusive of the secular and the sacred, is always oriented in the direction of freedom. That the Exodus story, therefore, became a significant re-telling in the life of Black people is not a surprise. Indeed, it provided a means to "make sense" of the material world and lay the groundwork for the formation of a national identity.

The religious imagination within the biblical drama of Exodus provides a way of reading Black religious and political history. For several Black religious groups including the Black Coptic Church, the story of Exodus illustrates a mode of religious activity that lends itself to a conception of identity. When collapsed in the modern world, this conception allows for the construction of descriptive categories and vocabularies that define Black identity, through the lens of the people of Israel.

Exodus, then, as a foundational saga in the imaginative and historical memory of Black people, points toward what is possible within the context of social and religious death. Its plot is the starting point for thinking and performing *otherwise*. From Christians to Black Jews, from church edifices to the streets of the Civil Rights movement, Exodus has been appropriated as a text that speaks to the national consciousness of Black folk in search of identity, a homeland, and freedom. Certainly, as Jacob Dorman offers, "in the late nineteenth and early twentieth centuries, the Exodus narrative was not simply a sacred text, a parable, or a religious metaphor for African American deliverance from slavery. Exodus was a sign of God's deliverance, a central organizing principle for the rise of Black national consciousness, and concrete process of migration."[58] In the BCC, Exodus serves this purpose, and also provides a basis for the creation of Black identity. In short,

> Exodus is a metaphor for a conception of nation that begins with the common social heritage of slavery and the insult of discrimination—the psychical and physical violence of white supremacy in the United States—and evolves into a set of responses on the part of a people acting for themselves to alleviate their condition. What sets it apart from the ideas of nation that have come to dominate black political debate is its

moral component; that is, the nation is imagined not alongside religion but precisely through the precept of Black Christianity.[59]

When Prophet David appealed to the Exodus account for his explanation of the "400-year Passover," two things were accomplished in that moment: Prophet David collapsed history and employed imagination to speak about national Black deliverance and identity. Through the lens of Israel, Prophet David made a claim about Black identity that included an argument similar to that of Black Hebrew Israelite traditions; that is, members of the BCC assert that they are of the "household of Israel," or "Royal Jews."[60] The historical collapsing of time assists with this claim, as members interpret the Black experience of liberation as God's act of deliverance working on their behalf, as it did for the children of Israel. Moreover, in a further rhetorical move, Prophet David imaginatively constructed an historical arc between the Exodus story and the story of Black Americans, such that the two events mirror and interpret each other. By this means, a collective identity is forged in the community, one connected to that of Israel, which proved "that God is mighty in battle and chooses the oppressed people to set free."[61] In the BCC, Passover is a commemoration of history or, more concretely, an immediate experience of human bondage in which God rescues the nation from social misery. For Priest Meshach, "this is why we refer to our tradition as the Coptic nation. We are a nation of people with an identity that God gave us since the beginning of time. Our Passover is our way of never forgetting that God chose this nation to enjoy a special relationship with him [sic]."[62]

The performance of Passover in the BCC illustrates a Black religious tradition committed to asserting its divine relationship with God while performing Blackness such that Blackness, as well, is asserted as divine. Dressed in all black holy garments and a crown "because Black is a divine power,"[63] believers march from outside of the temple to the inside, behind a young man carrying the Ethiopian flag, while a Queen in the temple sings a song with the lyrics, "I am the light of the world."[64] This ritual is significant on two fronts. By wearing all black, "we seek to disrupt the notion that white is pure and Black is evil. On our Passover, we wear all black as a symbol of God's divine power, because God comes out of the darkness, and to say to the world, Black is not just beautiful, but Black is powerful and a reflection of God."⁶⁵ Additionally, "we march in carrying the Ethiopian flag and singing 'I am the light of world' because, as God's holy and chosen Ethiopians, contrary to popular belief, our beautiful Black bodies are the lights of God that shine brightly to bring forth the Black Messiah."⁶⁶

As the pinnacle of the religious life of believers in the BCC, the Passover signifies "coming out of the wilderness into the promised land, which is way of saying it is our birthing—being born again—into the kingdom of God."⁶⁷ The wilderness language employed by Queen Maryann is noteworthy in that it echoes the biblical drama of Exodus, the children of Israel's deliverance from the wilderness experience. For the BCC, Black folk in North America, from chattel enslavement to the present day, have experienced a wilderness or exilic experience. Indeed, "many [Black] people," asserts Queen Michal, "are still in the wilderness awaiting to be delivered from the harsh conditions of mental and psychological slavery."⁶⁸ Passover is about deliverance from wilderness and the coming of joy and freedom, as announced by Prophet Cicero, who is a Moses-like figure—one sent to proclaim their freedom. The celebration of Passover, therefore, is an annual remembrance of the end of chattel slavery, but also a celebration for new converts who have been initiated into the faith, which officially happens on the final day of Passover, which the BCC recognizes as the Day of Pentecost, or the birthing of the Church through new members.

The Day of Pentecost is the summit of Passover in the BCC. It is the fiftieth day of a seven-week-long Passover "season," in which believers, especially new converts, partake in fasting of various sorts, including an abstention from sexual activity, to "prepare their bodies to receive the holy spirit."⁶⁹ The seven-week Passover period follows a one-year new members' class, which the church calls the "School of Wisdom." Priest Eli notes:

> Prophet Cicero set up the Church . . . so that new members, which we call "students," would sit under a teacher in the temple for a period of at least one year. My teacher was Mother Rebekah. For one year, the teacher pulls the student from the wilderness or the valley of dry bones; a place of despair or lack of hope. It's bondage or slavery. We call this teaching the student back to himself [sic]. After one year, the student is baptized and

then sealed with the gift of the Holy Spirit, which happens on Pentecost through the laying of hands by the leader."[70]

Followers bridge two moments in Biblical history: the Passover, described in Exodus; and the Pentecost, described in Acts, the latter of which marks the birth of the church as the Holy Spirit falls upon believers.[71] In the Black Coptic faith, the Day of Pentecost, as the conclusion of Passover, indicates a follower's deliverance from the vestiges of slavery and an entrance into a new identity. Indeed, it is not until a new convert has undergone the Pentecost experience that he or she receives a royal title in the Church, symbolizing their relinquishing of the negro and their acceptance of their royal birthright or new identity.

Passover is the culmination of the religious life of members of the BCC. As noted, it is a "holy season" that includes the Church's annual baptism, which is pointed in the direction of a new Black being. When Prophet Cicero instituted the baptism as part of the holy season, it was held on July 4th in Lake Michigan. He selected the 4th of July as a performance of a double hermeneutic. On one hand, he sought to "wage a critique of the country's celebration of independence," while also affirming "a new identity that commences with the baptism."[72]

Echoes of Frederick Douglass' July 5th, 1852, keynote address, "What to the Slave is the Fourth of July?" given at Corinthian Hall, Rochester, New York, rings in this religious observance. In this cultural and religious critique of the United States, Douglass highlights what he sees as the glaring hypocrisy of a nation that was concurrently committed to freedom and oppression, especially as it pertained to the life of the enslaved. For Douglass, the question was, how were enslaved Black folk to celebrate a nation's independence, in which the enslaved existed as an "object" deprived of a soul, devoid a dignity, and, indeed, not free? To this, Douglass writes:

> What, to the American slave, is your 4th of July? I answer: a day that reveals to him, more than all other days in the year, the gross injustice and cruelty to which he is the constant victim. To him, your celebration is a sham; your boasted liberty, an unholy license; your national greatness, swelling vanity; your sounds of rejoicing are empty and heartless; your denunciations of tyrants, brass fronted impudence; your shouts of liberty

and equality, hollow mockery; your prayers and hymns, your sermons and thanksgivings, with all your religious parade, and solemnity, are, to him, mere bombast, fraud, deception, impiety, and hypocrisy—a thin veil to cover up crimes which would disgrace a nation of savages. There is not a nation on the earth guilty of practices more shocking and bloody than are the people of these United States, at this very hour.[73]

Like Douglass, the BCC maintains that

the 4th of July is a problem for black people in America. Prophet Cicero understood that such a day also revealed the deep hypocrisy about Christianity in America, and therefore sought to implement the process of a spiritual birth and the act of claiming a new identity and heritage on the 4th of July, as a means of rejecting the Country's celebration and offering us a real reason to celebrate being born anew.[74]

Baptism in the Black Coptic group aims to not only integrate new believers into the community, but to dislocate notions of citizenship and the nation. The selection of July 4th as their original baptism day announces a religio-social and indeed political theological critique of a nation that, on one hand, celebrated its liberation from England, while maintaining a slavocracy that reduced the enslaved African to "object" status lacking claims to citizenship. Baptism on July 4th functioned as both a critique and a counter-cultural construction; one that pushed back against a romanticization of the nation's independence and announced a new citizenship and identity not reliant upon an American imagination. It inaugurated citizenship in the earthly spiritual kingdom. The fact that religion became the vehicle through which to perform this imagination demonstrates the function of religious performance in the search for identity and personhood.

Standing outside on a warm July morning in 2018, at the 79th Street Beach in Chicago, I observed the sacrament of baptism. New converts, dressed in black holy garments with black scarfs on their heads, gathered to be immersed by BCC ministers. Singing "Take Me to the Water to Be Baptized," there was a sense of solemnity among the members. One by one, the new converts were ushered into Lake Michigan's water, where they were baptized "in the name of the Father, Son, and the Black

Figure 3.7. Baptism 2018, Black Coptic Church Series, Chicago, IL, January 2021. Credit: Iwona Biedermann Photography.

Holy Spirit." As one convert departed the water, I asked her how she felt after her baptism. She noted, "I have waited all year for this. I feel good. Black Jesus has made me whole. I was lost but now I am found." She continued, "For me, this is like a new beginning. My queen [teacher] told me I am no longer a nigga, but I am a royal princess and God made me in his [sic] image. So today is my freedom. I am a new person and I am Black and beautiful."[75] This young woman's characterization of the baptism as a cessation of "negro" details its function in identity formation and meaning making. In many Christian circles, baptism marks one's admission into the Christian faith and purification from the sins of the past. In the BCC, baptism not only symbolizes entrance into the faith, but a social intervention in the life of the believer who, after having been called from the "wilderness," rejects and denounces the life of the negro, and performs a new religio-racial identity that commences with a turn toward Blackness as a turn towards freedom.

What are we to gather from the rituals and observances, such as the adoption of spiritual names, the wearing of holy garments, and the observance of Passover and baptism, of the BCC? They bring together the imaginative and performative functions that stand at the foundation of Black religion; that is, interrupting social conditions of the absurd by means of religious imaginaries that perform *otherwise* or radically different modalities of Blackness. Blackness *otherwise*, in the theology and performances in the BCC, is an identity that includes divine Blackness. The performed imaginaries, such as the assumption of a new name and holy garments, model an identity that is not the production or property of the material order, but rather locates Blackness within the realm of the divine. Adherents in the BCC understand their ritualistic activities as "acts of freedom and liberation that lead to liberated Black minds, and Black bodies that are not ashamed to be Black."[76]

When Priest Meshach laid hands on Princess Debra and changed her name to Mariyah, he admonished her that "if I change your name everything will be alright." Priest Meshach's connection between the ritual of assuming a new name and being "alright" is not merely about the changing of Mariyah's name. Rather, that change confers a new identity that

Figure 3.8. Black Coptic Men in Baptism Procession, Baptism 2007, Black Coptic Church Series, Chicago, IL, January 2021. Credit: Iwona Biedermann Photography.

is fundamentally transcendent, fugitive, and not bound by anti-Black imaginaries. When I asked Priest Meshach to elaborate on the name changing and other rituals of the BCC, he said,

> When we baptize, observe Passover, wear our garments, and change names, we are declaring that to be black is to be in the tradition of the divine reality of God. Everything we do in this tradition is to reconnect Black people to the divine source of our creator. That means letting go of the oppressive theologies and practices of standard Christianity and returning to the divine reality of Black God. In our walk of faith, returning to the divine source means letting go of negro, nigger, and colored, and claiming our royal birthright through the process of our baptism and Passover.[77]

Imagining *otherwise* in this tradition includes the construction of rituals and observances that narrate a story about the past yet lends toward Black futurism; Blackness unrestricted. Indeed, it is within such practices that the BCC locates hope within the fractured reality of the absurd and pronounces divine Blackness as both a theological and ontological fact.

4

"Somehow, Someway"

Black Coptic Women and the Politics of Gender

I sat with a group of Black Coptic women inside Coptic Nation Temple on a warm summer Chicago evening in 2019. Most of the women, whose ages ranged from 38 to 75, were in a position of leadership in their respective temples (i.e., "first lady" [pastor's wife] or spiritual teacher). Eager to discuss the place of women in the Black Coptic royal imagination, they gathered around a hollow square table, and greeted each other with hugs, smiles, and laughter. "Good to see you, queen," one of the women exclaimed to another. Echoes of similar greetings lingered as the women took their seats. It was apparent that they were enthusiastic about the forthcoming conversation.

Up to this point, my group discussions had been mixed-gender, with men often dominating the conversation. My purpose with this group was to interrogate how Black Coptic women understood their status in the BCC, through their own personal testimony. It was an opportunity for Black Coptic women to engage the subjects of race, religion, and identity from their perspective, and to share their own understanding of the religious imagination of Black Coptic believers. Their designations as Ethiopian queens, princesses, and empresses are titles of pride that impact both their spiritual and secular lives—their lives between Sundays. However, their interpretation of such titles is fraught with limitations within the BCC's spiritual hierarchy, as the male leadership exercises primary authority among believers. In this sense, the spiritual hierarchy of the BCC, one predicated on the idea of a Black royal nation in which the social divisions of the broader culture would be eradicated, presents a gender imbalance that has profound ramifications for women in the assembly. Plainly put, the promise of a spiritual nation of royal believers is an ideal within the BCC that is not yet actualized.

Figure 4.1. Black Coptic Queens, Black Coptic Church Series, Chicago, IL, January 2021. Credit: Iwona Biedermann Photography.

Empress Hatshepsut replied to a question about the support that Black women receive from society in general and within Black culture specifically:

> I don't think, historically, Black women were supported very much. More so, historically, Black women have carried the load of everything. And I would like to pinpoint that historically—not only were Black women responsible for their own community, their own families and children, [but] they were also responsible for other ethnic families, children [and] communities, and for *their* upkeep and *their* well-being. So, it is almost like a brainwashing to where the Black woman has been told this is what you should be, and this is what you should do. [. . .] But if I'm not good and healthy, then how can I take care of someone else?[1]

In a further delineation of the space that Black women occupy in society, Candace Queen Rachel, the sixth of eight siblings reared in a single-mother household in the Chicago South Side community of Englewood, noted:

> Historically, the jobs of Black women were to take care of white women's children. They would have to leave their homes to prepare for the white women's children to make sure you fed them, prepared them for school, sent them to school, and make sure you cleaned their house. That's how it used to be. So, while [Black women] were sending off [white women's] children they had to depend on someone else to take care of their children because she was not able to do that. That was oppression.[2]

Empress Hatshepsut's and Candace Queen Rachel's explanation of the historic realities of Black women fits the "superwoman" narrative of the selfless giving of Black women to their community and to that of others. This narrative is a story of Black women as sacrificial lambs, with little reward from a society that fails to acknowledge their worth. The superwoman motif is a legacy of chattel slavery, and has a historical relationship with the "mammy" character—a Black woman who cares for others while the self is neglected. As noted by sociologists Leeja Carter and Amerigo Rossi, "The mammy, jezebel, and sapphire are three well-known intersectional racial and gender stereotypes used to characterize Black women."[3] The mammy is a "self-sacrificing, mothering woman who happily cares for her slave owner and his family, her family, and community, seemingly unaffected or without fatigue."[4] The superwoman categorization of Black women, however, does not simply refer to their secular lives. Indeed, the spiritual lives of Black women within the Black Church often follow this pattern of bodily and mental self-sacrifice, while Black Church hierarchy, by and large, fails to include them in leadership, save in a few selected roles. Sociologists C. Eric Lincoln and Lawrence H. Mamiya captured this well in their landmark study *The Black Church in the African American Experience*, in which they contend:

> Women serve in a myriad of roles in black churches as evangelists, missionaries, stewardesses, deaconesses, lay readers, writers on religious subjects, Sunday School teachers, musicians, choir members and directors, ushers, nurses, custodians, caterers and hostesses for church dinners, secretaries and clerks, counselors, recreation leaders, and directors of vacation Bible schools.[5]

Empress Hatshepsut's assessment of the lives of Black women mirrors that of Lincoln and Mamiya. Her analysis is also in line with the superwoman motif, and provides a starting point for a critical conversation about women in the BCC's royal hierarchy and in the construction and performance of Black identity.

Religious constructions of racial identity are not divorced from issues of gender. To be sure, gender complicates narratives of racial liberation. This is the case because Black women's experience of oppression is multi-faceted. As outlined by womanist theologian Jacquelyn Grant, "racism and sexism are interrelated just as all other forms of oppression are interrelated. Sexism, however, has a reality and significance of its own because it represents that peculiar form of oppression suffered by Black women at the hands of Black men."[6] It is important, therefore, to see that a myopic focus on racial oppression may obscure the myriad and intersectional identities that individuals *already* bring with them. To this end, it is useful to ask, did the royal imagination of Prophet Cicero Patterson extend beyond a racial category, and what limitations are present in this imaginative community, considering its emphasis on racial identity?

This chapter explores the relationship between Black Coptic women and the imagination and performance of racial and gender identity as they come alive in the BCC. As illustrated, the BCC's attempt at identity reclamation is one in which members surrender their given identity in exchange for one predicated upon an idea of Black royalty. Followers, therefore, envision themselves as part of a "royal family" that connect them to their "true" identity. Notwithstanding the undercurrent of classism as well as essentialist assessments of Blackness present among Black Coptic believers, the appeal to a professed royal identity and hierarchical structure, one in which women do not experience their royalty in a manner equivalent to men, begs for analysis. This chapter probes the performance of the Black Coptic royal imagination and the ways that patriarchy complicates the claims of gender equality within the group. There is a belief among Black Coptic believers that women in the tradition occupy a more liberating religious space than they do in other Black Churches. In practice, however, Black Coptic women do not share in a royal experience that is egalitarian. Rather, the idea and performance of a royal hierarchy reinscribes notions of gender separation that leaves them both biologically and spiritually inferior to men in the group. Indeed, one does not get imaginations and performances of royalty without hierarchy, rank, and a subservient class. Black women, who themselves are also ranked among each other, are not at the top of the Church's royal arrangement. The Black Coptic women's experience, then, is caught between a haughty idea of Black royalty and the confines of a patriarchal structure, rendering the group's claim to liberation incomplete and narrow at best, and disingenuous at worse.

The crux of this conversation is the Day of Pentecost, the most sacred day of the Black Coptic liturgical calendar. On this day, leaders of individual Black Coptic churches perform a rite of laying hands on the heads of the new converts, who have concluded their studies in the School of Wisdom and have undergone baptism, as a sign of their receiving the Holy Spirit. Historically, and through the present day, this ritual has been exclusively conducted by men known as the Prophets. There is a widely held belief among Black Copts that the laying of hands on the Day of Pentecost is reserved for men, thereby rendering senior leadership in the group unachievable for women. This exclusionary practice not only muddles the BCC's claim to liberation theology, but produces an environment in which racial identity often eclipses concerns of gender liberation.

Women in the Black Coptic Church

Since its founding, women have played an essential role in the BCC. It is not unusual to hear Black Coptic members testify how a particular "queen" is responsible for their salvation. It is also the case that the male hierarchy in the community were introduced to the theology and beliefs of the BCC by women who comprise the teaching arm of the organization. Notes Queen Huldah, "because women make up the vast majority of the congregation, and because the queens are the primary teachers, every leader in the BCC was taught by a woman. She was the one who introduced them to whatever salvation they now confess."[7] Candace Queen Rachel attests that Black Coptic women "are the key people in our churches. It is the queens in the temple who carry the service. In many cases women are the reason why people are attracted to the church. When people visit and attend a bible class, they are captivated by the queens who are teaching the classes."[8] Women have been the crucial channel through which individuals who converted to the BCC were instructed in the theology and rituals of the faith. As in other Black Church traditions, the educational division of the BCC is one in which women bear the brunt of the responsibility.

In addition to their role as teachers, Black Coptic women have participated in the governance and maintenance of the BCC. Since women are the largest demographic among Black Coptic churchgoers, they are also the largest economic bloc in the community. In most cases, "women are the church cooks, the main source of fundraising, the choir directors, and the childcare providers during church services, and are also responsible for the cleaning of the temples."[9] Undoubtedly, notes Priest Eli, "the queens are the backbone of the church."[10] Yet, while the notion of the "backbone" has been used by men in Black churches to compliment the women for their untiring service, "the telling portion of the word backbone is 'back.' [. . . .] What they really mean is that women are in the 'background' and should be kept there. They are merely support workers."[11] While it is true, then, that Black Coptic women share the burden of leadership in certain roles, with respect to pastoral leadership there is an ambivalence that overshadows the promise of equality; an ambivalence that is not unlike present in mainstream Black churches.

In *If It Wasn't for the Women: Black Women's Experience and Womanist Culture in Church and Community*, sociologist Cheryl Townsend Gilkes traces the historic role of women in African societies and demonstrates the continuity and discontinuity that exists between Black women and their African female ancestors in sacred and secular spaces. Indeed, argues Gilkes, "In Africa, the themes of female independence and self-reliance were reflected in the organization of economic, family, and political roles. In numerous West African societies, women were persons, in their own right, with responsibilities and privileges not derived from husbands and fathers."[12] Historian Letitia Woods Brown maintains that, as a result, "African women achieved considerable economic independence; in religious ceremonies, women were priests, even leaders of some cults. Women also maintained their own secret societies."[13] In fact, relates Gilkes, "one African queen, Candace, led military campaigns of such ferocity that all later queens have born the same generic name."[14]

Despite the strong, independent, and critical roles that women played in traditional African societies, gender relationships in the Black church have an ambivalent tone.

To be sure, "women have emerged in every African-American religious tradition as persons with significant power in spite of overwhelming resistance of the largest church bodies to women's ordination."[15] Black Church women known as "mothers" are symbols of such authority. As Gilkes illustrates, "mothers" are women who, considering their age, wisdom, or both, have gained the admiration and respect of those within community and church. Gilkes suggests that "the roles of church and community mothers represent impositions of familistic and pseudo-familistic ties upon social organizations and the process of social influence."[16] While the responsibilities of these church mothers are comparable to their function in the community, there are differences between the community mother and the church mother. On the one hand, "Mothers in communities have carried on the roles of elders in traditional West African societies where accumulated wisdom is power. They have occupied positions of leadership in women's organizations and local branches of national organizations."[17] In essence, community mothers have been effective in helping to produce "real changes for 'the race.'"[18]

On the other hand, the place of the church mother is more complicated and paradoxical due to the fact that uncertainty concerning "the appropriate roles of women in public life are more obvious within the churches."[19] Further, the Black Church is not a monolith, but rather composed of various denominations in which the role of the church mother differs from church to church. Notes Gilkes:

> Within larger Baptist and Methodist denominations, women are organized under a system of relatively unyielding male authority. Baptist and Methodist church mothers tended to be influential and venerable elders. Within the sanctified churches, those Pentecostal and holiness denominations which were founded and managed by black people and which have retained more of the traditional Southern African elements of black religious worship and liturgy, there is a broader range of attitudes and practices concerning the position of women. Church mothers are not only role models and venerable elders. According to some ministers, "women

are important for moral guidance within our congregations—but also older, venerated, spirit-field women who hold considerable power within a nearly autonomous and well-organized, parallel women's world."[20]

Although the position of church mothers varies among Black churches, from influential elders to women with great authority, Gilkes highlights a critical component that reveals a tremendous paradox in the Black Church. The Church of God in Christ (COGIC), for example, one of Gilkes' case studies, acknowledges the administrative and spiritual roles of church mothers. However, there is a significant demographic within the COGIC that takes the position that "nowhere can we find a mandate to ordain a woman to be an elder, a bishop or pastor. Women may teach the gospel to others . . . have charge of the church in the absence of its pastor . . . without adopting the title of elder, bishop or pastor."[21] Nonetheless, Lucille Cornelius, who composed a history of the COGIC, maintains that women have been a critical demographic in its history and organization—that the history of the COGIC is, in fact, a history of women.[22] Such a paradox is reminiscent of the history and narrative of women in the BCC.

The Black Coptic royal imagination is at the center of the search for identity among believers. The allure of a religious world in which individuals entered an imagined royal family was the pull factor for many who converted. Queen Maryann, for instance, left the spiritualist church in part because "the [Black] Coptic Church had a monarchy of queens who were healing, teaching, and raising the dead from a dead state to a living person." Moreover, "women were queens and held positions of authority in the Church."[23] Without question, women have been important to the expansion of the BCC. At its origin, says Priest Eli, Prophet Cicero "built the Church on women. He did not start with seven men; he started with seven women. These women were given the authority to teach both women and men. The women were the first people to lay hands on the new converts."[24] Priest Eli contends that "women have great power and authority. We see them as doctors, lawyers and teachers. They light the people's minds. They even have the authority to teach and preach. If something happens to the leader, they have the authority to lead in his absence."[25] In fact, argues Priest Meshach, the BCC is constructed on a matriarchal system in which the pillars of the Church, known as the

"Head Queens," play a critical role in maintaining governance and order within individual churches. These women, who are pastors' wives or other women of notable standing, are considered the spiritual parallel to the male leaders of the church, contributing to the idea within the community that Black Coptic women are distinctive in their religious roles.

Black Coptic believers share a sense that the role of women in their church is not only liberative, but distinct from that in other traditions. Candace Queen Rachel describes the distinction this way:

> I think it varies depending on the religious denomination. I understand where some churches, like in the Baptist church, wives take a docile role. They really sit, and they have on a big hat. That's it. Unless they have a women's day program, then they may speak at that time. So, this is really the only religion I can compare to, I have never really been in any other. But as I see it our roles as women are very different.[26]

Queen Shiphrah agrees:

> I have been to a lot of churches, but have not been under the tutelage of different faiths. I agree with Candace Queen Rachel regarding the positions. Many times, the Baptists, or any other of the other churches like the Methodists, and what have you. Those women are basically first ladies, and those are the ones that operate within the jurisdictions of special programs, like women's day or something like that. And in the [Black] Coptic Church, of course, it is totally different. You have many different hats to wear. I think that depending on where you are and your position, I find that women really have to assume a lot of positions because they are the backbone of the Church. And so, their visibility is much more defined within the church structures. Even though it may say that man is the head, it is women who are really working behind the scenes to keep things flowing.[27]

Similarly, Empress Hatshepsut, Queen Shiphrah's daughter, states that she has

> had the privilege of being exposed to many different denominations. I would say that I agree with [Queen Shiphrah] and Candace Queen Rachel.

I noticed that women in other denominations basically get in where they fit in. So, if you fit in being an usher, than that is when you have your time to shine in the service, because you're ushering and you're escorting people and you're kind of mandating and keeping the order in the church. When I level my experiences with those in other denominations, there is a level of empowerment, but I like to say the word empowerment because the women in [the Black Coptic Church] that are prominent and active in the Church, it's more than simply empowerment.[28]

The above testimonies suggest that there is an apologetic deportment with respect to the location of Black Coptic women in the larger group. Queens Rachel and Shiphrah, and Empress Hatshepsut, evaluated the role of Black Coptic women relative to women's roles in other Black Church traditions, despite having admitted very little interaction with other such religious communities. What we encounter, then, is an idealizing of the place of women in the BCC. Such idealism—indeed, such a sense of nostalgia—is in line with the broader heroic imagination that surfaces in the BCC vis-à-vis the construction of Black identity, permitting those within the group to read their tradition transcendentally, beyond the margins of the wider Black Church and Black culture. In practice and theology, however, this idealized discipleship of equals runs up against a patriarchy that, through a closed religious system mounted behind the appearance of a matriarchal structure, performs not very differently from the Black churches as described by Gilkes. In short, a rhetoric of equality and agency is at odds with the Church's practice. Still, among Black Coptic believers there is a sentiment that women have long enjoyed a position of leadership that outpaces other traditions. On this point, the community highlights two women who have been consequential in Black Coptic history.

Queen Capernaum and Queen Rebekah: Sisters in the Spirit

Among Black Coptic believers, Queen Capernaum, wife to Prophet Peter Banks, is a pioneer. After the death of Prophet Cicero, she was instrumental in the transition of the BCC from a small, fledgling, and fragile community to a thriving organization. While Prophet Peter was the spiritual leader after Prophet Cicero's death, Queen Capernaum was influential in holding the movement together and its evolution to a larger society. Queen Huldah, who was a spiritual pupil of Queen Capernaum, notes:

> After the passing of Prophet Cicero Patterson, many of the people wanted Prophet Peter as the leader but did not necessarily want Queen Capernaum as the First Lady. Queen Capernaum left the Universal Prayer House and Training School and began ministering in her home to members of her class. After Prophet Peter left the Universal Prayer House and Training School to initiate his ministry, he joined with Queen Capernaum and together they built the True Temple of Solomon.[29]

Queen Huldah remembers Queen Capernaum as a "spiritually in-tune woman who would captivate anyone who entered into her surroundings."[30] For Black Coptic devotees, Queen Capernaum was not merely the wife of Prophet Peter; she was an example of the authority and prestige women can have within the group. Yet her position as the wife of the group's longest serving, and arguably most admired, spiritual leader was not only consequential in relation to her function in the community, but also sheds light on how the spiritual hierarchy of the community reinforces classism and an imbalanced performance of equality among Black Coptic women. That is, Queen Capernaum's standing among Black Coptic believers is not representative of the larger community of women who comprise the BCC. Indeed, insists Prophet Hiram, Queen Capernaum was a member of the "royal family" which, in this sense, is a reference to the biological family of Prophet Peter. In essence, within the BCC there is a "royal family within the royal family." Members of Prophet Peter's family were afforded certain privileges and honors that were not available to ordinary believers. As the wife of Prophet Peter, for example, Queen Capernaum was known as the "Candace Queen," a title reserved for the wives of spiritual leaders, as a reference to the Candace Queens of Meroe. "Candace Queen" can be translated as "Queen Regent."

Queen Capernaum's biological sister, Mother Queen Rebekah (1923–2005), an early follower of Prophet Cicero, is another Black Coptic woman of great influence. Mother Rebekah was known as a "Moses" figure, given her role in "delivering many lost souls and bringing them to

God."³¹ I interviewed Mother Rebekah in 2005, shortly before her death. She told me about her first encounter with Prophet Cicero. She recalled that, prior to joining the BCC, she was searching for a religious institution that would benefit her and her children. Her path to conversion followed a dream in which "Black Jesus led [her] to the [Black Coptic Church]."³² This narrative is enshrined in the oral tradition of the BCC. Candace Queen Rachel recounts the story in this way:

> Prior to her joining the church, Mother Rebekah was in a coma. While in a coma, Mother Rebekah had a dream about a man. After she awoke from her coma she went looking for this man that was in her dream. As she was walking down Cottage Grove Avenue in Chicago, she passed by the Universal Prayer House and Training School. As she looked inside, she saw the same man who was in her dream. The man was Prophet Cicero. As she introduced herself to him, he told her, "I was waiting for you." So, I regard Mother Rebekah as the matriarch of the Black Coptic Church.³³

During my interview with Mother Rebekah, she leaned into the characterization of a "Moses" who had been "sent to deliver the people of God." She said that God had "sent me on a divine mission to assist Prophet Cicero in elevating the consciousness of Black people who had been rejected by the world."³⁴ Mother Rebekah contended that North American Blacks were in the "condition they were in because they had been led away from their God and the image of God in which God created them."³⁵ Therefore, she maintained, "Black people needed to be told that they were somebody and that they were God's chosen people."³⁶ She reported that, during his lifetime, "Prophet Cicero taught me many things that he hadn't taught other people because it was my job to teach the people from the 'nigger' and 'negro' degree to the truth that they were somebody."³⁷ In describing herself as Moses, Mother Rebekah communicated the idea that her role in the BCC was to help "Black people reach the promised land," which she described as "a land of peace and freedom."³⁸ Such a characterization, or Moses typology, also indexes the Exodus narrative, a story that, as we have seen, is significant in both the theological and ritual world of the BCC. A promise of divine deliverance is the focal point of the Exodus narrative and, in my interview, a woman, Mother Rebekah, self-identified as the conduit of a message of deliverance.

For Candace Queen Rachel, Mother Rebekah was one of the greatest spiritual teachers in the history of the BCC. She verbalized "that there were many testimonies of people who were sick or who had been given a certain amount of time to live by doctors who were unable to heal them. God used Mother Rebekah as a vessel to perform healings."[39] Throughout her lifetime, she said, Mother Rebekah taught well over 600 converts to the BCC.[40] Says Candace Queen Rachel, "most of the spiritual leaders who are pastors over churches were taught by Mother Rebekah."[41]

Throughout the leadership of Prophet Peter, Mother Rebekah held the title of "Head Queen." I asked Mother Rebekah what this meant. She said that, as Head Queen, "I was in charge of them all."[42] She reported that it was her job to keep order and governance in the True Temple of Solomon. In the absence of Prophet Peter and Queen Capernaum, Mother Rebekah was the leader pro tempore. Candace Queen Rachel recalled that when Mother Rebekah spoke, her word was not challenged.[43] Moreover, according to Prophet Hiram White, Mother Rebekah was one of Prophet Peter's most trusted advisers. Whenever confusion arose in the church, "Mother Rebekah would get things in order."[44] In the final analysis, Mother Rebekah enjoyed an authority and respect in the organization that has yet to be matched by any other woman.

For Black Coptic believers, the aforementioned stories reveal that Black Coptic women are uniquely positioned in leadership, in contrast with Black Church women more generally. During my interview with the church's highest-ranking women, it was evident that they wanted to make the case that the space afforded to Black Coptic women was revolutionary and trailblazing in relation to the broader Black Church. Priest Meshach maintained that in giving women a central role in the ministry, "Prophet Cicero did something beyond the feminist movements."[45] Queen Maryann argued that the "roles of women in the Black Coptic Church were quite different from the roles of women in other churches. We were given a more active role."[46]

However, while select women in the BCC, most notably wives of Church leadership or those have who reached a certain rank in the tradition, have been afforded high status, the situation of Black Coptic women is not as revolutionary as believers think. While women have been instrumental in the Church's history and continued expansion, there is a glass ceiling that prevents the full and unrestricted leadership of women. My interview participants established that the central function of women in the BCC is to "teach." This phenomenon of being relegated to teaching is similar to what Gilkes found in other traditions. However, the role of women in the BCC represents a paradox that calls into question the concept of identity and "liberation" in the Church's theological program. That is, like other Black Church traditions, the BCC is a gender ambivalent religious world, in which the flourishing of women is not organic or independent, but regulated and defined by a male hierarchy which maintains gender inequality under a theological vision.

As we have seen, there is a perception in the BCC that women, who are in the majority in the group, enjoy a significant degree of leadership and notoriety. Yet there was a consensus among those interviewed that women traditionally do not hold the office of spiritual leader or pastor. For some women in the group, interestingly, this did not describe the religious groups that they engaged with prior to joining the BCC. Indeed, many of the women had been members of religious organizations in which women thrived and shared leadership with men. Queen Shiphrah, for instance, who was born in Mississippi and moved to Chicago as a young child to live with her grandmother after her mother fell ill, was introduced to the practice of religion early in life. Her grandmother, whom Queen Shiphrah described "as a devoted servant [who] was very rigid in her faith . . . was a singer, and in the choir, [and] was a prophetess." She continued that at her spiritualist church, in which she was raised, she "was under the tutelage of women in the ministry and a woman pastor." However, in her present role, as first lady at Faith Temple Coptic Church on Chicago's far South Side, her understanding of women leadership is shaped by a theological positioning that limits the extent to which women can lead the organization.

The absence of women at the helm of the BCC is connected to the question of "who" the Church prepares for future leadership positions within the group. With respect to the possibility of the BCC preparing and supporting women to serve as spiritual leader or pastor of a BCC, Queen Shiphrah maintained that she doesn't see this happening "because of the fact that, from the foundation of the [Black Coptic]

Church, it has been shared that a women cannot lead this setup. That is what has been handed down. So no, I don't see women being prepared for that particular role."[47] In a further elucidation of the issue of female leadership—not metaphorically or symbolically, but in actual practice—Candace Queen Rachel neatly articulates the ambivalence that surrounds the matter:

> I have to agree with Queen Shiphrah in those aspects. . . . I think that as far as leadership, it has never really been a thought of mine to want to be a leader of the Coptic Church because I feel that leadership or pastor is a title which has duties to fulfill, but I feel that I am already a leader and a pastor in the work that I do. I don't have to be in that particular role. No one has to call me out to designate me to that role to say that is what I can do. As Queen Shiphrah said, the foundation is what we have to build upon. Sometimes people change things and add things, but I think that we keep the foundation that has been set before us, and that is that men will lead this faith. So no, I don't feel bad about it. I have never given thought to it because there are no limits to the role that a woman could play in the Black Coptic Church, per se. You may say leadership, but I feel like I am a leader. I feel like my husband and I are co-pastors. And I feel that as a woman in this faith that I would be the best teacher there could ever be. So, I feel like I am a leader in my own right because I am the one who is bringing [new converts] into the church and teaching them.[48]

Both Candace Queen Rachel and Queen Shiphrah understand the question of women leadership in the BCC to be governed by the "foundation" of their tradition, as introduced by Prophet Cicero. That is, there is a reluctancy among believers to advance theological propositions or promote religious practices that, in their own estimation, are misaligned with the thinking of their founder. This originalist hermeneutic at work among Black Coptic believers is connected to the notion explored in chapter one, that for Black Coptic followers Prophet Cicero was on a divine mission and operated as a messianic figure. The construction of ideas that contradict, directly or in appearance, his ideas are viewed with suspicion. Indeed, highlights Priest Meshach, "I am not totally sure if women will lead the Church and have the ability to lay hands on the Day of Pentecost. I have a hard time going against the prophet, and I have to trust his wisdom. Will the day come in the future? Perhaps. I just need to make sure that what we do doesn't go against the prophet."[49] However, in line with others' vacillation about women and spiritual leadership, Priest Meshach acknowledged that "our tradition is built on men and women. On the day of Pentecost, the (male) leader cannot lay hands without a woman assisting him. So, it takes both of us to perform the job."[50] Yet, the centrality of the act is reserved for men.

Women Are Teachers, Men Are Leaders: On Phallic Spirituality

The religious world of the BCC is one in which the royal imagination promises a recovery of a Black identity rooted in dignity and social salvation. As we have seen, "Hail to the queens of Ethiopia" is a symbol that points toward what is possible within the material world. Indeed, the BCC is suspicious of soteriological discussions that are divorced from what Black people experience within the matrix of the absurd; that is, anti-blackness as imagined and performed without end. Yet the social salvation idealism of the community is constrained within a space, and confirmed in practices, that do not extend full holistic salvation to women. On the contrary, believers propose an ordering of unique roles within the religious group on account of one's biology. Priest Meshach contended that "there is something distinct about a man and a woman in terms of what God has given us. God has given women something and the man something. In our training and understanding, there is an essential part of certain key elements within healing and certain kinds of spiritual work, that men are given and women are not."[51] In an elucidation of Priest Meshach's contention, Queen Huldah noted that "role identification, provided that there is mutual respect for one another's role, doesn't necessarily undermine the value of women or the idea that they are liberated to be all that they can be."[52] The gesture toward a biological argument in defense of Black Coptic women's inability to fulfill the spiritual work of the BCC is striking and invites deliberation.

As we have explored, the ritualistic world of the BCC includes an observation of the "Day of Pentecost" as the climax of new converts' study in the tradition. Recounting the scene in Acts 8 when Peter and John laid hands upon the people of Samaria and they received the Holy Spirit, the Day of Pentecost in the BCC recovers this practice and includes the laying of hands on new converts. Within the BCC, however, this ritual is performed by the spiritual leaders of individual temples, and is a practice reserved for men. The spiritual imagination of a new Black person whose identity is steeped in divinity is therefore limited in the case of Black Coptic women. Black Coptic followers uphold the notion that the laying on of hands is a spiritual practice limited by biology, or what I identify as "phallic spirituality."

The performance of patriarchy within the BCC is not confined to the hierarchy of the group—a hierarchy that enforces a heteronormative approach, in which a cis-male is placed at the epicenter of the royal imagination with respect to leadership. More than this, the patriarchy is experienced in the ritualistic life of the community, wherein cis men are thought to possess a genetic makeup that renders possible the performance of Pentecost, or the laying of hands. The logic that informs this practice is related to a heteronormative understanding of sexual activity. Notes Empress Selah, "Women are receptors. What I am physically I am also that spiritually. Men are projectors. They are that physically and they are that spiritually."[53] To the extent that the Day of Pentecost involves projecting the seal of the Holy Spirit upon converts via the laying of hands, men perform this task because of their physical and biological constitution. Correlating Empress Selah's attestation with scripture, Priest Meshach argued that "we do have the records to say that Peter gave the Holy Ghost; it has something to do with the genetic makeup."[54] Therefore, "because man was given the power to lay hands, like Peter of the scriptures, we follow this model."[55] Queen Huldah affirmed this position, namely that "the physical nature of man and woman is reflective of their spiritual nature."[56] Accordingly, reasoned Queen Maryann, "Prophet Cicero wanted men to be men and women to be women. He wanted men to take responsibility of [their] home and women to hold [their] role."[57] The physical nature of men, contended Queen Maryann, is to lead the home. Queen Michal argued this point plainly: "Within the Church there are different bodies of leadership. The prophet is the leader over the temple. In his role, he delegates heads over different degrees and ministries within the church."[58] Finally, Candace Queen Rachel declared, "When Prophet Cicero set the organization up, he gave women critical roles. In the social order of his day, men were the head of the home, and he probably never thought that there would be a need for the woman to lead because there would always be a man."[59] Queen Huldah's testimony regarding the physical and spiritual nature of man and woman proposes that man, as leader of the home, is naturally head of the church.

The above statements reveal that Black Coptic women have found an avenue through which to reconcile these exclusionary practices with the role of women in other Black churches. As noted above, Black Coptic women perceive their religious organization as offering a distinctive brand of liberation, seemingly oblivious of the progress in other Black Church traditions such as the African Methodist Episcopal Church (AME), who elected their first female bishop, Bishop Vashti McKenzie, in 2000. But more than this, their acceptance of gendered roles illustrates how Black Coptic women negotiate identity in relation to the broader claims of the BCC concerning Black liberation. For these women, there is a sense of relinquishing roles such as spiritual leader because they discern an equality rooted in an understanding of the scriptural place of women. Candace Queen Rachel articulates that, biblically, "women were co-workers in the ministry. On the Day of Pentecost, the prophet cannot seal the Holy Spirit unless there are women present with him to assist in the process."[60]

The teleological reconciliation of the BCC's new identity and new being with a glass ceiling based on human biology and proof texting of scripture, often leads to a notion of flight. When asked about the possibility of young women ascending to spiritual leadership, women in the group presented the option to depart the tradition rather than urge a different path. Empress Hatshepsut reflected:

> Well, I would support her in that she should continue to have aspirations in whatever it is she wanted to be. However, there is a realistic side I would have to bring out to balance her. I might say, "Well, baby, this may not be the particular sect or way of life for you to fulfill those dreams or aspirations in the way you want." I would still remain optimistic.[61]

In a similar vein, Queen Magdalene noted that "I just don't think that kind of aspiration would come from one of our homes because they learn that in their tradition, they can be called in other ways. They have the ability to preach, to teach, or to heal. But they would already see that in their faith women do not typically lay hands on the Day of Pentecost."[62]

These statements reveal much about the relationship of Black Coptic women to their tradition, how they negotiate their search for identity and meaning, and the ways that the BCC's desire to foster and cultivate a Black identity not regulated or determined by cultural production is limited. The tradition, despite its belief that it transcends other Black Church traditions, reinscribes the superwoman motif, while prohibiting women's full and uninhibited ascent to leadership in the community. More than this, the BCC bolsters tropes that relegate a woman's position based on her gender. Their inability to lay hands on the Day of Pentecost is based on a heteronormative understanding of sexual function. Yet, for Black Coptic women, there is a sense of hope and meaning within the tradition that is expressed in their testimony and revealed in their service to the community. Theologian and ethicist Keri Day states that

> while black churches do empower some black women to use their religious activism for community well-being, other black women experience gender oppression within black churches and are often related to the background through celebration of their "backbone": service. While their persistent and ongoing "backbone" services and efforts have enriched black church life, this reality aggravates persistent sensitives about the strength of and sustainability of black women.[63]

This describes the situation of Black Coptic women. The paradox is revealing. As described earlier, there is a shroud of mystery around Prophet Cicero. He is read throughout the group as one whose divine mission was above culture, and one who presented a way of being Black through a retrieval of a forgotten past. Yet there is also an admission that he was informed by his social context and a man of his time. In the social order of his day, noted Queen Rachel, "men were the head of the home, and it is likely that he never thought that there would be a need for the women to lead because there would always be a man."[64] Like his contemporaries, such as Elijah Muhamad and Marcus Garvey, Prophet Cicero was a race-man. He privileged racism over-against other forms of oppression, including gender. While he allowed women in the movement to participate in defined roles, his version of the BCC nonetheless advanced biological and genetic distinctions in spiritual practices that distort claims of freedom. While the BCC offers Black women a space within with to locate joy and meaning, it is also a complex world of contradictions. An engagement with womanist theology is helpful in understanding the situation.

Enter Womanist Tradition

Black theology matured within a North American social context that included systemic oppression that denied basic human rights to Black people. White theologians' failure to address the discrepancy between racism and the Christian gospel rendered urgent the birth of a theology that highlighted the original sin—racism—that molded the American experiment. Black theology, in its earliest expression, grappled with the paradox of being Black and Christian in North America. The focus of the first generations of Black theologians was the problem of racism in relation to the Christian gospel.

While the social context of the American Sixties demanded the eruption of theological voices from below, the narrow focus of early Black theologians on the problem of racism advanced an essentialist understanding of that particular oppression, rendering other forms of oppression invisible or inconsequential. Stated otherwise, oppression is not uniquely the suppression of a group on account of their racial identity. It is the dehumanization of an individual or a group on the basis of race, gender, sexual orientation, social class, economic status, or other identities that manifest in the human experience. In this regard, it is critical to bear in mind that, over the centuries, groups and individuals have been castigated and labeled as the ontological other for reasons that extend far beyond race. Therefore, the significant contribution of both feminist and womanist theologians is their skillful articulation of the problem of gender in the history of religions and, in the case of womanist theologians and ethicists, their scrutinization of the brutal history of oppression concerning Black women in the Black Church and society more generally. Religious scholar and cultural theorist Tamura Lomax notes that

> while the Black Church provides hope and guidance for many of today's maladies, in some cases it dispenses the illness, diagnosis, and prescription. That is, the Black Church sometimes mirrors the antiblack, sexist, classist, homophobic, transantagonistic violence experienced in the rest of the world. And for black women and girls, it can be a battleground for simultaneous erasure and stereotype seeing, or, more explicitly, marginalization and sexual discrimination on some days, and sexualization, clandestine catcalling, unblinking stares, name calling, sexual harassment, and sexual violence—emotional physical, epistemological, and otherwise—on others.[65]

Lomax's analysis of the situation lays bare the reality of the Black Church as an institution that, on the one hand, provides hope and refuge from an unforgiving world, while conversely emulating the structures that it seeks to destroy. In this sense, the Black theological project of the American sixties situated the Black Church at the center of liberative discourse, while failing to critique the organizational realities that render suspicious broad claims to liberation. Although at its origins Black theology provided a theological and social investigation of racial oppression, womanist theological reflection offers a path forward not merely for the academic study of religion and theology, but also for the practice and performance of Black religions as a lived experienced grounded in liberation for the whole of the Black community. This reflection is grounded in the experience of Black womanhood, yet accounts for the communal lives of all Black people. Womanist theologian Jacquelyn Grant notes that:

> Black women must do theology out of their tri-dimensional experience of racism/sexism/classism. To ignore any aspect of this experience is to deny the wholistic and integrated reality of black womanhood. When black women say that God is on the side of the oppressed, we mean that God is in solidarity with the struggles of those on the underside of humanity, those whose lives are bent and broken from the many levels of assault perpetrated against them.[66]

Womanist theology articulates the shortcomings of both feminist and Black theologies. It is not merely a critique of racism within feminist theology, or a "calling out" of negligence on the part of Black male theologians to construct a truly holistic liberating Black theology, one that reflects the various experiences within Black life and culture. On the contrary, the emergence of womanist theology represents a theological venture of Black women in which the fullness of racial identity and gender are woven together toward an imagination and performance of freedom vis-à-vis the truly liberating God who enters human history on behalf of the harmonyha. Process and womanist theologian Monica Coleman describes womanist theology in this way:

> Womanist theology is a response to sexism in black theology and racism in feminist theology. When early black theologians spoke of the black experience, they only included the experience of black men and boys. They did not address the unique oppression of black women. Feminist theology, on the other hand, unwittingly spoke only of white women's experience, especially of middle- and upper-class white women. They did not include issues or race and economics in their critique. [...] The term womanist allows black women to affirm their identity as black while also owning a connection with feminism.[67]

Womanist theologian and anthropologist Linda Thomas affirms womanist theology as "critical reflection upon black women's place in the world that God has created; it takes seriously black women's experience as human beings who are made in the image of God; it affirms and critiques the positive and negative attributes of the church, the African American community, and the larger society."[68] Therefore, in womanist theology, one encounters a reflection on God, humanity, and culture, in which the Blackness of one's identity is not prioritized over the experience of womanhood. Accordingly, womanist theology is both corrective and constructive. As a corrective, womanist theology first calls into question the primary structures in which black and feminist theologies are conceptualized; constructively, womanist theology advances nuanced theological reflections and biblical interpretations that mediate an intersectional conversation between race and gender, and examines the ways such identities converge in the lives of Black women.

Womanist theology provides the context within which one can imagine a holistic Black theology of liberation, that expresses the hope of freedom for all oppressed persons. By studying the social context from which Black theology emerged, womanist theologians and ethicists expand our vision of Black theology. Womanist ethicist Emilie Townes maintains that "black theology has articulated a strong doctrine of sin in relation to racism and an equally strong doctrine of virtue on the part of those who oppose racism."[69] However, she is careful to note that "womanist theology cannot and must not merely accept methodologies or constructs of theological reflection that do not consider with ongoing rigor the experience of African-American women and the diversities found within black womanhood."[70] Therefore, "race is only one consideration for womanist theo-ethical thought. Race is joined with a host of other materialities of black life in a hermeneutic of liberation and transformation."[71]

In her womanist theological presentation, Kelly Brown Douglas offers a critique of the iconographic Black God and Black Christ that were ubiquitous in classical Black theological writings and their impact on Black women's liberation. Her analysis contends that the images of God and Jesus as Black symbolize a divine presence that stands in solidarity with those who are racially oppressed. However, she argues, divine images that showcase solidarity along racial lines must be more expansive, to express solidarity with those who are both black *and* female. Douglas contends:

> Shaped by the Black Power/civil rights movement out of which it emerged, black Theology focused only on one dimension of black oppression—white racism. Its failure to utilize black women's experience further prevented it from developing an adequate analysis of black oppression. It did not address the multiple social burdens, that is, racism, sexism, classism, and heterosexism, which beset black men and women. Consequently, it presented an image of God and Christ that was impotent in the fight for black freedom. A black God, one concerned only with the battle against racism, could not sustain and liberate the entire black community. This God could not affirm or empower black women as they confronted sexism.[72]

Although Douglas is critical of Black images of God to the extent that such images seemed to be mostly interested in combatting white racism, she maintains that "black theology opened the door for black people to further explore the richness of their own experience in their efforts to understand the meaning of God's presence in human history."[73] A womanist lens is helpful in framing a critique of the position of Black Coptic women in relation to church leadership.

Prophet Cicero Patterson was a religio-race-man. His religious imagination, which promised a recovery of Black identity through the introduction of a royal Black monarchy, was indebted to a particular interpretation of his cultural milieu. Much like his contemporaries, and even later generations of Black theologians, Prophet Cicero did not present a nuanced pronunciation of the role of women in the Black Church. While he gave his rigid attention to the problem of the negro, his performative imagination was one that also performed patriarchy. He was not alone in this limited vision of the Black church. As James Cone has argued, after his own silence on this matter,

> The Black Church, like all other churches, is a male dominated church. The difficulty that black male ministers have in supporting the equality of women in the church and society stems partly from the lack of a clear liberation-criterion rooted in the gospels and in the present struggles of oppressed peoples.... It is truly amazing that many black male ministers, young and old, can hear the message of liberation in the gospel when related to racism, bur remain deaf to a similar message in the context of sexism....[74]

Cone's description of the liberation lens that dominated early Black freedom struggles, one that was focused on race, extended beyond Black churches and Christian-oriented groups. Indeed, in her work on women in the NOI, historian Ula Yvette Taylor highlights the conundrum of women in the movement. Without question, argues Taylor, women joined the NOI for a variety of reasons with full knowledge of the patriarchal structure of the organization. She notes:

> Black women attracted to these teachings faced a choice. Joining the NOI meant entering a process of remaking; for women, it involved shaping a puritanical feminine identity, in marked contrast to the supposedly masculinized woman who took root during North American slavery.

> Proscriptions regarding appropriate feminist behavior were linked with self-sacrifice, self-love, and loving others, and ultimately, agreeing to build a separate black Islamic nation.[75]

In similar form, women who joined the BCC entered a world prefaced on an idea of Black royalty. Joining the BCC meant becoming part of a nation within the nation that harnessed conceptional ideals of Black life that contradicted the American narrative of Black identity. It meant that one was able to fashion an existence outside constructed notions of a ghettoized Black life. Women who joined the BCC found the spiritual hierarchy to be psychologically transformative, permitting them to assert a sense of Black pride that they did not find in other traditions. Yet, they joined with an awareness of the organization's male dominance. Indeed, in the physical center of Black Coptic temples, on a rostrum, exists a throne in which the male leader sits, with senior ranking women on either side. Analogously, Taylor writes with respect to women in the NOI:

> ... the NOI provided a space for women who had been disrespected, abused, and who had struggled to find a "home" in racial America. How each woman sought to make meaning of her NOI membership is of course impossible to capture in full. There exists, nonetheless, uniform declaration by female believers that ring loud in the ears of all who care to listen. Securing husbands under obligation to provide, respect, and protect was intrinsic to their Nationhood choice: the NOI leadership promised responsible patriarchs for the betterment of the nuclear family and, ultimately, the black nation.[76]

The question remains, how do women in the BCC respond to the tension between racial liberation and gender oppression?

Somehow, Someway: A Concluding Note

When I sat with the group of Black Coptic women that summer evening in Chicago, it was clear to me that they were fiercely connected to their faith and that they were aware of the complex relationship of gender, race, and faith in the BCC. They offered reflections on their struggles and joys of faith, which were neatly captured in the phrase, "somehow, someway." They revealed that their spiritual world, despite its complexities, was racially redemptive, even if ambivalent with respect to gender.

The leadership status of women presents challenges to the BCC's far-reaching claim of identity formation. As we have seen, the recovered identity for women includes a notion of royalty. Yet, this is confronted by a definition of royalty in the community that leans toward classism and sexism. Indeed, the women are not merely ranked in relation to the men, but they are also ranked among each other (i.e., there are various forms of queens in the group that are ranked on seniority). Moreover, the patriarchy within the BCC shows itself not just in the leadership, but also in the logic used to justify the male-dominated hierarchy, including the undermining of women's biological and genetic makeup. Yet there is a devotion to the group, despite these challenges, that reveals the resilience of Black Coptic women. This was made clear by Empress Hatshepsut, who summarizes the relationship between the superwoman motif, Black women invisibility, and faith in this way:

> ... through this struggle, what I have gathered ... is always somehow, someway, things work out. God always seems to help black women make a way of out no way. The woman always finds a way to lighten the load of the community, to find room for those who might need a place to stay, to carry the church, to sing in the choir, or to make ends meet. She holds the community in place even though the community doesn't always hold her up.[77]

Empress Hatshepsut's reference to "making a way out of no way" summarizes the faithful struggle Black Coptic women, which is not unlike that of other Black women in relation to their faith traditions.

Womanist theologian Delores Williams, in her *Sisters in the Wilderness*, interprets "making a way out of no way" as a function of the personal relationship between Black women and God: "Many times, as a little girl, I sat in the church pew with my mother or grandmother and heard the black believers, mostly women, testify about 'how far they had come by faith.' They expressed their belief that God was involved in their history, that God helped them make a way out of no way."[78] In her reflection on "making a way out of no way," Monica Coleman is careful to not situate Black women as passive in the making of that way. Rather, she contends, "making a way out of no way" acknowledges God's role in providing options that did not appear to exist in the past. It is a weaving of the past, future, and possibilities offered by God—a weaving that leads to survival, quality of life, and liberating activity on the part of black women."[79] Plainly put, "making a way out of no way" is a nod toward human—particularly, Black female—agency in transforming the present for the sake of self and community. Empress Hatshepsut was clear that "making a way out of no way" describes how God *helps* Black women in their pursuit of justice and salvation. Black Coptic women navigate the murky waters of race, gender, and faith, not as empty slates onto which their destiny is drawn. Rather, the group of women with whom I met were aware of their choices, made their decisions, owned their narrative of faith, and constructed their Black Coptic identity despite the many challenges of patriarchy that come alive in the BCC.

5

Divine (Primordial) Blackness

Imagination, Hope, and a Word on Afro-Pessimism

What emerges in the desire that constitutes a certain proximity to that thought is not (just) that blackness is ontologically prior to the logistics and regulative power that is supposed to have brought it into existence but that blackness is prior to ontology; or in a slight variation of what Nahum Chandler would say, blackness is the original displacement of ontology, that it is ontology's anti- and ante foundation, ontology's underground, the irreparable disturbance of ontology's time and space.[1]
—Fred Moten

A man is either free, or he is not. There cannot be an apprenticeship for freedom.[2]
—Amira Baraka

Moses approached the thick darkness, where God was.
—Exodus 20:21 (NRSV)

Observation

Chicago. Sunday afternoon. Black History Month. Coptic Nation Temple. Priest Meshach approaches the podium on the church's rostrum. He says that he has enjoyed the speakers who preceded him. He says, "I would like to have a few remarks about so-called Black history. [. . .] Many churches and groups across the country are celebrating Black history." He continues,

> But if you want to study Black history you can't begin that study with Jamestown. You can't begin with slavery. We are not the sons and

Figure 5.1. Priest Meshach at Podium, Black Coptic Church Series, Chicago, IL, February 2021. Credit: Iwona Biedermann Photography.

daughters of slaves. We are the descendants of a Black God and a royal people. So, if you wanna talk about Black history, you have to go back even further than Ethiopia as the cradle of civilization. You have to go back to the beginning of time itself, when God created and shaped the first people as Black people, in the divine image of God.[3]

The community responds with "Amen," "That's right," and "Speak the truth."

* * *

I arrived at the Chicago South Side home of Priest Meshach and Candace Queen Rachel at 5:30 in the evening. It was a hot day in July. I had scheduled follow-up interviews with several members of the community. Candace Queen Rachel, who is married to Priest Meshach, offered their home as a more welcoming and, perhaps, more relaxed meeting space. For this follow-up conversation, I invited several queens in the community who had been active participants in the research, and Priest Meshach. I was the first of the guests to arrive. When Priest Meshach opened the door, he seemed happy to see me. "How's the family" he asked. Candace Queen Rachel, who was preparing glasses of iced water, stopped to give me a hug. "Good to see you," she said. As I sat at their kitchen table to unpack my meeting notes and prepare for the session, Priest Meshach stood up from his seat, glanced outside toward the backyard and offered, "Why don't we meet outside today? It's a nice evening." I agreed. As we sat on their patio by the pool, surrounded by greenery, I took note of their clothing. She wore a shirt with the inscription "Black Queen," and he, a Bob Marley t-shirt with an emblem of an Imperial Ethiopian flag (the version with the lion of Judah in the center). As the conversation unfolded, I asked Priest Meshach how he defined Blackness. In a prior session, he had alluded to an idea of Blackness that was intriguing and, in my estimation, deserved more interrogation. Unlike other interview sessions in which Blackness and discussions of race were centered on the imaginative performance of the community, this time he shifted to an abstract description that seemed to summarize Church teaching about Blackness and the body:

> In the [Black] Coptic Church, Prophet Cicero taught us that Black is divine. We are not focused on a color, but a power. The scriptures tell us that God abides in the thick darkness outside of space and time.[4] We believe that is the divine Blackness where God abides. And for us, as Copts, Blackness is the beginning of all creation. God creates out of Blackness; it is the womb of creation. And so, when we think about God, before anything else was made or existed, we think about God in the thick blackness of the dark void. And because God occupies space, the space is divine because God is not governed by anything but consumes all time and space. So, before slavery, before white people created the nigger and negro, or colored person, Blackness existed as a divine entity in the universe. Like Jesus taking on human flesh, we believe that the darkness, or Blackness, that was before all other creation, has been imparted onto our Black bodies as representations of that divine reality of Blackness. So, we believe, in our identity is our divinity. That identity is divine blackness. Everything we do in the Black Coptic Church is related to our bodies as living presentations of divine Blackness. This is why we can say that Black history does not begin in slavery or Jim Crow. Blackness is a divine history. We are walking representations of that divine history.[5]

There is much to unpack in Priest Meshach's description of Blackness, which includes gestures toward Christology, ontology, and other thematic considerations within the Black Coptic belief system. But in that moment, I pondered how Ethiopia, which occupies a weighty space in the Church's religious imagination, factored into this seemingly abstract turn. Other accounts of the Church's retrieval of a divine racial identity focused on Ethiopia as a divine geography, and on the performance of women in the community as Ethiopian queens. I was unable to make an immediate connection between Priest Meshach's response and those earlier accounts. We will return to this question toward the end of this chapter but, for now, a summation of our earlier discussions and a nod toward where I intend to land seems apropos.

Thus far we have focused on the relationship between performative imagination and identity construction within the Black Coptic religious world. I have argued that the BCC is an imaginative community that aims to recover an ideal of Black life that is deeply rooted in a heroic and grandiose read of a revered African civilization, namely Ethiopia, with traces and gestures toward ancient Egyptian culture. Indeed, this has been the cornerstone imagination of the BCC since its inception. This particular read and performance of Blackness contributes to an amalgamation of race and religion that also lends toward the performance of resistance; that is, the BCC not only sees itself as elevating Black culture and Black life, but also, as demonstrated in ritual and performance, contests notions of Blackness that are diminished to a confrontational read, in which Blackness is merely relational or defined by the vestiges of white supremacy. Such remnants, for Black Coptic believers, are epitomized in the invention of the negro—and within anti-Black imaginaries manifested in the form of the present-day Black person—which only appears as a fragment of the human and as a tool of the State from which labor is extracted. In this, I have positioned the BCC as a religious movement in which adherents understand their religious performances, which I identified as fugitive, as representative of Black life that is free, uncontrolled, and unconditioned by material realties. In short, I have argued that Blackness *otherwise* is a cornerstone performance among Black Coptic devotees. This performative imagination, that is, a sense and performance of Black life that aims to jettison anti-Black imaginaries, is observable in the posture toward Ethiopia, rituals such as adopting spiritual names, and performances such as wearing holy garments. At this stage, I aim to probe identity formation as a foundational feature—if not the kernel—of Black Coptic belief and performance, indeed the engine that drives the Church's theology and rituals. To accomplish this, I theorize divine Blackness as the epistemological starting point of the Black Coptic belief structure.

The Thick Darkness

Before investigating the articulation of Blackness espoused by Priest Meshach, it is helpful to consider, briefly, Black Coptic theology—specifically, a "Black God" as the theological underpinning of the divinization of Blackness, which is a principal conviction among Black Coptic followers. Priest Meshach's description of divine Blackness is not divorced from the Church's larger belief system. At the center of the BCC is an acceptance that God is not merely present in the thick darkness, thereby divinizing Black space, but rather God *is* Black. The theological expression "in the image of their God" has a profound impact on the imagination and performance of Blackness among Black Coptic followers in relation to embodiment and ontology. In short, the Blackness of God is not an abstract idea about God, distinct from the world of people. Black Coptic followers relate God's Blackness to their own disposition in the world, as they seek to reject anti-Black imaginaries and construct an identity that recovers Blackness as a divine and, as we have seen, a royal manifestation.

The origins of the BCC, as a religious movement that sought to thwart pessimistic and dehumanizing constructions of Blackness in the early and middle parts of the twentieth century, necessitated what was described in previous chapters as a hermeneutic of counter-indoctrination. A hermeneutic of counter-indoctrination in the BCC re-interprets scripture and re-imagines theology to recover and advance Black dignity. Prophet Cicero created a theology that established a relationship between the divine (God, Jesus, Holy Spirit, etc.) and "Black." We hear this when members of the congregation "give honor" to God before they speak in their religious services. As devotees approach the pulpit to make remarks, provide testimony, or address the congregation in any capacity, they begin with:

> I give honor to I Am the I Am God, a Black God
> His Son Black Jesus,
> And I give honor to the precious Black Holy Ghost[6]

This novel relationship between the divine and "Black" shaped their theological, social, and political understandings of what it meant to be Black in North America—which, for centuries, had been shaped by a religious empire that distinguished all things divine via white imagery, while excluding "Black" from their religious imagination. For Priest Eli, when he says "Black God," it reminds him that he is made in God's image. He notes: "Saying 'Black God' is personal for me. It is not about a racial category. God made me in his image. God can reveal himself in many ways. But to me he revealed himself as Black God. Serving a God who looks like me lets me know that I am somebody. I am in the image of my God."[7] Therefore, the BCC's emphasis on "Black" in its doctrine should not be read as a negative nationalism, or even necessarily in a political manner. Rather, the BCC's Black doctrine functions as a catalyst whose purpose is to counter disparaging acuities of Black being, interrupting the shame often associated with Blackness, and annihilating theologies that suggest God is not concerned about the well-being and the future of Black people. Declaring the Blackness of things divine, for Empress Selah, "is an extreme proclamation for an extreme indoctrination,"[8] which "immediately dismantles . . . what was a violent many years of generational indoctrination."[9] If one visits a BCC on any given Sunday, jubilant expressions such as "Thank you, Black Jesus!" are readily heard.

White Jesus, for Black Coptic followers, indicated that Black bodies were less aesthetically appealing than white bodies, which were always portrayed in images of the divine. Indeed, in a 1969 *Ebony Magazine* article, "The Quest for the Black Christ," Alex Poinsett captures the spirit of the day, as the National Committee of Black Churchmen pushed for a radical transformation in divine imagery. The Black churchmen, maintains Poinsett, were "seeking a theology tailored to the suffering, sorrow and survival of black people. They quest after a theology into which can be woven, for instance, the black Christmas and black Easter proposal of Chicago's imaginative Jesse Jackson. The Christ they had always known was white, blond and blue-eyed so that by subtle implication they were condemned for their blackness, for their flat noses, [and] for their kinky hair. . . .[10] In the BCC, Black God and Black Jesus communicate a sense of the body as united with the divine, thereby shattering conceptions of relational Blackness married to a normative whiteness.

The announcement of Black God is therefore an attempt to reduce the radical "otherness" of God, or God as removed from the human condition. In contradistinction, the Church's appeal to an idea of a God who is Black functions as a method by which the Church declares that God is interested in the human condition, and that the universality of God is best seen in the particular. Black theology has long argued that the Blackness of God as revealed in Jesus positions God as one who participates in the suffering and liberation of Black people. James Cone states:

> What we need to ask is this: "What is the form of humanity that accounts for human suffering in our society? What is it, except blackness? If Christ is truly the Suffering Servant of God who takes upon himself the suffering of his people, thereby reestablishing the covenant of God, then he must be black. To get to the meaning of this and not get bogged down in racial emotionalism we need only ask, "It is possible to talk about suffering in America without talking about the meaning of blackness. Can we really believe that Christ is the Suffering Servant if he is not black?" Black Theology contends that blackness is the one symbol that cannot be overlooked if we are going to take seriously the Christological significance of Christ.[11]

The Blackness of Jesus as the suffering servant exposes the character and essence of a God who manifests among the most oppressed who, for Cone, are Black people. In similar fashion, when Black Coptic believers assert a Black God and Black Jesus, they claim that the divine is present with them, allowing them to imagine *otherwise* impossible narratives of Black dignity.

In the BCC, the supposition of Black is a cultural and theological claim about the status of Black bodies in relation to God. As we have seen in preceding chapters, at the Church's founding, Prophet Cicero's teaching that Black people were formed in the image of God was a challenge to prevailing perceptions of Black people, who were deemed as non-human. Cornel West has argued that the notion that Back people are human is a relatively new invention.[12] The BCC's assertion of Black God makes a decisive break with religious imaginaries that advance anti-Black narratives.

Primordial Blackness

The question is appropriate: what is it about Blackness for Black Coptic believers that renders belief and performance around Blackness divine? In part, as we have discussed, the elevation of Blackness is about the construction of a racial identity. Yet, as Priest Meshach noted above, Blackness does more than name a color or racial category. For followers, Blackness reveals their understanding of the divine. Blackness, therefore, as metaphor, discloses knowledge about God and knowledge about Black bodies, which are clothed in divinity. In other words, Blackness is framed as a site of theological activity. In his only written pamphlet about beliefs in the Black Coptic Church, *Here Comes the Shadow of the Sun*, Prophet Peter, successor to Prophet Cicero, maintains that

> It has been said on many occasions the Black Nation is nothing and never will be nothing. That is a mistranslation according to the Bible. . . . There are many of the Black Prophets in the Bible that speak on Black. You will find that Solomon was a Black man. Solomon said, "I am Black but Beautiful. . . . You will find in the Book of Lamentations 5:10, "Our skins were Black." You will find in the Book of Jeremiah 14:2, "They are black." You will find in the Book of Lamentation 4:9 . . . , "Their faces are blacker than coal." . . . the Book of Nahum 2:10 [reads] "The faces of all gather blackness." . . . Book of the Song of Solomon 1:6 [reads], "Look not upon me because I am black." The Book of Joel 2:6 says, "All faces must gather blackness." Jeremiah 8:21 speaks again on blackness saying, "I am hurt. I am black; astonishment hath taken hold of me."[13]

Notwithstanding the absence of an exegetical treatment of the selected passages, Prophet Peter's promotion of biblical stories that feature Blackness discloses efforts of the Black Coptic community to situate Blackness within a divine context. Indeed, Prophet Peter's calling attention to these "Black passages" suggests a tri-fold purpose. First, as we have observed in the Black Coptic Church's celebration of Passover, he imaginatively employs Blackness as a national/racial category that connects North American Blacks to biblical history. In other words, he imagines a single and unified racial and cultural idea of Blackness, such that biblical passages like those he chose to highlight narrate a divine story about Blackness—one that disproves the assumption that "the Black Nation is nothing." Second, he seeks to counter such a narrative by engaging in a sort of proof texting around biblical passages that, for him, speak to a positive postulation about Blackness. Third, in grounding his read of Blackness in biblical passages, Prophet Peter constructs a relationship between Blackness and divinity, making Blackness the hermeneutical lens through which the theological and religious practices of the BCC are read.

In the BCC, the turn toward divine Blackness as a turn toward the mystical is an act of fugitivity. The appeal toward divine Blackness is an intentional departure from—or fleeing—Blackness as moderated by imaginaries that conflict with their understanding of divine Blackness. As a fugitive performance, the turn toward divine Blackness is also a turning away from, or rejection, of symbols that perpetuate and maintain Blackness within material boundaries or, what I referred to earlier as a ghettoization of Blackness. When members of the community assert divine Blackness, they are making a declaration that Blackness is not measurable within human or material metrics. Instead, there is a belief in the Black Coptic community that Blackness, as a substance and essence, precedes all forms of matter. So, the turn toward divine Blackness is an orientation beyond the world; not as in escapism, but as in the fullness of Blackness that cannot be understood by or limited to the physicality of location in time (*kronos*). Accordingly, among Black Coptic believers, Blackness, like their attention to and claims regarding Ethiopia, shatters presumed borders that attempt to stall Blackness within a specific time and place. Queen Huldah, recounting the teaching of Prophet Cicero, said that "as Black Copts we are in the world but not of the world. The world, the world created by white people, cannot contain Blackness. The resiliency of Blackness liberates itself from the imprisonment of false idols and false images of Blackness. Blackness desires to be free."[14] Fugitive Blackness, then, is Blackness uninhibited by "the world" of terror and white supremacy, but present as gift, a concept we will explore later in this chapter.

In the extended quote that opens this chapter, Priest Meshach wrestled with a notion of Blackness that undergirds the theology of the Black Coptic community. He intertwined an interpretation of Blackness with a conception of God as the origin of thought and performance of Blackness—first as a substance, then as an embodiment or enfleshment upon Black bodies. It is worth noting that we see this type of theological procedure in the Church's Christology, in relation to the Black body of Jesus. For present purposes, however, Priest Meshach's account of Blackness in the BCC illuminates several principal features of the religious imagination at work in the community, and displays how the BCC contributes to a wider discourse on imagining Blackness as *otherwise*. That is, as an extension of Prophet Cicero's admonition that Blackness is the "cradle of civilization" and the "fossil of thought,"[15] Priest Meshach offers a metaphysical and, indeed, mystical, read of Blackness as *a priori* to the material horror of ontological terror, to borrow a phrase from Calvin Warren, that threatens the very being of Black people in North America. This read has a profound impact on how we see Black people anthropologically, and shapes the ontological interpretation of what I will describe in this chapter as *BlackBeing*; that is, I propose to theorize the conception of Blackness in the BCC. I argue that their conception of Blackness, as one grounded in the mystical, offers a way forward, because it locates its being in the reality of the divine, in contrast to Blackness defined by structural, ontological, and existential threats to being itself, or what I have simply referred to in earlier chapters as the absurd. I suggest an ontological description not divorced from experience, which was the concern of Fanon[16], but rather one that takes seriously the pathology of whiteness and its attempt to reimagine Blackness as that which lacks being and therefore operates as a slave and object of its (whiteness's) performance.

Priest Meshach invokes a theology and cosmology that commences with Blackness as the genesis, indeed, as the origin of thought. Noteworthy in his description, however, is the caveat: for Black Coptic believers Blackness is not a concentration on color, but rather on the condition in which Blackness is shaped and derives its essence—what he refers to as "power." That is, Blackness as *already* formed in a divine reality, insofar as Blackness—in the thick darkness—is the atmosphere in which God exists prior to the creation of the exterior world. There is a focus in the BCC on the *anteriority* of God, as God exists prior to creation. This emphasis is not foreign to Christian theology. Indeed, in mainstream Christian theology, immanent trinity, in contrast to the economic trinity, designates the *ontos* of God, as God subsists prior to the process of creation and salvation. The interior life of the Christian God is one that resides in permanent darkness or radical *nothingness*. Yet, for the BCC, the void—or nothingness of the darkness—is not equivalent to "absence." On the contrary, as advanced by Priest Meshach and expressed in the teaching of the BCC, "the darkness in which God exists is an essence itself. It is a substance made divine by the presence of God."[17] For Priest Meshach, all creation is traceable to a divine starting point which cannot be separated from the Black substance (i.e., Black and Blackness) that precedes the material world. For him, such substance, the darkness before material reality, "is the same Blackness that has been placed upon Black flesh."[18]

What are we to glean from this imagination of Blackness? The BCC's performative imagination is not limited to an archeological approach or retrieval of material and social history, like the artifacts of a revered culture (i.e., Ethiopia) that are appropriated in the religious life of believers—though these elements are important. They are significant as the community performs its idea of a Black person that is free and autonomous. But Priest Meshach's construal of Blackness as a divine reality, indeed substance, renders a nuanced approach toward understanding the intersection of race and religion. That is, the performative imagination among Black Coptic believers commences with a sort of incarnational view of Blackness, interpreting Blackness as an essence that precedes materiality, and assumes the bodies of Black persons, profoundly impacting their anthropology and giving rise to what I identity as a Blackontology, which seeks to reject the problem of the negro and de-stabilize notions of ontological Blackness as earlier described by Victor Anderson. This expression of Blackness, then, not only helps to concretize the Church's performance of Blackness, but enters in, and sheds light on, modern discourse on the question of Black being. The expression of Blackness in the BCC challenges us to ask whether and to what extent we may talk about Black being as opposed to Black non-being. In the BCC performative imagination is primarily the presentation and execution of Blackness as divine and as symbol, toward which Black bodies point and in which they participate. One may think of Blackontology as the starting point of both theological reflection and religious practice. Divine Blackness, in this sense, is the imagination of Blackness unrestrained, *a priori*, and not the property of the colonial settler or his religion.

The turn toward primordial Blackness aims to disentangle Blackness from the fetishized focus on anti-Black imaginaries, as well as from the possession (object), as in ownership, of Black people. It is an assertion of Blackness as a mystical reality, indeed transcendent. This is not to suggest that *anyone* can lay claim to Blackness, as American cultural theorist and Black studies scholar Fred Moten articulates in his phenomenology of Black Spirit,[19] but rather an assertion that Blackness is too mysterious and too divine to be possessed by any group; Blackness is therefore the foreword thought. It is the stuff *before* the stuff. This method of reading Blackness signals that Blackness is a gift. Indeed, in his own turn toward mysticism, Moten offers a similar movement. Calvin Warren's summation of Moten's articulation of Blackness is helpful here. Notes Warren:

> [For Moten] Black people are 'touched by blackness' (blackness is presented to them much like Being is presented to *Dasein* for Heidegger), but blackness is not the property of black people. Blackness becomes what philosopher Mary Jane Rubenstein might call "strange wonder" (cf. Rubenstein 2010)—a wonder that Heidegger described as the groundlessness of Being. Because it is without ground, this wonder cannot be objectified or owned as the property of this or that group of persons. The relationship between black people and blackness is not one that Moten explicitly articulates, primarily because he is attempting to detach blackness from black people and conceptualize blackness as a mystical abstraction appearing to the world.[20]

As is true for Moten, the turn toward the Black mystical in the BCC is a bearing toward an abstraction that appears as gift. Yet, as we shall see, there is an attempt in the tradition to ascribe Blackness to Black people, not as in custody, but rather as incarnational. In sum, within the context of the absurd, Blackness is a performance of the fugitive; Blackness unleashes itself from the perceived grip of modernity. This chapter interrogates the aforementioned imagination, and offers ways that such claims intervene in contemporary discourse in Black Studies and Black religious scholarship.

The Negro and the Ontological Dilemma

I have argued throughout this text that, at the core of the search for identity in the BCC, there is a rejection of negro and its legacy as a racial description for Black people. This denunciation is made clear in the various performances and rituals observed in the tradition. What we ascertain from the religious world and practices of the BCC is an effort to recover and imagine the possibility of *otherwise* via a postulation of divine Blackness as a mode of being that counteracts and rejects the construction of the negro and other pejorative classifications of the Black person. This type of performative imagination is routine in the BCC, as manifested in the glance toward Ethiopia and the construction of an imagined homeland, the assumption of a spiritual name, and the religio-self-fashioning of the body and the person. Such practices, although they offer insights and are critical to the formation of the person in this community, are best understood through the lens of the mystical, or the turn to *divine* Blackness.

The turn toward divine Blackness is a pivot away from negro and a denunciation of its festering imaginaries, namely, religious and social performances that deny the being and value of Black bodies. Most notably, as we have seen, for Black Coptic believers, the problem of the invented negro or anti-Black constructions of Blackness, is not reducible to a social problem that is solved merely by social and political measures. Quite the contrary, among believers, the idea and performance of negro—i.e., an anti-Black world—is a religious and theological problem that commands an orientation toward the divine in the quest for a definition and performance of the Black person that does not succumb to anti-Blackness. *Otherwise*, in this formulation, is the performance of divine Blackness; it is a practice of the imagination.

The BCC's emphasis on the divine as the starting point for interpreting Blackness reflects Prophet Cicero's efforts to fundamentally rebuff anti-Black imaginaries, primarily observed in the invention of the negro and its being defined against the divinization of whiteness, or what I call relational Blackness. As Fanon observes, "Not only must the black man [sic] be black; he must be black in relation to the white man [sic]."[21] This type of relational Blackness, a way of measuring, defining, and assigning aesthetic value to Blackness and Black bodies, argues Priest Gehazi, "means that black people and black culture only mean anything when they are seen through the standard of white people and white culture."[22] For the BCC, the creation of the negro, and the world in which the negro is required to sustain an anti-Black project (i.e., a cosmological reality in which the negro/Black person lacks being is a *necessary* precondition) damage the dignity of Black people and reduces Black bodies to mere tools of the State; indeed, property of an imagination. Prophet Hiram, a Black Coptic spiritual leader, notes:

> To be black in the United States is to always be a negro or a nigger. We may have moved from that period of history, but the laws in the country and the way Black people are treated still speak to what it means to be a negro. So, for some, the language might be dated, but the reality is still real for Black people. You look at our schools, our neighborhoods, our income status, and the way police target young Black boys, then you know we are still living as negroes. Prophet Cicero and Prophet Peter taught us that the negro and the condition of our people was an attempt to destroy us and kill our spirits. So, when I think of negro and the condition of Black people, I think about a people who are actually not people.[23]

Prophet Hiram's contention that to be Black (negro) is non-existence (i.e., not to be a person) creates a situation in which members of the BCC, like members of Black religions worldwide, assert their existence (being) while perceived as non-persons. Non-person as a descriptive category of the Black person is an anthropological and ontological space that members of the community must cross in quest of an *otherwise* history and identity. This space, one in which the onto- and anthro-possibilities of Black people are questioned, or, at worst denied, is summarized by Queen Maryann, an early convert to the BCC:

> Prophet Cicero knew the shape we were in. Many people had accepted that they were nothing. After so long hearing people call you nothing and treat you like nothing, you start to believe it. And when Prophet Cicero

was teaching, he had more people who joined the church who thought they were really a negro. But we didn't have anything or own anything because we accepted the negro degree. Prophet Cicero taught us the negro would lead us nowhere because the negro was nobody. Nobody loved the negro. Nobody respected the negro. Nobody wanted the negro to be around. We were not living; we were just there. Like things on a wall or tools waiting for somebody to use us. But Prophet Cicero came back to take us back to our true self; the people of God.[24]

Prophet Hiram and Queen Maryann's description of a negro, or the Black person—that is, the Black person as imagined in a culture of racism—is the product of anti-Black imaginaries in which Blackness is reduced to the status of a thing and, more relevant to this chapter, a notion of Blackness that is ontologically damaging—as Prophet Hiram says, to occupy space as a non-person.

Prophet Hiram and Queen Maryann's interrogation of the modern world and the place of the Black person in it echoes what literary theorist Christina Sharpe refers to as living in the wake. Living, or laboring, in the wake means living in the aftermath of slavery, suffering slavery's continued earthquakes that dislocate Black bodies, stifle Black imagination, and threaten to destroy Black life. It is the condition in which the negro is created, placed, and policed by terror. Sharpe notes: "Living in the wake means living the history and present of terror, from slavery to present, as the ground of our everyday Black existence; living the historically and geographically dis/continuous but always present and endlessly reinvigorated brutality in, and on, our bodies. . . ."[25] Prophet Hiram's contention of everyday terror that haunts Black boys and girls describes living in the wake. As Sharpe notes, it is the foundation of Black existence; an existence that is often defined and recognized by attempts to dodge the ever-present realities of the wake. The negro, Queen Maryann notes, is the category in which Black people are placed (sans existence) in the wake.

For the BCC, the problem in imagining the negro as the free Black is that negro negates existence. It is more than the problem of double consciousness described by Du Bois. Moreover, insofar as "things" are not thinking or rational beings, the problem of the negro is not solved by Descartes' turn toward the subject, i.e., *cogito ergo sum*. It is to wrestle with Shakespeare's "To be, or not to be." It is a question of either affirming and performing "being" or succumbing to the station of the negro, which impedes being itself. Such oscillation between non-being (the absurd) and the possibility of being (*otherwise*) frames the situation in which divine Blackness, for the BCC, seeks to emerge. Divine Blackness, as an ontological turn, seeks to negate the negation; it imagines *otherwise* unimaginable possibilities and tries to perform the same, such that the Black person is not relegated to non-being status in the wake, but rather affirms dignity and personhood. The paradoxical problem, then, of the negro, is that the negro—or Black person as non-being, devoid of an ontological ground, and the property of the imagination of the colonial settler—is, in the summation of Queen Maryann, unwanted but required for the project of colonialism (the absurd), to persist and survive, neither of which are options for the negro.

The BCC, from its inception to present day, has grappled with the place of the negro in an anti-Black world, accomplishing a stunning and, indeed, painstaking task in their religious imagination; that is, not merely asserting identity, but imagining and performing *being* itself. Indeed, Sharpe notes, "living in . . . the wake is living the 'afterlife of property' and living the afterlife *partus sequitue venrtrem* (that which is brought forth follows the womb), in which the Black child inherits the non/status, the non/being of the mother. That inheritance of a non/status is everywhere apparent now in the ongoing criminalization of Black women and children."[26] Stated differently, the BCC's theology recognizes a higher problem: the negro chiefly presents as an ontological problematic contradictory to being, and therefore precludes any claim to the category of the human. Such a paradox means that this religion must both imagine the possibility of being and assign an identity to being that does not entrap itself in the paradox—the problem—of the negro. Critical to this contradiction, however, is that members of the BCC do not capitulate to the threat of—or performance of a world that requires—Black nonbeing and loss of identity for the negro. Rather, the BCC imagines a pathway for thinking through the weeds of the ontological dilemma as presented in an anti-Black world via various attendant imaginaries, including religious, social, political, and economic. At this juncture, Calvin Warren helps to frame the problem even more concretely.

Ontological Terror in the Aftermath

It is appropriate to ponder to what extent it is possible to construct, recover, or resurrect a Black identity not bound by the enduring artifacts of enslavement the world maintains. Cultural and performance studies theorist Saidiya Hartman outlines slavery's rejection of Black humanity in this way:

> If slavery persists as an issue in the political life of black America, it is not because of an antiquarian obsession with bygone days or the burden of a too-long memory, but because black lives are still imperiled and devalued by a racial calculus and a political arithmetic that were entrenched centuries ago. This is the afterlife of slavery—skewed life chances, limited access to health and education, premature death, incarceration, and impoverishment. I, too, am the afterlife of slavery.[27]

The afterlife of slavery is the absence of life for the negro. The absence of life is maintained by a denial of the sources and tools that contribute to human flourishing. It is at this intersection, of the afterlife (negro) and an awareness of the afterlife, that the BCC's turn toward the divine seeks to intercede. Indeed, Sharpe notes, "if we are lucky, we live in the knowledge that the wake has positioned us as no-citizen. If we are lucky, the knowledge of this positioning avails us particular ways of re / seeing, re / inhabiting, and re / imagining the world."[28] Imagination in this sense in an intervention.

The apex of the Black Coptic religious imagination and world, then, is the rejection of negro—afterlife—as a valid descriptor for Blacks while simultaneously performing *otherwise* to recover identity. This is an onerous task, certainly, given the assumptions of the tradition as espoused by several key figures. Moreover, the interpretation of stolen Black life, or Black life as property and captive, in the BCC, finds partial resonance with Afro-Pessimism, particularly in Calvin Warren's *Ontological Terror*. Do Black persons possess being? Is there is a legitimate claim to personhood and agency, considering the existential absurdity that shaped the historical context in which the BCC was birthed? Simply put, when members of the BCC make the declaration that Black life is divine and therefore, in contemporary form, "matters," what in fact are they asserting, given that the negro—the modern Black in the imagination of white culture—is an invention of white supremacy? In other words, as Warren poses, "these questions of value, meaning, stability, and intelligibility lead us to the terror of the declaration, the question it conceals but engages: what ontological ground provides the occasion for the declaration? Can such ground be assumed, and if not, is the declaration even possible without it?"[29]

The declaration of *Black-as-person* at first glance appears as paradox, given the way that the BCC interprets the categories negro and Black as two sides of the same coin within the cosmological imagination of the colonial settler. That is, within the social order of the colonial settler and his religion, Black people are merely negroes, and thereby, devoid of being and humanity. Analogous to the thinking in the BCC, Warren commences with an acknowledgement of an antithesis; namely:

> The Negro is black because the Negro must assume the function of nothing in a metaphysical world. The world needs his labor. This obsession, however, also transforms into hatred, since nothing is incorrigible—it shatters ontological ground and security. Nothing terrifies metaphysics, and metaphysics attempts to dominate it by turning nothing into an object of knowledge, something it can dominate, analyze, calculate, and schematize. When I speak of function, I mean the projection of nothing's terror onto blackness as a strategy of metaphysics' will to power. How then, does metaphysics dominate nothing? By objectifying nothing through the Black Negro.[30]

Warren is an important conversation partner with the BCC insofar as his contribution helps to concretize the problem of the negro, which has been an important element of the BCC's theological positioning since its inception. As we have seen, there is consensus that the insidious creation of the negro was necessary in order to accomplish the imagination of those who presumed themselves to have being or, even more, to be divinized in the image of God, while the negro's task is, as object, to labor for the State. For Warren, then, while Blacks have function, given the ordered and performed imagination of white supremacy, they do not possess being. To be sure, "the world needs Negro, even as the world despises it."[31] Ontological ground and anthropological possibilities, then, are not within reach of the negro. The cosmological and earthly orientation of the negro is not toward a joyful place-in-the-world. Rather, the negro as problem exists or, is placed within the world—invented—as human machinery. Warren deliberates, then, the efficacy of an imagination of Black being not beholden to anti-Blackness, given the ontological terror in which the Black was invented. Warren argues:

> Black ~~being~~ becomes a site of projection and absorption of the problem of metaphysics—a problem that the captor would like to ignore or neglect by imposing it onto black ~~being~~. Thus, black ~~being~~ is not only necessary or involuntary labor pornotroping, but also necessary ontologically; it inhabits the problem of metaphysics. This inhabitation is the ~~space~~ and ~~place~~ of the Negro Question—our proper metaphysical question.[32]

The negro, then, is entangled in a muddled form of the *being not*; specifically, the paradox of perceived or shadow existence, lacking any real claim to existence itself, but rather, only present as a "form" of the human but projected as a thing. Such entanglement demands the question that Warren rightly asks, one that the BCC seeks to answer: "One must take a step backward and ask the fundamental question: is the Black, in fact, human? Or can Blackness ground itself in the *being* of the human? If it cannot, then on what bases can we assert the mattering of Black existence? If it can, then why would [Black Lives Matter] need to be repeated and recited incessantly?"[33] So, the question of an ontological ground for identity among Black people endures. That is, what are the ontological conditions that permit Blacks to claim status as *human* beings, and thereby assert an identity resultant from it? While the BCC shares certain conceptions of the world and the place of the Black person in it with Afro-pessimists like Calvin Warren, they diverge on how this question is answered. Whereas Warren views Blackness as tethered to an ontological project meant to hopelessly destruct Black people to things, the BCC offers a path forward, indeed a certain grammar, for working through the malaise of what Warren deems as ontological terror.

Warren's project, particularly his read of the ontological terror that haunts the negro, especially the "Free Black,"[34] is indispensable in comprehending the station of Blacks worldwide. To be sure, there is a fundamental dread and fear that preoccupies [free] Black persons as they strive to maintain a sense of dignity within the context of cosmological absurdity, rendering the concept of freedom suspect. For Warren,

> "Free Black" is a grammatical and syntactical battlefield upon which dead bodies—Trayvon Martin, Renice McBride, Michael Brown, among countless others—are displayed. We can also call this disaster the "metaphysical holocaust," as Frantz Fanon describes. It is the systemic and relentless wiping out of black cosmologies, histories, and frames or reference/orientation. The metaphysical holocaust is violence without end, violence constitutive of a metaphysical world. It is a "violence that continuously repositions the black as a void of historical movement," as Frank Wilderson describes it. This void and stasis of temporal linearity is precisely the nothing blacks incarnate. The term *free black*, then, is the syntactical reflection of the metaphysical holocaust, the violence between the terms of free and black that is unresolvable.[35]

Warren's attention to anti-Blackness is significant, therefore, because he foregrounds the constant struggle of Black folk to negotiate between nothingness and their assertion of somebodiness within a context that defines Blackness as that which is relegated to the periphery of society and reduced to non-being. Warren's analysis, however, is deeply fatalistic and succumbs to Black non-being as not only necessary, but an inescapable invention of modernity. Indeed, "the world needed a being that would bear the unbearable and live the unlivable; a being that would exist within the interstice of death and life and straddle Nothing and Infinity. The being invented to embody Black as nothing is the Negro."[36] In a further demonstration of the fatalistic turn, at a gathering that considered the killing of Ferguson, Missouri unarmed Black teenager Michael Brown by Officer Darren Wilson and the police state, Warren recounts what he told those in attendance:

> I told the audience there was not a solution to the problem of antiblackness; it will continue without end as long as the world exists. Furthermore, all the solutions as presented rely on antiblack instruments to address antiblackness, a vicious and tortuous cycle that will only produce more pain and disappointment. I also said that humanist effect (the good feeling we get from hopeful solutions) will not translate into freedom,

justice, recognition or resolution. It merely provides a temporary reprieve from the fact that Blacks are not safe in an antiblack world, a fact that can become overwhelming. The sort of antiblackness might alter, but antiblackness will remain a constant—despite the power of our imagination and political yearnings.[37]

While Warren's attention to the absurd is useful and indispensable, his notion of Black being, or a free Black being, as unattainable, indeed an impossible feat, invites further deliberation. The ontological construction presented in his argument yields to an ontology that is merely socially constructed and therefore the property of anti-Blackness or the colonial settler. One is thus left wondering about the possibility of hope, of Black identity, and the possibility of *otherwise*. That is, if Black existence and Black identity are apprehended by a confrontational read of history, whither Black joy? The promise of Afro-Pessimist thinkers such as Calvin Warren is their unapologetic and necessary work of uncovering the predicament of the negro or the "free-Black." However, the lacuna in the project is a lack of language that provides a conduit through which to imagine Blackness without succumbing to white supremacy. I argue that Black religious discourse opens new possibilities and frontiers for reading Black existence and identity that pushes the conversation in different directions. Moreover, Black religion, since its beginnings in the imagination of enslaved persons, has opened new routes to a distinct theological tradition birthed within the invisible institution, and has provided a vocabulary that allowed participants to wrestle with the absurd while refusing to yield their being and personhood to nothingness. Whereas Warren, for instance, and the broader turn to Afro-Pessimism, does not envision a world in which Black life has meaning and value, the turn toward Black religion unseals new potentials for grammars that deliberate the affirmation of Black life and Blackbeing.

Through their performative imagination, followers of the BCC offer a retort to Afro-Pessimism. In similar fashion, many mainstream as well as understudied Black religions contend with anti-Black racism via the construction of religious worlds, performances, and practices that fight the temptation to succumb to nothingness. From the ring shout of enslaved Africans to the "holy dance" and shout among modern-day

Black Christians, from religio-self-fashioning in the Nation of Islam to the turn toward divine Blackness among Black Coptic devotees, Black religions have imagined and performed joy and thereby retained hope within structures that maintain the absurd. As I have argued throughout this text, the possibility of *otherwise* is captured in religious performance. In the remaining pages we will examine the BCC as a religious response to pessimism.

Throughout this book, we have shared the testimony of Black Coptic believers who understand their religious practices as not only constructive in their search for identity, but also as providing hope. That is, religious practices in the BCC are not fixated on preparation for the next life, but also, as we have seen, affirm and perform hope in the now. Therefore, when members of the BCC appeal to a heroic read of Africa, adopt spiritual names, and partake in other rituals of identity formation they are performing their imagination of Blackness as transcendent and, as argued above, mystery. Indeed, the intervention seen in the BCC is an intervention that was burgeoning as a cultural and religious spirit of the times. Other religio-racial movements like the Nation of Islam and the Moorish Science Temple also wrestled with the meaning of Blackness in the face of absurdity. Their religious response to racism included the recovery of divine geographies and divine histories. In the case of the BCC, it also included a notion of divine Blackness that addresses questions of ontology.

Blackontology

This chapter opened with a question posed to Priest Meshach about "Blackness," to which he offered the following:

> The scriptures tell us that God exists in the thick darkness outside of space and time. We believe that is the divine Blackness where God abides. And for us, as Copts, Blackness is the beginning of all creation. God creates out of Blackness; it is the womb of creation. And so, when we think about God, before anything else was made or existed, we think about God in the thick Blackness of the dark void. And because God occupies that space, the space itself is divine as God is not controlled by but consumes all time and space.

Priest Meshach's description of Blackness as divine and as the space that God occupied before time, suggests a Blackness that is not, in contrast to an Afro-Pessimist approach, the social or material production of modernity. Indeed, while negro is rejected in the BCC as a legitimate identifier for Black people, the turn to divine Blackness is understood as a turn to Blackness that is not containable by the objectified negro. In this sense, while negro is a contraption crafted for social utility, "Black and Blackness supersede negro."[38] Further, for Priest Stephen, "when we as Black Copts talk about Black and Blackness, we are talking about a mystical reality that is the essence of God. When white people came up with the term negro as a substitute for Black, they tried to hijack our Blackness by imposing negro and nigger on us. But Prophet Cicero came to teach us back to our original identity, which is a divine Black identity."[39] The BCC rejects an ontology in which Black being is imprisoned to the imagination of the constructed negro. This turn to divine Blackness, then, is a metanoia that forefronts Blackness as a divine source which materializes—becomes flesh—in Black people, shattering conceptions of the negro. The ontological imagination of the BCC provides resources, indeed a vocabulary, for the performance of what I call Blackontology, that is, an articulation of Blackness in which Blackness already, as in *a priori*, is an essence that flows from the divine.

What might it mean to imagine Blackness as an essence, indeed, as an indispensable quality or nature? In the BCC, Blackness is imagined as an intricate reality of God's nature. As we have seen in preceding chapters, the Church declares that God, as Black, is the source of all being, to be sure, being itself. As I sought to understand how this belief guides the Church's theology and religious practices and thereby how the community interprets Black identity, I gathered the following from Mother Queen Rebekah:

> Prophet Cicero taught us about Black God and Black Jesus. When he came from the South to the North, he put a sign outside the church that said, "come and learn about a Black God and a Black Jesus." White peoples [sic] told us that black was dirty. But Prophet Cicero told us that God is Black. And if God is Black, and we are Black, we share that with God. We are not talking about a color, you understand, we are talking about the

power of a Black God. People hear black and automatically thinks [sic] of a color. But the spirit of God is a black spirit. It is the spirit that make [sic] God who God is. Black spirit is the creation of all things, you see. Out of darkness come [sic] the light; out of darkness come the peoples [sic]; out of darkness come everything that is. The darkness is the Blackness.[40]

Similarly, in a continuation of his explanation of divine Blackness, Priest Meshach notes that:

The Blackness of God signifies the space of darkness from which all creation flows, including Black bodies. When we read in the scripture that God is to be found in the thick darkness, or the triple darkness, we understand that it is impossible to separate God from the darkness that he [sic] inhabited before the ages. So, while some people may think about a dark "void" where nothing existed, we understand that nothing to be something. The something is the being of God as found in the darkness, the womb of all creation. For us, this means the being, or the nature of God, is only understood if we begin with the Blackness of God. God is Black because God chose to exist in the darkness before anything else. So, the Blackness is the nature and the essence of God.[41]

Mother Rebekah and Priest Meshach's reflections turn toward the transcendental. The transcendental provides the structure for a mystical read of Blackness as a nature and ontological existence that precedes other (material) forms of existence, especially social and political death. Indeed, for the BCC, Blackness as an essence and nature, is the substance that originates outside of time as the "stuff" of divinity. Insofar as the divine encompasses the thick darkness, or Blackness, such space is divinized. More critically, however, within both interpretations of Blackness rests the contention that Blackness is the space or essence from which "all creation flows, including Black bodies." This theological posture lends itself toward the development of Blackontology as a way of interrogating Black life and offers an intervention in the conversation of Black being and Black identity.

Blackontology as a mode of thinking about Blackness assists Black Coptic believers wrestling with questions of identity and being, and offers differentiation from the ontological critique found in the work of

Afro-Pessimists. Moreover, Blackontology as presented in Black Coptic religion escapes the trap of ontological Blackness described by Victor Anderson, and that also is found within the Afro-Pessimist thought. Whereas ontological Blackness is predicated upon, indeed indebted to, forms of Blackness created by the colonial settler, Blackontology imagines Blackness as the essence of a divine source. Indeed, there is a kind of woeness mired in pessimism in that ontological Blackness concedes to white supremacy and denies Black life; it denies Black imagination; it reduces Black being to nothingness and interprets Black life as the antithesis to whiteness. Blackontology, however, as elucidated by my informants, asserts that Blackness is *prior to* the social and political displacement of Black life. Blackontology asserts that, because Blackness precedes the ontological terror of white normativity, Blackness is not the property of an anti-Black world, but rather Blackness is the property of divinity. Such is the religious and theological point of departure among Black Coptic believers.

During my fieldwork in the BCC, an idea that was persistently repeated is that Black "history," or the history of Blackness, does not begin with struggle. In the opening of this chapter, I introduced Priest Meshach's contention that Black history exceeds temporal limitations and includes a *time before time* This stands in contradistinction to the work of Afro-Pessimist thinker Frank Wilderson, who states:

> To put it bluntly, blackness cannot be separated from slavery. Blackness is often misconstrued as an identity (cultural, economic, gendered) of the Human community; however, there is no black time that precedes the time of the Slave. Africa's spatial coherence is temporally coterminous with the Arab, and then European, slave trade. The time of blackness is the time of the paradigm; it is not a temporality that can be grasped with the epistemological tool at our disposal. The time of blackness is no time at all, because one cannot know a plenitude of blackness distinct from Slaveness.[42]

For the BCC, imagining Blackness as radically *otherwise*, that is, Blackness as the material of divinity, allows for a Blackness not bound to nor conditioned by anti-Blackness, but rather, in the tradition of philosopher Fred Moten's para-ontology, Blackness as "ontologically prior to the to the logistic and regulative power that is supposed to have brought it into existence ... [and] prior to ontology. ..."[43]

What might it mean, then, to imagine Blackness as flowing from the essence of divinity? A sort of Black time before slavery. In the BCC, the intersection of Blackness and divinity sets the stage for the community's claim about embodiment. Contends Queen Huldah,

> When we consider the Black body, we are talking about a body that bears the essence of God. We believe that because God created in blackness and persisted in blackness, that blackness transmits the mark of divinity. Blackness is God and God is blackness. Prophet Cicero taught us that to be Black is to be in the image of God, not necessarily in color, but in that we are the bearers of the original substance in which God presented himself [sic]. Blackness is not merely a by-product of divinity; blackness flows from divinity like rivers flow from oceans. They are one and the same.[44]

Blackontology, then, asserts a Blackness that is being itself, unconditioned, undetermined, and prior to the dislocation and misapprehension of Blackness by the colonial settler. It allows a performance of Blackness that it is unable to be held captive by oppressive imaginations. Insofar as the BCC contemplates Blackness as flowing from the divine essence, Blackness is not merely an abstract reality that remains in a state of radical otherness. Rather, as Queen Huldah asserts, the Black body bears the (Black) essence of God, indeed, it is a body that enfleshes divinity.

What we glean from Queen Huldah's words is that the BCC's deportment toward divine Blackness is not merely a theoretical or theological imagination wanting of human implications. It aims at the recovery of Black being and the assertion of a new Black person. Theoretical abstractions far removed from the human experience are not considered useful in the community. Prophet Judah, a spiritual leader in the BCC, notes that "everything we believe and do in this Church is about empowering [Black] people to know that Black is beautiful and that they are a holy people."[45] Divine Blackness as a theological starting point is therefore concretized in the Church's theological anthropology, which contemplates the Black body as a sacred site of God's divine activity. Such is evidenced in the various forms of religio-self-fashioning presented in previous chapters. The formalization of this contention is best understood in Priest Meshach's statement quoted earlier, that "like Jesus taking on human flesh, we believe that the darkness, or Blackness, that was before all other creation, has been imparted onto our Black bodies as representations of that divine nature of Blackness. So, we believe, in our identity is our divinity."[46]

Priest Meshach's correlation between Black bodies enfleshing divinity and the mainstream Christian belief in the incarnation was intentional, but he also recognized differences. When asked if he could elaborate on his statement, he replied,

> The point here is not to obscure or weaken the incarnation story. When we in the [BCC] talk about our bodies bearing the image of God, we don't mean that we are God. We do want to make the case that as God chose Jesus to become the incarnate word, God chose Black bodies as the vehicles of his [sic] divine essence or Blackness. So, Black bodies incarnate Blackness in the way that Jesus incarnates the logos.[47]

The position inherent in the statement is that Black bodies are the recipients of divine material or divine substance, otherwise known as Blackness. Black bodies, then, per this line of argument, enflesh divinity in the sense that their bodies incarnate Blackness—or divinity. Accordingly, enfleshing divinity is a performance of Blackness predicated on the assertion that Black bodies, as sacred sites, are not reducible to the social materiality and invention of anti-Blackness. Indeed, Blackness is not determined by crisis or sustained by the absurd. Rather, Black bodies point to *otherwise* in that Black bodies are symbols of divinity.

For Black Coptic believers, the assertion of enfleshed divinity disrupts a long history of pseudo-biology, -anthropology, and -theology, that defined Blackness as deviant, out of control, and unworthy. The new anthropological claim is necessary precisely because, for

> far too long, black people have been taught to hate our bodies. We have been indoctrinated to believe that somehow our bodies were less than white bodies. Our noses too broad, our hips too wide, our lips too big. We have basically been taught to believe that black bodies are ugly, and we should strive to be like someone else because they, white people, are

beautiful. Our images on television are often made to look unappealing. Our hair is too nappy and so we must straighten it to have so-called "good hair." We have been taught that the black sex is nasty. I mean, when you think about the history of beauty in the world as told by the dominant culture, it's a history of black hate. Prophet Cicero says, look, to hell with what they say about our black bodies. The fact that God chose God's son to appear in a black body in North Africa cannot be disregarded. So, when we talk about our bodies as the presence of God, it dispels all the myths about blackness that we have been told. It is a radical indoctrination to reject an extreme history of black hatred that many Black people have internalized.[48]

The BCC's theological position—here articulated by Queen Huldah—supports the performance of *otherwise* Blackness outlined in preceding chapters. The performance of royal titles and adoption of spiritual names are part of so-called "myth busting" and the performance of Blackness not determined by white normativity. In their assertion that Blackness is an anthropological manifestation of the divine, Black Coptic believers disrupt the reading of Blackness in contrast to the so-called purity of whiteness. Their belief in the enfleshing of divinity permits the BCC to emphasize Blackness as transcendent; that is, the mystical reality and nature of Blackness in the flesh of Black persons as conveyors of that which is true and that which is beauty. Priest Meshach's conviction that their identity is in their divinity is helpful in thinking about Blackness in flesh, or enfleshing divinity.

When Queen Rebekah and other members of the Black Coptic community reference their understanding of history and Blackness as not a production of anti-Blackness, they appeal to a sense of identity that foregrounds Blackness in the mystical. Commencing with the numinous, that is, the ontological and anthropological argument, believers maintain that Black identity is only understood correctly by "placing Blackness in its proper context. And the context for us is the divine origin of Blackness."[49] The unification of the divine and the so-called mundane, for believer Queen Huldah, means that

> as Black Copts, we vehemently reject any theological and religious position that attempts to demarcate the body from the spirit. Many

> forms of Christianity have historically talked about the spirit is of God and the body is of the world, and therefore it's wicked, unclean, and not pure. But the reality is that such beliefs have been far more detrimental for Black bodies, as our bodies are the bodies that's [sic] really seen as unclean and wicked. So, when we talk about Black identity we are returning to an African centered worldview, in which this western distinction of the sacred and profane is rejected, and all things are sacred. The spirit is sacred and the body is sacred. So, our identity is one in which the divine reality of blackness is in direct contact with our divine bodies.[50]

The turn to the mystical, then, is not merely for the purpose of fashioning an ontological claim about Blackbeing—it also assists the BCC in understanding the Black body as sacred. Accordingly, for Black Copts "the religious practices and sacraments performed within Black Coptic settings are demonstrations of our divine identity."[51]

This particular rendering of Blackbeing suggests an important point about the Black body. I argue that the theological and ontological assertions within the tradition move beyond the rejection of human classifications about Blackbeing. That is, affirming an incarnational Blackness, such that Black bodies have been imprinted with a divine substance (Blackness), and are therefore not reducible to racist constructions, offers a new way to think about Black spirit in the flesh. Queen Huldah encapsulates it: "Black bodies are more than what the physical eye can see. We are both body and spirit. And to understand our identity we must talk about both."[52]

Hope in Black

When I sat with interview participants on a summer Wednesday evening in August 2018, I wanted to better understand how the Church understood the relation between identity construction and hope. We saw earlier that Queen Magdalene, a teacher in the community, said that recovery of identity in the BCC is not merely a claim about personhood or being; rather, "an emphasis in our tradition on identity is to provide a sense of hope for Black people who have basically been told to hate their body and their existence. And this hate of being Black means that racism wins and we might as well throw in the towel."⁵³ In a similar vein, Prophet Judah said that

> My church is in what most people would consider a bad area. There are drug dealers, prostitutes, gangbangers, and school dropouts. When I look at my community where the church is, I am reminded of the community that Prophet Peter's church, the True Temple of Solomon, was in. It also was a so-called bad area. But Prophet Peter taught us that our people are not bad. They are lost; they don't know who they are, and so they respond to how the world treats them: like dogs, or Negroes and Niggers. But Prophet [Peter] taught us that when people know who they are and who they are not, they can find hope. So, my job, as a leader in the Church, is to rescue the lost sheep and give them what they need to wake up and live.⁵⁴

Finally, Mother Rebekah made the point that "[Black] people are lost because they don't know who they are. They think they are niggers, negroes, and so-called colored peoples. But if I can let them know that they are God's divine people, then they will change their world."⁵⁵ From these statements, one can extrapolate the connection between epistemology, identity, and hope that is present in the BCC. That is, competing epistemologies yield contrasting views on Black ontologies and anthropologies, and greatly impact the degree to which one imagines and performs otherwise impossible possibilities. Blackontology underlies the performance of what I identified earlier as a heroic identity; that is, the potential of assembled identities to perform social and personal salvation.

In the BCC, Blackontology is a belief about Blackness as *otherwise*. It views Blackness as a divine essence, prior to the material world, prior to the absurd, and prior to an existential threat of non-being. The turn to divine Blackness, this movement toward the mystical darkness as the "something" of divinity, marks a significant contribution to how we think about Blackflesh and Blackbeing. The BCC's generative postulation concerning Blackness as a divine substance which becomes incarnate, or enfleshed, in Black bodies, indicates that Black being is not conditional or determined by imaginations that seek to negate being. To the contrary, Blackbeing cannot be negated insofar as Blackness is the ground of being. It is the Spirit in the dark that accomplishes *otherwise* as it [Blackness] becomes enfleshed. The anthropological condition of Blackness, then, is one in which Black bodies share in the mystical reality of Blackness. In their turn to divine Blackness, members of the BCC are making a radical turn back to their original identity; they are asserting Blackbeing as uncontained by the materiality of racism.

For that reason, it is also a refusal of Afro-pessimism. Suspicious of the claim that Black lives matter, Afro-pessimists don't believe that Blacks can have life or identity apart from the State; indeed, Black identity is tethered to white supremacy. Vincent Lloyd notes that, for Afro-Pessimists, "the oppression of Blacks may be an empirical condition, but it is also much deeper, so addressing that oppression requires much more than reducing present suffering. Altogether, Afro-Pessimism is so labeled because it points to the depth and gravity of Black oppression, and it suggests that efforts at ameliorating that oppression over the years and decades have been in vain."[56] Such a position capitulates to white supremacy. Their view denies the earliest religious imagination of enslaved Africans who organized the invisible institution, and the spirituals tradition of the same, which express joy and hope, and a refusal to yield their being to social misery. Similarly, for Black Coptic believers, divine Blackness is the imagination of *otherwise* in the presence of the absurd. The assertion of divine Blackness is not merely a rejection of the negro. It is a contention of *a priori* Blackness; Blackness as the original thought and performance of the divine.

* * *

This chapter began with an extensive quotation of Priest Meshach, as he mused on the idea of Blackness among Black Coptic believers. Blackness, Priest Meshach implies, precedes performance. He says that Black Coptic believers see Blackness as the "thick darkness"—the divine space in which God exists prior to the divine imagination and performance of the material world. Blackness, as space, says Priest Meshach, is divinized by the presence of God. The religious imagination of Black Copts commences with a turn toward the transcendental, defining Blackness as prior to the ontological terror and absurdity that renders Black life as no-thing. This chapter has examined the implications of this cosmology and theology for Black Coptic devotees, including ontological considerations, as well an engagement with Calvin Warren. The question becomes, then: whither Ethiopia? Since we have already learned that Black Coptic believers see Ethiopia as a starting point for constructing Black identity, how does primordial Blackness relate to Ethiopia? Prophet Cicero offers a connection between the two that is worth a brief consideration.

When Prophet Cicero Patterson imagined the thought and performance of divine Blackness in relation to a divine economy—that is, God outside (exteriority) the immanent and abstract space of the thick darkness (interiority)—he imagined Ethiopia, and the broader African continent, as God's playground. In *Black I Am That I Am God*, Prophet Cicero writes that, "it seems to me that if God was going to bake cookies in the form of men, he would need a hot oven to start the baking. Ethiopia is the hot oven."[57] He cites the work of archeologists Louis and Mary Leakey demonstrating that humans originated in Africa, all of which he refers to as the "Land of the Ethiopians."[58] For Prophet Cicero, Ethiopia, as the cradle of civilization, enjoys a unique relationship with God; it is the source of enfleshed divine Blackness, or humans who bear the mark of divinity. God "is the one who gave the Ethiopians that beautiful black skin . . . and out of all the races determined that they would have the hair as sheep—wooly hair, like Jesus."[59] Coptic, for Prophet Cicero, is the religious and cultural bridge between the past and the present. Indeed, in his writing, Prophet Cicero claims to have received revelation and inspiration from God.

This religious approach to Blackness differentiates itself from approaches that focus on pessimistic interpretations of Blackness. This is significant to the extent that an examination of Blackness via a religious lens grounds the conversation in a particular vocabulary, namely that of hope, which has been consistent across those traditions that constitute the Black sacred cosmos, including Christianity, Islam, and new religious movements such as the BCC. This is seen in Black Pentecostal traditions, which execute *otherwise* as hope in their performance of the "shout," and in the NOI's attention to self-fashioning Blackness and claiming an identity not bequeathed to them by white supremacy. In the BCC, hope commences with a turn toward the mystical assertion of Blackness, whereby the Blackness of the dark abyss sustains Black being (Blackontology), enfleshes Black bodies, and divinizes Blackness in the flesh. That hope continues with the recovery of an assembled heroic identity; believers look toward the biblical country of Ethiopia as the home of divine Blackness enfleshed. Via a performative imagination, believers claim an identity not beholden to Western culture or the vestiges of white supremacy, but rather one captured in their weekly recitation of Solomon 1:5: "I am Black and beautiful."

Conclusion

Imagination and the Future of Black Coptic Religion

The expansiveness of Black religions cannot be captured in any single manuscript. The religious lives of African Americans have always been complex and nuanced, telling the story of one group's desire to make sense of the absurd. Still, within the diversity and complexity of Black religions, we find a common yearning to traverse the isolation and exile of a world predicated on anti-blackness. Black religions showcase various attempts to construct religious worlds that result in human and social transformation.

This book began with the metaphor of earthquake to describe the context within which Black religions, particularly Black new religious movements, have imagined and performed *otherwise*. The BCC emerged from a racial earthquake and the tremors that followed. Prophet Cicero Patterson imagined a religious world in which followers would reassemble their lives with a gaze toward Ethiopia. What we encounter, then, in the BCC, is a longing for Zion, a desire for a homeland. On the South Side of Chicago, Prophet Cicero created a religious society that reflected his vision of Black identity; an identity steeped in Black royalty, with a court of queens, princesses, empresses, princes, and others. The telos of this imagination was a recovery of divine Blackness, a mystical turn toward a reality of Blackness not bound by the materiality of social death. For BCC followers, this imagination, and the performance of a royal spiritual hierarchy, inculcated a sense of pride that enabled them to rebuild and assert dignity in the earthquake's aftermath.

Without question, those who converted to the BCC saw it as a religious space that not only contradicted "the world," but that permitted them to worship their God on their own terms, attentive to notions of Black liberation. Rituals such as baptism and Passover connected them to a spiritual foundation while they maintained a focus on social salvation through a divinely inspired history as God's chosen people. Indeed, the rituals of liberation and freedom that are practiced in the BCC are as much about connecting to the unseen realm as they are about social redemption. Still, within this imaginative community, questions remain about the type of society that they imagine and perform.

Essentialist conceptions of Blackness, classism, and sexism are manifest in the BCC. One must ponder, therefore, to what extent current followers are curious about the enduring questions relative to BCC's future. The religious and social landscapes have changed since the Church's founding. For new religious movements like the BCC, the impact of the social gap between its founding and present practices remains to be seen. The future of the BCC, in particular its potential for growth and sustainability, requires a modernization of its theology and practices to reflect the current world. In essence, the BCC emerged as a response to earthquakes of racial terror against Black bodies and Black existence. The challenge to the BCC now is maintaining its relevancy and crafting a message for the modern hearer. In its current state, the BCC is a tradition in trouble.

What began as a missionary effort by Prophet Cicero Patterson evolved into a thriving religious movement in Chicago, alongside peer organizations tackling similar concerns. The Church transitioned from a religious movement to a religious organization under the leadership of Prophet Peter Banks. However, since the passing of Prophet Peter, the BCC can be characterized as a community in search of its identity. The disintegration from a single church headed by a charismatic figure to a scattered group has had several consequences. The most pressing of these is the apparent lack of growth within the organization. Since the demise of Prophet Peter in 1989, the BCC has experienced a lack of new converts, as well a steady decrease in membership. Accordingly, the BCC is functioning within a paradigm of survival.

The membership that the Church maintains today is not the result of organic intake of new members. On the contrary, the Church's membership is sustained by current adherents and their offspring, who theoretically comprise the future of the group. For the BCC to remain a viable religious option in the years ahead, the organization will need to mount a unified front in order to examine the BCC from within. The Church's spiritual leaders must engage in a critical analysis of their theology and religious practice. They must ask the "tough" questions.

One of those questions, and arguably the most demanding, is related to women in the BCC. While the BCC has sought to address the question of liberation relative to the issue of race, it must broaden its understanding of oppression. The status of women in the BCC undermines the Church's overarching message of Black identity and freedom. Womanist scholars have painstakingly demonstrated the failures of Black churchmen who seemingly employ the master's tools to build the Black Church. Such framing is important to name. We must identify the fallacy of Black churches that are guided by ideologies and theologies rooted in misogyny. Modernizing the Church on issues relating to gender will lend credibility to the liberation theology at the center of its mission.

The BCC expands our understanding of Black religious imaginations. It shows us other forms and practices available to Black Americans in their effort to make sense of the unimaginable. In a state of Black emergency, the BCC materialized as a religious alternative in which its followers claimed identity, imagined other worlds, and performed differently from mainstream Black religions. Believers were not looking to leave the United States, but rather to construct a community that allowed them to sing the Lord's song in a strange land.

ACKNOWLEDGMENTS

The Black Coptic Church: Race and Imagination in a New Religion is in the world because of extraordinary support from family, friends, a cloud of witnesses, ancestors, and institutions, without whom this work would not be possible. I am therefore indebted to a community of individuals who believed in this project, and who periodically checked in to make sure I was still on task. This book represents a ten-year labor of love that chronicles a missing piece in the history of Black religions. I am thrilled to share this story with you.

To begin, I would like to thank my family for their untiring encouragement of me and this project. Books are not easy to write. The writing process requires time. Often, this means time away from home, late nights, early mornings, during sporting events, at the dinner table, in church, or while riding in the car. For me, all the above is true. Yet, none of this would have been possible without steadfast love from those who make my world complete. Because of that, I thank Tamitha, my wife, for holding down the home while I traveled for research, conferences, writing retreats, or when I simply needed space to think. She has been a steadfast rock, a praying partner, one who provided ideas about the writing process, and one who has made many sacrifices for this book. My children, Sofia, Olivia, Leonard, and Gabriel are the heartbeats for whom I write. Their love of "da-da" is the purest thing in the universe. They would often ask, "how many more pages do you have to go until you are finished?" They sacrificed daddy time for this project, and did so with grace because they, too, wanted *The Black Coptic Church: Race and Imagination in a New Religion* to enter the universe. My mother, Cynthia Gardner, and my stepfather, John Gardner, along with my sister and brother-in-law Nicole and Leonard George, often provided support for us so that I could write. We are forever grateful for the many weekends they babysat our children or just visited our home to free up time for my writing.

My *Doktorvater*, Jon Nilson, has unswervingly believed in this book and the need to tell this story. Over the years since I completed graduate school, Jon has been a major source of inspiration for this project in its current form. Without his support this project would not have come to fruition.

There are many institutions to acknowledge. Funding for *The Black Coptic Church: Race and Imagination in a New Religion* was provided by the following entities. The University of Illinois at Urbana-Champaign, where I am on faculty in the Departments of African American Studies and Religion, provided research funds and supported an academic year leave for the final writing of this project. Jonathan H. Ebel, Head of Religion, and Ronald W. Bailey, Head of African American Studies, honored my time away and encouraged me, without fail, to finish writing. My University of Illinois colleague, Bobby J. Smith, and I spent many hours in each other's office talking about our respective projects. Bobby provided a listening ear toward the conclusion of writing this manuscript. His feedback was invaluable. Candice Jenkins and Merle Bowen helped me to think through the final tasks of manuscript submission, including searching for subvention funds and locating indexing services.

While on faculty at Saint Louis University (SLU), I was awarded a Summer Research Award as well as Mellon faculty development funds for ethnographic research and the hiring of a research assistant, Abby Block, who traveled with me for field work and who completed countless hours of transcribing research sessions. I was also granted a semester research leave by the Office of the Provost at SLU, which afforded me the space to write without teaching or advising commitments. Elizabeth Block, Rachel Lindsey, and Emily Dumler-Winkler, who were colleagues at SLU and remain dear friends, read and provided feedback on early chapter drafts. Other SLU colleagues Jay Hammond, Peter Martens, Randall Rosenberg, Christopher Tinson, and the late Jonathan C. Smith provided support in various ways. I am appreciative of their friendship.

In 2020, I was awarded a Louisville Institute Sabbatical Grant for Researchers, which provided the funding for an academic year leave. I am grateful to my Louisville cohort, who offered feedback on the overall project during our winter meeting. I was also supported by the American Academy of Religion with an individual research award that provided funding for the final ethnographic portion of this project.

The Society for the Study of Black Religion (SSBR) is a sacred space for Black scholars of religion. It provides the space in which to think critically about Black religions with a community of scholars who are invested in your success. For me, SSBR has been a reminder of why we do what we do, and that the study of Black religions is not merely an academic exercise, but is done for the preservation of culture. The study of Black religions is a "soulful" study. For these reasons, I am eternally grateful to my SSBR sponsor, Eboni Marshall Turman, whose recommendation for admission into the SSBR permitted me access to a world of scholars who have become friends for a lifetime. Melva Sampson, Herbert R. Marbury, and Kimberly D. Russaw, are part of my SSBR "conference crew." Our conversations, evening encouragement sessions, and their support from afar has meant the world to me. SSBR provided me the space in which to interact with scholars I have always admired. Not enough can be said about Victor Anderson and Stephen Ray. Engaging these intellectual giants during SSBR conferences was life changing for me. My ideas were tested, sharpened, and made better because they pushed me to be a better scholar. Finally, it would take another book to talk about my friendship with Michele Watkins. Michele and I shared many moments during SSBR gatherings talking theology, debating ideas, raising questions about the other's project, and offering much-needed feedback about our work. Michele is a scholar par excellence and friend for a lifetime. I am deeply grateful for the friendship we have created.

The Black Coptic Church: Race and Imagination in a New Religion is a book because Peter Paris saw its potential during an annual SSBR conference. Peter and I had a conversation over lunch about my ideas and the book I desired to write. He told me that day that he wanted me to submit a proposal to New York University Press for possible inclusion in the Religion, Race, and Ethnicity series. Peter remained committed to this work and encouraged me throughout the process to complete the manuscript. Judith Weisenfeld, Wallace Best, Vincent Lloyd, and Ashon Crawley read the proposal, and each offered critical feedback. I appreciate their reading of the proposal in its early stages and their encouragement to submit it.

Marla Frederick is not only my former professor, but she is also a friend. I have admired Marla since my first course with her at Harvard

Divinity School. Marla inspired me to do ethnographic research. Her *Between Sundays* is a masterpiece, in which she invites ordinary believers into the world of ideas and demonstrates why the voices in the pews are so important. I desire to model that type of scholarship. Marla read the manuscript proposal for this book. She sent feedback, raised questions, and reminded why the world needed it.

Jeffrey McCune has been in my corner since day one. His counsel, pushback, and friendship has been a source of strength throughout this writing process. Jeffrey was instrumental in bouncing ideas as I navigated between chapters and reading various parts of the manuscript. We all need friends who are also constructive critics. For me, that person is Jeffrey.

Jennifer Hammer. Where do I begin? Jennifer, my NYU Press editor, has made the writing process an enjoyable one. Jennifer reads *everything* that is sent to her. She responds thoughtfully, pointedly, and with the care and concern of someone who is truly interested in your success. Jennifer epitomizes the best of what it means to be an acquisitions editor. She is truly building something magical around race and religion at NYU Press, and I am thrilled to be in the mix. Finally, I would be remiss if I did not mention Veronica Knutson, Jennifer's very capable editorial assistant, who was instrumental in the publication process. She is a generous human with whom to work.

Iwona Bidermann, who provided many of the photographs for this manuscript, is an extraordinary human being. Her attention to detail and to perfection is unmatched. Iwona spent many hours working on photographs from the BCC that were initially unusable in this manuscript. I cannot say enough about Iwona's diligence, her patience, and her work ethic. I am grateful to call her friend.

I have been blessed to have extraordinary graduate students and research assistants throughout the writing of this book. I am grateful for Calandra Warren, who helped assemble this manuscript for proper submission to NYU Press. She paid attention to the small details and helped keep me on track. I could not have finished the book without David Justice. David assisted with gathering research, securing photograph permissions, reading chapters, and assembling the manuscript. His thoughtfulness in relation to this project has been appreciated more than he will ever know. I am truly grateful for his commitment to academia, his being a good colleague, and his perseverance in his own research.

Several people have provided insight into the writing process or some form of support over the course of this project. I extend warm thanks to J. Kameron Carter, Dwight Hopkins, Irvin Hunt, Leah Jordan, Desireé McMillion, and Jeannette Arbuckle.

Religion is personal. That my research participants made themselves vulnerable in our discussions, and persisted to the end, is something I do not take for granted. I am deeply grateful to my research group for making this project possible. We spent hundreds of hours in interviews over the course of ten years. Their knowledge of the Black Coptic tradition enabled this project to leave the launch pad and manifest beyond an idea. To Candace Queen Rachel, Queen Huldah, Queen Shiphrah, Queen Mikal, Queen Hosanna, Queen Mary Ann, Queen Abigail, Queen Magdalene, Queen Bethel, Queen Zion, Queen Selah, the late Queen Rebekah, Empress Hatshepsut, Priest Meshach, Prophet Jacob, Prophet Hiram, Priest Eli, Prophet Hosea, the late Priest Stephen, and the late Prophet Judah, I say thank you. Each of these persons provided substantive information for the completion of this manuscript.

Finally, everyone needs a solid group of friends. Larry Perry, my dear brother and friend, has been an ongoing source of support for my work. He and I have often discussed our projects and sharpened each other's ideas. Larry has become one of my closet friends in academic spaces and, for that, I am grateful. My "crew," Seth Wilson, Vernard Burton, Brandi Murain, Brittney Burton, and Zerrick Burton have been a force of love and encouragement during the writing of this book. They celebrated the good times, provided support in the difficult moments, and have demonstrated the power of friendships that transform into family. I am stronger, wiser, and more focused because of their demonstration of what friendship looks like.

NOTES

EPIGRAPH
1. Saidiya Hartman, *Lose Your Mother: A Journey Along the Atlantic Slave Route* (New York: Farrar, Straus, and Giroux, 2008), 6.

INTRODUCTION
1. Prophet Hosea Belcher, "Christology of the Black Coptic Church," interview by Leonard C. McKinnis, Chicago, IL, January 20, 2009.
2. Sylvester Johnson, *African American Religions, 1500–2000: Colonialism, Democracy, and Freedom* (Cambridge: Cambridge University Press, 2015), 26.
3. Hartman, 6.
4. I use the term "Black religions" to highlight the complexity of Black religious life in North America. That is, while I accept the term "Black religion" to describe the Black religious practices that evolved, in one way or another, from the religious practices of enslaved Africans, I assert that it fails to capture the diasporic nature of Black religious imaginations. By employing "Black religion(s)," I hope to articulate a rich world of Black religious practices that share a common history yet are also very different.
5. Empress Zilpah, *The Rise of a Black Woman* (Chicago: New Heaven Coptic Temple church archives, unpublished).
6. Ibid., 26.
7. Orlando Patterson, *Slavery and Social Death: A Comparative Study* (Cambridge: Harvard University Press, 1982).
8. Cornel West, *Prophesy Deliverance! An Afro-American Revolutionary Christianity* (Louisville: Westminster John Knox Press, 1982), 55–56.
9. Prophet Jacob, "History of the Black Coptic Church," interview by Leonard C. McKinnis, Chicago, IL, September 5, 2016.
10. Priest Meshach, "Theology of the Black Coptic Church," interview by Leonard C. McKinnis, Chicago, IL, June 15, 2009.
11. Priest Meshach, "History of the Black Coptic Church," interview by Leonard C. McKinnis, Chicago, IL, September 5, 2016.
12. Edward Curtis, *Black Muslim Religion in the Nation of Islam, 1960–1975* (Chapel Hill: The University of North Carolina Press, 2006), 16.
13. Priest Eli, "The History of the Black Coptic Church," interview by Leonard C. McKinnis, Chicago, IL, June 22, 2009.

14. Queen Huldah, "The History of the Black Coptic Church," interview by Leonard C. McKinnis, Chicago, IL, June 22, 2009.
15. For example, Judith Weisenfeld, *New World A-Coming: Black Religion and Racial Identity during the Great Migration* (New York: New York University Press, 2018); Jacob Dorman, *Chosen People: The Rise of American Black Israelite Religions* (Oxford: Oxford University Press, 2013); and Edward Curtis, *Black Muslim Religion in the Nation of Islam, 1960–1975* (Chapel Hill: The University of North Carolina Press, 2006).
16. Prophet Cicero Patterson, *Black I Am That I Am God* (Chicago: Coptic Nation Temple archives, 1959).
17. Phillis Wheatley, "To the University of Cambridge, in New England," in Henry Louis Gates and Nellie McKay, eds., *The Norton Anthology of African American Literature* (New York: W. W. Norton & Co., 1997), 71.
18. Paul Laurence Dunbar, *The Complete Poems of Paul Laurence Dunbar* (New York: Dodd, Mead, and Company, 1913).
19. Charles Reavis Price, "Expressions of Ethiopianism in Jamaica," *New West Indian Guide* 77, no. 1/2 (2003): 31–64.
20. Victor Anderson critiques what he calls a problem of "ontological blackness" in Black theology. For Anderson, Black theology is caught in an ontological trap because its system, or creation of a new Black person, is contingent upon the idea of racism and other social factors—against which Black theology defines itself as a sort of "corrective." Prof. James Cone's usage of history and privileging of categorical experience presents a significant problem and challenge for Black theology. That is, to the extent that Cone's structure of knowledge vis-à-vis God's plan for divine freedom and liberation from existential suffering is dialectical in nature, Black theology is thereby a conditional reflection on God, lacking any transcendental possibilities. That is, Black theology is held captive to a confrontational reading of history that necessitates a theological foe (white supremacist theology), and one that collapses epistemology and ontology into a radical state of contingency; one that doesn't situate existence and knowledge in the Image of God, but rather against the backdrop of human wretchedness. Victor Anderson captures the essence of the problem in his *Beyond Ontological Blackness*. Anderson argues that, given the reliance on "dialectical structures that categorical racism and white racial ideology bequeathed to African-American intellectuals," the structures on which Cone constructs the Black theological project, "the new being of black theology remains an alienated being whose mode of existence is determined by crisis, struggle, resistance, and survival—not thriving, flourishing, or fulfillment. Its self-identity is always bound by white racism and the culture of survival." The tragedy of this crisis, for Anderson, is "blackness has become a totality of meaning. It cannot point to any transcendent meaning beyond itself without also fragmenting. Because black life is fundamentally determined by black suffering and resistance to whiteness (the power of non-being), black existence is without the possibility of transcendence from the blackness that whiteness created." Anderson's ontological critique of Black theology is significant on several fronts.

Most notably, as argued above, the mainstream ontological construction of the "person" in Black theology lends itself to a definition of person whose knowledge and existence is radically shaped by external factors, in a determinative way, such that oppression is both a theological and an existential necessity. See Victor Anderson, *Beyond Ontological Blackness: An Essay on African American Religious and Cultural Criticism* (New York: Continuum, 1999), 86–104.

21. Hans Baer, *The Black Spiritual Movement: A Religious Response to Racism*, 2nd ed. (Knoxville: University of Tennessee Press, 2001), 147.
22. Cited in Robert Hill, ed., *Marcus Garvey and the Universal Negro Improvement Association Papers*, vol. 7: November 1927–August 1940 (Berkeley and Los Angeles: University of California Press, 1990), 442.
23. Ibid. 24.
24. Rugare Rukuni and Ena Oliver, "Africanism, Apocalypticism, Jihad, and Jesuitism: Prelude to Ethiopianism," *HTS Teologiese Studies/Theological Studies* 75, no. 3, (2019): 1.
25. Priest Meshach, "History and Identity in the Black Coptic Church," interview by Leonard C. McKinnis, Chicago, IL, June 8, 2017.
26. I use normative here in the tradition of Cornel West. In *Prophesy Deliverance! An Afro-American Revolutionary Christianity,* West maintains that, contextually, the situation of the early African in America was one of "exile." That is, in the DuBoisian sense, early Africans in America were "away" from home via a process of forced migration, otherwise known as enslavement. Theirs, however, was a particularly precarious situation in that their attempt to make sense of their "whoness" was eclipsed by the search of a nation in its embryonic stage for its own soul and distinct identity apart from its European parents. It is within this social and historical context that the search for identity of the African in America commences. Other factors made the Africans' search even more complex, including: 1) the dominant narrative of what constitutes "human" and "person" is deeply rooted in the racist ideology of pre- and post-Enlightenment thinkers in Europe and America, and thereafter secretes itself within the social fabric of North America; 2) the dominant metaphors and vocabulary of beauty, truth, etc. are couched in the social construction of what West calls the "normative gaze"—that way of looking at the world that normalizes and legitimizes whiteness as the standard of truth and beauty; 3) the black body is understood as physiologically, anthropologically, and ontologically "other"; and 4) in the tradition of DuBois, the Black body is a "problem"—that is, it is between two realities and two worlds. The Black body is essentially in an exilic state. The search for identity, then, originates as fugitivity. Black religion, then, is fugitive at its core.
27. Priest Meshach, "The History of the Black Coptic Church," interview by Leonard C. McKinnis, Chicago, IL, June 22, 2009.
28. Dorman, 56.
29. Ibid.
30. Eddie Glaude, *African American Religion: A Very Short Introduction* (Oxford: Oxford University Press, 2014), 6.

31. Arthur Huff Fauset, *Black Gods of the Metropolis: Negro Religious Cults of the Urban North* (Philadelphia: University of Pennsylvania Press, 1944), 1–12.
32. Ibid., 7.
33. Milton Sernett, *Bound for the Promised Land: African American Religion and the Great Migration* (Durham: Duke University Press, 1997), 154.
34. Albert Raboteau, *Canaan Land: A Religious History of African Americans* (Oxford: Oxford University Press, 2001), 25.
35. Sernett, 155.
36. Ira De Augustine Reid, *In a minor key: Negro youth in story and fact* (Westport, CT: Greenwood Publishers, 1940), 83.
37. Ibid., 84.
38. Thomas F. DeFrantz and Anita Gonzalez, eds., *Black Performance Theory* (Durham: Duke University Press, 2014), 1.
39. Ibid.
40. Ibid., vii.
41. Emily Raboteau, *Searching for Zion: The Quest for Home in the African Diaspora* (New York: Grove Press), 2013.
42. Nadine George-Graves, "Diasporic Spidering: Constructing Contemporary Black Identities," in Thomas F. DeFrantz and Anita Gonzalez, eds., *Black Performance Theory*, 37.
43. George-Graves, 37.
44. Ibid.
45. George-Graves, 41.
46. Gayraud S. Wilmore, *Black Religion and Black Radicalism: A Religious History of African Americans*, 3rd edition (Maryknoll, NY: Orbis Books, 1998), 22.
47. Anderson, 86–104.
48. Wilmore, 23.
49. Albert Raboteau, *Slave Religion: The "Invisible Institution" in the Antebellum South*, updated edition (Oxford: Oxford University Press, 2014).
50. See Albert Camus, *The Myth of Sisyphus*, translated by Justin O'Brien (New York: Knopf Doubleday Publishing Group, 2018).
51. Wilmore, 55.
52. See Nat Turner and Thomas A. Gray, *The Confessions of Nat Turner: The Leader of the Late Insurrection in Southampton, Va., as fully and voluntarily made to Thomas R. Gray, in the prison where he was confined, and acknowledged by him to be such when read before the Court of Southampton; with the certificate, under seal of the Court convened at Jerusalem, Nov. 5, 1831 for his trial. Also, an authentic account of the whole insurrection, with lists of the whites who were murdered, and of the negroes brought before the Court of Southampton, and there sentenced, &etc.* (Baltimore: Thomas A. Gray, Lucas & Deaver, 1831), 7–11.
53. Wilmore, 33.

54. I use the term christianity with a lower case "c" to contrast the organic development of Christian theology pronounced and performed by enslaved persons, with the "christian theology" of slave apologists.
55. Frederick Douglass, *Narrative of the Life of Frederick Douglass, An American Slave*, (Boston: Anti-Slavery Office, 1845), scanned 1999, Documenting the American South, University of North Carolina at Chapel Hill, www.docsouth.unc.edu.
56. C. Eric Lincoln and Lawrence H. Mamayia, *The Black Church in the African American Experience* (Durham, NC: Duke University Press, 1990).
57. Reid, 84.
58. Fauset, 7.
59. See Rev. R. C. Keller, "Coptic Heritage Seen in King Solomon's Temple," *The Chicago Defender*, March 10, 1973, and "Catching the Spirit: A Celebration of Chicago's Storefront Churches," *The Chicago Tribune Magazine*, Sunday edition, June 7, 1987.
60. Su'ad Abdul Khabeer, *Muslim Cool: Race, Religion, and Hip Hop in the United States* (New York: New York University Press, 2016), 2.
61. William Young, "The Shape of Reflexivity: A Pragmatist Analysis of Religious Ethnography," *American Journal of Theology and Philosophy* 35, no. 1 (January 2014): 1.
62. Marla Frederick, *Between Sundays: Black Women and Everyday Struggles of Faith* (Berkeley: University of California Press, 2003), 19.
63. Gladys Daniel and Claire Mitchell, "Turning the Categories Inside-Out: Complex Identifications and Multiple Interactions in Religious Ethnography," *Sociology of Religion* 67, no. 1, (2006): 4.
64. Frederick, 20.
65. Queen Maryann, "History of the Black Coptic Church," interview by Leonard C. McKinnis, Chicago, IL, June 22, 2009.
66. Ibid.
67. Calvin Warren, *Ontological Terror: Blackness, Nihilism, and Emancipation* (Durham, NC: Duke University Press, 2018), 39–58.
68. Statement of Faith, Black Coptic Church, in "Student Handbook," Coptic Nation Temple, Chicago, IL, 2010.

1. THE ORIGINS OF A PROPHET

1. Field notes.
2. My emphasis.
3. Empress Hatshepsut, "History in the Black Coptic Church," interview by Leonard C. McKinnis, Chicago, IL, August 4, 2018.
4. I use the term "brush harbor" here as a way of shedding light on the clandestine and fugitive nature of Black religions in general, and the BCC in particular. For Black Coptic followers, worshiping in secrecy allowed the group to maintain agency and control over their religious lives, much like enslaved Africans who

retreated into the woods to worship away from the watchful eye of their overseer.

5. Hebrews 7:3 (NRSV).
6. Queen Maryann, "History in the Black Coptic Church," interview by Leonard C. McKinnis, Chicago, IL, January 19, 2009.
7. Queen Huldah, "History in the Black Coptic Church," interview by Leonard C. McKinnis, Chicago, IL, January 19, 2009.
8. "United States Census, 1900," database with images, FamilySearch (https://familysearch.org: accessed 10 April 2021), Louis C. Patterson in household of Primus Patterson, Amelia Township (north, west part) St. Matthews village, Orangeburg, South Carolina, United States; citing enumeration district (ED) 48, sheet 5A, family 107, NARA microfilm publication T623 (Washington, D.C.: National Archives and Records Administration, 1972); FHL microfilm 1,241,537.
9. Burr Oak Cemetery, Alsip, IL, Louis. C. Patterson tombstone photographed July 9, 2018.
10. "United States Census, 1920," database with images, FamilySearch (www.familysearch.org: accessed 3 February 2021), Lewis Patterson, 1920.
11. Queen Maryann, "History in the Black Coptic Church," interview by Leonard C. McKinnis, Chicago, IL, January 19, 2009.
12. Ibid.
13. Henry Lyman Morehouse, "The Spirit and Policy of the American Baptist Home Mission Society in its Work For the Colored People in the South," *Baptist Home Mission Monthly* 17, no II (November I 1895): 412–22, 414.
14. Queen Maryann, "History in the Black Coptic Church," interview by Leonard C. McKinnis, Chicago, IL, January 19, 2009.
15. Queen Rebekah, "History of the Black Coptic Church," interview by Leonard C. McKinnis, Chicago, IL, October 2003.
16. "History of the House of Prayer," Church archives, Universal House of Prayer and Training School, Atlanta, 2000.
17. Stephanie H. Davis, "Hattie Tolbert, 82, church leader, spiritual adviser, radio evangelist" (obituary), *Atlanta Constitution*, January 20, 2001, www.newspapers.com.
18. Baer, 164.
19. "Prophet Charged with Swindle," *Atlanta Constitution*, November 24, 1948, www.newspapers.com.
20. Ibid.
21. Ibid.
22. Yvonne P. Chireau, *Black Magic: Religion and the African American Conjuring Tradition* (Berkeley: University of California Press, 2006), 91.
23. *Atlanta Constitution*, 1948.
24. "$1000 A Week: 'Doctor-Prophet' Arrested on Patient Complaints," *Atlanta Constitution*, October 24, 1948, www.newspapers.com.
25. Queen Rebekah, video interview on spiritual autobiography, Chicago, July 2005.

26. Hans Baer and Merrill Singer, *African American Religion: Varieties of Protest and Accommodation* (Knoxville: University of Tennessee Press, 1992), 112.
27. Priest Gehazi, "Theology and Doctrine of the Black Coptic Church," interview by Leonard C. McKinnis, Chicago, IL, June 2017.
28. Queen Magdalene, "Theology and Doctrine of the Black Coptic Church," interview by Leonard C. McKinnis, Chicago, IL, June 2017.
29. Prophet Hiram White, "History of the Black Coptic Church," interview by Leonard C. McKinnis, Chicago, IL, July 2017.
30. Arthur Huff Fauset examines a set of Black religious movements in Philadelphia in *Black Gods of the Metropolis.*
31. Jean Beaman, *Citizen Outsider: Children of North African Immigrants in France* (Berkeley: University of California Press, 2017).
32. W. E. B. DuBois, *The Souls of Black Folk* (Reprint, South Kingstown, RI: Millennium Books, 2014).
33. West, 27–46.
34. Ibid.
35. Eddie Glaude, *In a Shade of Blue: Pragmatism and the Politics of Black America* (Chicago: University of Chicago Press, 2007), 47–48.
36. Ibid.
37. Weisenfeld, 8.
38. Sernett, 165.
39. Julius Bailey, *Down in the Valley: An Introduction to African American Religions History* (Minneapolis: Fortress Press, 2015), 124.
40. For a case study on Chicago soulful preaching, see Zach Mills, *The Last Blues Preacher: Reverend Clay Evans, Black Lives, and the Faith that Woke the Nation* (Minneapolis: Fortress Press, 2018).
41. Sinclair Drake and Horace Clayton, *Black Metropolis: A Study of Negro Life in a Northern City*, enlarged edition (Chicago: University of Chicago Press, 2015), 380.
42. Ibid., 388.
43. Ibid.
44. Fauset, 6.
45. Ibid.
46. Queen Maryann, "History of the Black Coptic Church," interview by Leonard C. McKinnis, Chicago, IL, June 22, 2009.
47. Empress Selah, "History of the Black Coptic Church," interview by Leonard C. McKinnis, Chicago, IL, June 22, 2009.
48. Prophet Jacob, "Identity in the Black Coptic Church," interview by Leonard C. McKinnis, Chicago, IL, August 12, 2017.
49. Queen Huldah, "Identity in the Black Coptic Church," interview by Leonard C. McKinnis, Chicago, IL, August 12, 2017.
50. Priest Meshach, "The History of the Black Coptic Church," interview by Leonard C. McKinnis, Chicago, IL, June 22, 2009.

51. C. Eric Lincoln and Lawrence H. Mamiya, *The Black Church in the African American Experience* (Durham, NC: Duke University Press, 1990), 17.
52. Baer and Singer, 59.
53. Ibid., 124.
54. Nadia Nurhussein, *Black Land: Imperial Ethiopianism and African America* (Princeton, NJ: Princeton University Press, 2019), 5.
55. Robin D. G. Kelley, *Freedom Dreams: The Black Radical Imagination* (Boston: Beacon Books, 2003), 19.
56. Kelley, 16.
57. US census data and war registration records show that L. C. Patterson was in Ohio between 1920 and 1940. During his arrest (1948) in Atlanta, he reported having been trained as a minister 27 years prior to his arrest, placing him in Ohio during his ministerial training. This is significant in that it places Patterson in the center of Black Spiritualist activity, especially as organized by Prophet George Hurley, founder of the Universal Hagar's Spiritual Church, who was likely a big influence on Prophet Cicero, and who organized various spiritualist communities throughout Ohio. "United States Census, 1920," database with images, FamilySearch (www.familysearch.org, accessed February 2021), Lewis Patterson, 1920; "United States Census, 1940," database with images, FamilySearch (www.familysearch.org, accessed January 9, 2021), Louis Patterson, Cincinnati, Hamilton, Ohio, United States; citing enumeration district (ED) 91–142, sheet 7A, line 16, family 191, Sixteenth Census of the United States, 1940, NARA digital publication T627. Records of the Bureau of the Census, 1790–2007, RG 29. Washington, D.C.: National Archives and Records Administration, 2012, roll 3191.
58. Father G. W. Hurley, *Aquarian Age*, Newsletter publication of the Universal Hagar's Spiritual Church, April, 1940.
59. Baer, 94.
60. Weisenfeld, 30.
61. Dorman, 58.
62. Queen Huldah, "Identity in the Black Coptic Church," interview by Leonard C. McKinnis, Chicago, IL, August 12, 2017.
63. Ibid.
64. Priest Gehazi, "Identity in the Black Coptic Church," interview by Leonard C. McKinnis, Chicago, IL, August 12, 2017.
65. Fred Moten, *Stolen Life* (Durham: Duke University Press, 2018), 131.
66. Empress Selah, "Identity in the Black Coptic Church," interview by Leonard C. McKinnis, Chicago, IL, August 12, 2017.
67. Empress Hatshepsut, "Identity in the Black Coptic Church," interview by Leonard C. McKinnis, Chicago, IL, August 12, 2017.
68. Chicago Committee on Race Relations, *The Negro in Chicago: A Study of Race Relations and a Riot* (Chicago: University of Chicago Press, 1922).
69. Nurhussein, 4.

70. Priest Meshach, "Identity in the Black Coptic Church," interview by Leonard C. McKinnis, Chicago, IL, August 12, 2017.
71. Queen Huldah, "Identity in the Black Coptic Church," interview by Leonard C. McKinnis, Chicago, IL, August 12, 2017.
72. Calvin Warren prefers this way of writing nothingness (that is, crossed out) as a way of expressing the lack of ontological ground of Black folk who, in his thought, do not possess being, and are only present as a creation of those who claim their being because they desire Black folk to carry out laborious tasks.
73. Black Coptic Church Archives, "True Temple of Solomon Church service, Passover, July 1986," Chicago, New Heaven Coptic Temple, 2020.

2. "ETHIOPIA SHALL SOON STRETCH FORTH HER HAND UNTO GOD"

1. Field notes.
2. Reverend Keller, "Coptic Heritage Seen in King Solomon Temple," *Chicago Defender*, March 10, 1973, 14.
3. Prophet Peter Banks (1929), also known in the community as King Peter, led the Black Coptic Church from the death of Prophet Cicero Patterson in 1968 until his own demise in 1990.
4. Queen Huldah, "Identity in the Black Coptic Church," interview by Leonard C. McKinnis, Chicago, IL, August 12, 2017.
5. Candace Queen Rachel, "History and Identity in the Black Coptic Church," interview by Leonard C. McKinnis, Chicago, IL, June 8, 2017.
6. Weisenfeld, 6.
7. Candace Queen Rachel, "History and Identity in the Black Coptic Church," interview by Leonard C. McKinnis, Chicago, IL, June 8, 2017.
8. Gulick, 394.
9. Paul Tillich, *Dynamics of Faith* (Reprint, San Francisco: Harper One Books, 2001), 48.
10. Gulick, 394.
11. Queen Huldah, "History and Identity in the Black Coptic Church," interview by Leonard C. McKinnis, Chicago, IL, June 8, 2017.
12. Ibid.
13. KQED Channel 9, "Take this Hammer," interview with James Baldwin, YouTube video, 3:02, April 24, 2010, www.youtube.com.
14. Tom Brune, "Vrdolyak gets endorsement at black church," *Chicago Sun Times*, March 23, 1987, 7.
15. Coptic Nation Temple, "Statement of Faith," Chicago, 2020, www.copticnationtemple.net.
16. Empress Hatshepsut, "History and Identity in the Black Coptic Church," interview by Leonard C. McKinnis, Chicago, IL, June 8, 2017.
17. Empress Selah, "History and Identity in the Black Coptic Church," interview by Leonard C. McKinnis, Chicago, IL, June 8, 2017.

18. Coptic Nation Temple, "Statement of Faith," Coptic Nation Temple, www.copticnationtemple.net.
19. Prophet Jacob, "History and Identity in the Black Coptic Church," interview by Leonard C. McKinnis, Chicago, IL, June 8, 2017.
20. Empress Selah, "Theology in the Black Coptic Church," interview by Leonard C. McKinnis, Chicago, IL, January 16, 2009.
21. Baer, 94.
22. Ruth Landes, "Negro Jews in Harlem," *Jewish Journal of Sociology* 9 (1967): 185.
23. Baer, 94.
24. Queen Huldah, "History and Identity in the Black Coptic Church," interview by Leonard C. McKinnis, Chicago, IL, June 8, 2017.
25. Priest Meshach, "Theology in the Black Coptic Church," interview by Leonard C. McKinnis, Chicago, IL, January 16, 2009.
26. Prophet Judah, "History and Identity in the Black Coptic Church," interview by Leonard C. McKinnis, Chicago, IL, June 8, 2017.
27. James Cone, *Black Theology & Black Power* (Maryknoll, NY: Orbis Books, 1968), 121–122.
28. Abyssinian Baptist Church, Dr. Calvin O. Butts III, "Give me that Old Time Religion?" YouTube, March 19, 2020, www.youtube.com.
29. Priest Meshach, "History and Identity in the Black Coptic Church," interview by Leonard C. McKinnis, Chicago, IL, June 8, 2017.
30. Baer, 96.
31. Curtis, 19.
32. Queen Huldah, "History and Identity in the Black Coptic Church," interview by Leonard C. McKinnis, Chicago, IL, June 8, 2017.
33. Queen Huldah, "Theology of the Black Coptic Church," interview by Leonard C. McKinnis, Chicago, IL, January 12, 2009.
34. Priest Stephen, "Theology of the Black Coptic Church," interview by Leonard C. McKinnis, Chicago, IL, January 12, 2009.
35. Empress Selah, "Theology of the Black Coptic Church," interview by Leonard C. McKinnis, Chicago, IL, January 12, 2009.
36. William Jones, *Is God a White Racist? A Preamble to Black Theology* (Boston: Beacon Press, 1973), 40.
37. Prophet Hosea, "Theology of the Black Coptic Church," interview by Leonard C. McKinnis, Chicago, IL, January 12, 2009.
38. In *A Theology of Liberation: History, Politics, and Salvation*, Gustavo Gutierrez contends that through a process of conscientization, "the oppressed reject the oppressive consciousness which dwells in them, become aware of their situation, and find their own language. They become themselves, less dependent and freer, as they commit themselves to the transformation and building up of a society" (57). Essentially, for Gutierrez, non-persons must foremost recognize that their oppression is oppression, and this is achieved through a process of conscientization/

consciousness-raising. Elisabeth Schüssler Fiorenza defines conscientization as "a process in which an individual or group names and understands structures of internalized oppression and begins to become free of them" (*Wisdom Ways*, 208). Since they had internalized this oppression and accepted it as God's will, freedom requires "them to reject this image and replace it with autonomy and responsibility" (Paulo Freire, *Pedagogy of the Oppressed*, 29). During this process of rejecting the oppressive consciousness, the oppressed are slowly recognizing that they are in fact oppressed and are capable of throwing off the chains of oppression and domination and claiming their freedom as the people of God.

39. Empress Selah, "Theology of the Black Coptic Church," interview by Leonard C. McKinnis, Chicago, IL, January 12, 2009.
40. Ibid.
41. Karl Barth, *Evangelical Theology: An Introduction* (New York: Holt, Rinehart and Winston, 1963), 125.
42. Tillich, 4–15.
43. Robert Anderson, *From Slavery to Affluence: Memories of Robert Anderson, Ex Slave* (Hemingford, NE: publisher unknown, 1927), 22–23.
44. Jurgen Moltmann, "God's Unfinished Business: Why it Matters Now," interview by Bob Scott, Tubingen, Germany, 2006, Trinity Church Wall Street, www.trinitywallstreet.org.
45. Ibid.
46. Queen Huldah, "Theology of the Black Coptic Church," interview by Leonard C. McKinnis, Chicago, IL, January 12, 2009.
47. Priest Stephen, "Theology of the Black Coptic Church," interview by Leonard C. McKinnis, Chicago, IL, January 12, 2009.
48. Gutierrez, 121–141.
49. Johann Baptist Metz, *A Passion for God: The Mystical Political Dimension of Christianity* (New York: Paulist Press, 1988), 121–133.
50. Jürgen Moltmann, *A Theology of Hope: On the Ground and Implications of Christian Eschatology* (New York: Harper & Row Publishers, 1967).
51. Gutierrez, 93.
52. Revelation 21:1–5 (NRSV).
53. Queen Huldah, "Theology of the Black Coptic Church," interview by Leonard C. McKinnis, Chicago, IL, January 12, 2009.
54. Royal Priest Meshach, "Christology in the Black Coptic Church," interview by Leonard C. McKinnis, Chicago, IL, January 20, 2009.
55. Queen Huldah, "Christology in the Black Coptic Church," interview by Leonard C. McKinnis, Chicago, IL, January 20, 2009.
56. Prophet Jacob, "Christology in the Black Coptic Church," interview by Leonard C. McKinnis, Chicago, IL, January 20, 2009.
57. Queen Huldah, "Theology of the Black Coptic Church," interview by Leonard C. McKinnis, Chicago, IL, January 12, 2009.

58. The term "Afrofuturism" was coined by Mark Dery who, in *Flame Wars: The Discourse of Cyberculture*, offers a chapter titled "Black to the Future: Interviews with Samuel R. Delany, Greg Tate, and Tricia Rose," in which he interrogates the relationship between science fiction and Black writers. There he writes, "Speculative fiction that treats African American themes and addresses African American concerns in the context of twentieth-century technoculture—and, more generally, African American signification that appropriates images of technology and a prosthetically enhanced future—might, for want of a better term, be called 'Afrofuturism.' The notion of Afrofuturism gives rise to a troubling antinomy: can a community whose past has been deliberately rubbed out, and whose energies have been subsequently consumed by the search for legible traces of its history, imagine possible futures?" I find this framing of Afrofuturism helpful in thinking with the Black Coptic Church, in that its members ground Afrofuturism, theoretically, in the dreaming and imagining of other worlds in their quest to construct a historical narrative. They make their future present in an ecclesial structure that, in search of a Black cultural past, gives regal titles to its members. They imagine a Black future in which Black life is autonomous and not rooted in Black social death.
59. Priest Meshach, "History and Identity in the Black Coptic Church," interview by Leonard C. McKinnis, Chicago, IL, June 8, 2017.
60. Priest Eli, "History and Identity in the Black Coptic Church," interview by Leonard C. McKinnis, Chicago, IL, June 8, 2017.
61. Candace Queen Rachel, "Identity in the Black Coptic Church," interview by Leonard C. McKinnis, Chicago, IL, July 25, 2019.
62. Empress Selah, "Identity in the Black Coptic Church," interview by Leonard C. McKinnis, Chicago, IL, July 25, 2019.
63. See Martin Luther King, Jr., "What is your Life's Blueprint," reprint, https://projects.seattletimes.com.
64. Queen Maryann, "Identity in the Black Coptic Church," interview by Leonard C. McKinnis, Chicago, IL, July 25, 2019.
65. Queen Huldah, "Identity in the Black Coptic Church," interview by Leonard C. McKinnis, Chicago, IL, July 25, 2019.
66. Ibid.
67. Empress Selah, "Identity in the Black Coptic Church," Interview by Leonard C. McKinnis, Chicago, IL, July 25, 2019.
68. Queen Bethel, "Identity in the Black Coptic Church," interview by Leonard C. McKinnis, Chicago, IL, July 25, 2019.
69. Ibid.
70. Ibid.
71. Ibid.
72. Ibid.
73. Priest Eli, "Identity in the Black Coptic Church," interview by Leonard C. McKinnis, Chicago, IL, July 25, 2019.

3. RITUALS OF FREEDOM

1. After this service, I asked Priest Meshach what he meant by "on trial." Insofar as the term finds resonance in other Black Church traditions, especially in relation to the "trial sermon" or initial sermon by a new minister, I was curious how it was employed in this community. In the Black Church, being "on trial" was a way for members to know that they have been truly called into the ministry. Signs of "being called" might include how the community responded with excitement or "talk back" during the sermon, with phrases such as "go 'head," "speak truth," or "preach, preacher!" In the Black Coptic Church, the term has similar meaning. The Church teaches that, prior to receiving one's spiritual name, the recipient undergoes a trial experience in which they will be "tested" by "the spirit" to make certain the person is worthy of the name. This might take the form of a difficult situation that requires faith to endure, possibly the loss of something (e.g., a job). At the time of these struggles, the believer is unaware they are on trial, but they express great jubilation when the moment arrives for them to receive their spiritual name, as they believe that they have "made it through," and the spiritual name is their reward for their endurance.
2. Field notes, Coptic Nation Temple, Chicago, IL.
3. Queen Huldah, "Identity in the Black Coptic Church," interview by Leonard C. McKinnis, Chicago, IL, June 22, 2016.
4. It is worth noting that the terms "chosen people" and "holy people" in the Black Coptic Church are not employed anti-Semitically or in a way to undermine Jews. Quite the contrary. When I asked what these terms meant, Queen Maryann Martin, an elder in the community, replied that every group of people has the option to identify themselves as the chosen people of God. She said it was necessary, given the condition of Blacks in America, to affirm that they were chosen and holy as a way to rebuke diminishing assertions of Black life. Her caveat was that, to be the people of God authentically, it was necessary for the group to exhibit the love of God. In this sense, there is an inclusivity and exclusivity in the phrase that seeks to capture a God who is God of all (field notes).
5. Empress Selah, "The History of the Black Coptic Church," interview by Leonard C. McKinnis, Chicago, IL, June 22, 2009.
6. Priest Stephen, "The History of the Black Coptic Church," interview by Leonard C. McKinnis, Chicago, IL, June 22, 2009.
7. Weisenfeld, 96.
8. Priest Gehazi, "Identity in the Black Coptic Church," interview by Leonard C. McKinnis, Chicago, IL, June 8, 2018.
9. Weisenfeld, 96.
10. Queen Michel, "Identity in the Black Coptic Church," interview by Leonard C. McKinnis, Chicago, IL, June 8, 2018.
11. Queen Huldah, "Identity in the Black Coptic Church," interview by Leonard C. McKinnis, Chicago, IL, June 8, 2018.
12. Ibid.

13. Priest Eli, "Identity in the Black Coptic Church," interview by Leonard C. McKinnis, Chicago, IL, June 8, 2018.
14. Candace Queen Rachel, "Ritual in the Black Coptic Church," interview by Leonard C. McKinnis, Chicago, IL, June 15, 2018.
15. Empress Hatshepsut, "Ritual in the Black Coptic Church," interview by Leonard C. McKinnis, Chicago, IL, June 15, 2018 (her emphasis).
16. Prophet Cicero Patterson, "Black I Am That Am God," Coptic Nation Temple church archives, Chicago, 1956.
17. Priest Eli, "Identity in the Black Coptic Church," interview by Leonard C. McKinnis, Chicago, IL, June 8, 2018.
18. Weisenfeld, 99.
19. Priest Meshach, "Ritual in the Black Coptic Church," interview by Leonard C. McKinnis, Chicago, IL, June 15, 2018.
20. Queen Huldah, "Ritual in the Black Coptic Church," interview by Leonard C. McKinnis, Chicago, IL, June 15, 2018.
21. Priest Meshach, "Identity in the Black Coptic Church," interview by Leonard C. McKinnis, Chicago, IL, June 8, 2018.
22. Queen Bethel, "Ritual in the Black Coptic Church," interview by Leonard C. McKinnis, Chicago, IL, June 15, 2018.
23. Stephen Greenblatt, *Renaissance Self-Fashioning: From More to Shakespeare* (Chicago: University of Chicago Press, 2005).
24. Lincoln and Mamiya, 8.
25. Curtis, 109.
26. Ibid.
27. Curtis, 110.
28. Curtis, 116–117.
29. Ibid.
30. Ibid., 117.
31. Weisenfeld, 122.
32. Empress Selah, "History in the Black Coptic Church," interview by Leonard C. McKinnis, Chicago, IL, July 6, 2016.
33. Field notes.
34. Priest Meshach, "Identity in the Black Coptic Church," interview by Leonard C. McKinnis, Chicago, IL, July 14, 2016.
35. Queen Huldah, "Women in the Black Coptic Church," interview by Leonard C. McKinnis, Chicago, IL, August 4, 2018.
36. Ibid.
37. Ibid.
38. Candace Queen Rachel, "Women in the Black Coptic Church," interview by Leonard C. McKinnis, Chicago, IL, August 4, 2018.
39. Queen Huldah, "Identity in the Black Coptic Church," interview by Leonard C. McKinnis, Chicago, IL, July 14, 2016.

40. Queen Bethel, "Identity in the Black Coptic Church," interview by Leonard C. McKinnis, Chicago, IL, July 14, 2016.
41. Queen "Sarah" is a pseudonym, as this interlocutor is masked in the project.
42. Field notes.
43. Field notes.
44. Field notes.
45. Field notes.
46. Field notes.
47. Field notes.
48. Field notes.
49. Queen Magdalene, "Ritual in the Black Coptic Church," interview by Leonard C. McKinnis, Chicago, IL, July 15, 2018 (speaker's emphasis).
50. Prophet Jacob, "Ritual in the Black Coptic Church," interview by Leonard C. McKinnis, Chicago, IL, July 15, 2018.
51. Prophet David, "Passover Service," New Heaven Coptic Temple church archives, 2 hours 15 minutes, July 27, 1986.
52. Priest Meshach, "Ritual in the Black Coptic Church," interview by Leonard C. McKinnis, Chicago, IL, July 15, 2018.
53. James Cone, *God of the Oppressed* (Maryknoll, NY: Orbis Books, 1975), 27.
54. Ibid.
55. Cain Hope Felder, ed., *Stony the Road We Trod: African American Biblical Interpretation* (Minneapolis: Fortress Press, 1991), 25.
56. Felder, 34.
57. Cone, *God of the Oppressed*, 28.
58. Dorman, 23.
59. Eddie Glaude, *Exodus! Religion, Race, and Nation in Early Nineteenth-Century Black America* (Chicago: University of Chicago Press, 2000), 6.
60. Black Coptic Church, "Statement of Faith," Coptic Nation Temple, www.copticnationtemple.net.
61. Prophet Hosea, "Doctrine in the Black Coptic Church," interview by Leonard C. McKinnis, Chicago, IL, November 2008.
62. Priest Meshach, "Doctrine in the Black Coptic Church," interview by Leonard C. McKinnis, Chicago, IL, November 2008.
63. Queen Huldah, "Doctrine in the Black Coptic Church," interview by Leonard C. McKinnis, Chicago, IL, November 2008.
64. Field notes.
65. Empress Selah, "Doctrine in the Black Coptic Church," interview by Leonard C. McKinnis, Chicago, IL, November 2008.
66. Queen Huldah, "Doctrine in the Black Coptic Church," interview by Leonard C. McKinnis, Chicago, IL, November 2008.
67. Queen Maryann, "Theology in the Black Coptic Church," interview by Leonard C. McKinnis, Chicago, IL, September 2008.

68. Queen Michal, "Doctrine in the Black Coptic Church," interview by Leonard C. McKinnis, Chicago, IL, November 2008.
69. Prophet Hiram, "Rituals in the Black Coptic Church," interview by Leonard C. McKinnis, Chicago, IL, November 2018.
70. Priest Eli, "Rituals in the Black Coptic Church," interview by Leonard C. McKinnis, Chicago, IL, July 2018.
71. Acts 2:1–4 records the coming of the Holy Spirit.
72. Prophet Jacob, "Ritual in the Black Coptic Church," interview by Leonard C. McKinnis, Chicago, IL, July 15, 2018.
73. Frederick Douglass, "What to the Slave is the Fourth of July?" Teaching American History, www.teachingamericanhistory.org.
74. Queen Huldah, "Ritual in the Black Coptic Church," interview by Leonard C. McKinnis, Chicago, IL, July 15, 2018.
75. Field notes.
76. Candace Queen Rachel, "Ritual in the Black Coptic Church," interview by Leonard C. McKinnis, Chicago, IL, July 15, 2018.
77. Priest Meshach, "Ritual in the Black Coptic Church," interview by Leonard C. McKinnis, Chicago, IL, July 15, 2018.

4. "SOMEHOW, SOMEWAY"

1. Empress Hatshepsut, "Gender in the Black Coptic Church," interview by Leonard C. McKinnis, Chicago, IL, June 7, 2018.
2. Candace Queen Rachel, "Gender in the Black Coptic Church," interview by Leonard C. McKinnis, Chicago, IL, June 7, 2018.
3. Leeja Carter and Amerigo Rossi, "Embodying Strength: The Origins, Representations, and Socialization of the Strong Black Woman Ideal and Its Effect on Black Women's Mental Health," in Wendi S. Williams, *WE Matter: Intersectional Anti-Racist Feminist Interventions with Black Girls and Women* (New York: Taylor and Francis, 2022), 289.
4. Ibid., 290.
5. Lincoln and Mamiya, 275.
6. Jacquelyn Grant, "Black Theology and the Black Woman" in Cornel West and Eddie Glaude, eds., *African American Religious Thought: An Anthology* (Louisville: Westminster John Knox Press, 2003), 837.
7. Queen Huldah, "Gender in the Black Coptic Church," interview by Leonard C. McKinnis, Chicago, IL, June 7, 2018.
8. Candace Queen Rachel, "Gender in the Black Coptic Church," interview by Leonard C. McKinnis, Chicago, IL, June 7, 2018.
9. Empress Hatshepsut, "Gender in the Black Coptic Church," interview by Leonard C. McKinnis, Chicago, IL, June 7, 2018.
10. Priest Eli, "Women in the Black Coptic Church," interview by Leonard C. McKinnis, Chicago, IL, February 2, 2009.

11. Jacquelyn Grant, "Black Theology and the Black Woman," in Cornel West and Eddie Glaude, eds., *African American Religious Thought: An Anthology* (Louisville: Westminster John Knox Press, 2003), 837.
12. Cheryl Townsend Gilkes, *It if Wasn't for the Women: Black Women's Experience and Womanist Culture in Church and Community* (Maryknoll, NY: Orbis Books, 2003), 64.
13. Letitia Woods, as quoted in Cheryl Townsend Gilkes, *It if Wasn't for the Women: Black Women's Experience and Womanist Culture in Church and Community* (Maryknoll, NY: Orbis Books, 2003), 64.
14. Townsend Gilkes, 65.
15. Ibid., 93.
16. Ibid., 63.
17. Ibid., 66.
18. Ibid.
19. Ibid., 68.
20. Ibid.
21. Ibid., 69.
22. Lucille Cornelius, *The Pioneer History of the Church of God in Christ* (Memphis, TN: COGIC Publishing House, 1973).
23. Queen Maryann, "Women in the Black Coptic Church," interview by Leonard C. McKinnis, Chicago, IL, February 2, 2009.
24. Priest Meshach, "Women in the Black Coptic Church," interview by Leonard C. McKinnis, Chicago, IL, February 2, 2009.
25. Priest Eli, "Women in the Black Coptic Church," interview by Leonard C. McKinnis, Chicago, IL, February 2, 2009.
26. Candace Queen Rachel, "Gender in the Black Coptic Church," interview by Leonard C. McKinnis, Chicago, IL, June 7, 2018.
27. Queen Shiphrah, "Gender in the Black Coptic Church," interview by Leonard C. McKinnis, Chicago, IL, June 7, 2018.
28. Empress Hatshepsut, "Gender in the Black Coptic Church," interview by Leonard C. McKinnis, Chicago, IL, June 7, 2018.
29. Queen Huldah, "Gender in the Black Coptic Church," interview by Leonard C. McKinnis, Chicago, IL, June 7, 2018.
30. Ibid.
31. Candace Queen Rachel, "Gender in the Black Coptic Church," interview by Leonard C. McKinnis, Chicago, IL, June 7, 2018.
32. Ibid.
33. Candace Queen Rachel, "Women in the Black Coptic Church," interview by Leonard C. McKinnis, Chicago, IL, February 2, 2009.
34. Queen Rebekah, "History of the Black Coptic Church," interview by Leonard C. McKinnis, October 2005 (video).
35. Ibid.
36. Ibid.

37. Ibid.
38. Ibid.
39. Candace Queen Rachel, "Women in the Black Coptic Church," interview by Leonard C. McKinnis, Chicago, IL, February 2, 2009.
40. Queen Rebekah, "History of the Black Coptic Church," interview by Leonard C. McKinnis, October 2005 (video).
41. Candace Queen Rachel, "Women in the Black Coptic Church," interview by Leonard C. McKinnis, Chicago, IL, February 2, 2009.
42. Queen Rebekah, "History of the Black Coptic Church," interview by Leonard C. McKinnis, October 2005 (video).
43. Candace Queen Rachel, "Women in the Black Coptic Church," interview by Leonard C. McKinnis, Chicago, IL, February 2, 2009.
44. Prophet Hiram, "Women in the Black Coptic Church," interview by Leonard C. McKinnis, Chicago, IL, February 2, 2009.
45. Priest Meshach, "Women in the Black Coptic Church," interview by Leonard C. McKinnis, Chicago, IL, February 2, 2009.
46. Queen Maryann, "Women in the Black Coptic Church," interview by Leonard C. McKinnis, Chicago, IL, June 15, 2009.
47. Queen Shiphrah, "Gender in the Black Coptic Church," interview by Leonard C. McKinnis, Chicago, IL, June 7, 2018.
48. Candace Queen Rachel, "Gender in the Black Coptic Church," interview by Leonard C. McKinnis, Chicago, IL, June 7, 2018.
49. Priest Meshach, "Women in the Black Coptic Church," interview by Leonard C. McKinnis, Chicago, IL, June 7, 2018.
50. Priest Meshach, "Women in the Black Coptic Church," interview by Leonard C. McKinnis, Chicago, IL, February 2, 2009.
51. Ibid.
52. Queen Huldah, "Women in the Black Coptic Church," interview by Leonard C. McKinnis, Chicago, IL, February 2, 2009.
53. Empress Selah, "Women in the Black Coptic Church," interview by Leonard C. McKinnis, Chicago, IL, February 2, 2009.
54. Priest Meshach, "Women in the Black Coptic Church," interview by Leonard C. McKinnis, Chicago, IL, February 2, 2009.
55. Ibid.
56. Queen Huldah, "Women in the Black Coptic Church," interview by Leonard C. McKinnis, Chicago, IL, June 15, 2009.
57. Queen Maryann, "Women in the Black Coptic Church," interview by Leonard C. McKinnis, Chicago, IL, June 15, 2009.
58. Queen Michal, "Women in the Black Coptic Church," interview by Leonard C. McKinnis, Chicago, IL, June 15, 2009.
59. Candace Queen Rachel, "Women in the Black Coptic Church," interview by Leonard C. McKinnis, Chicago, IL, June 15, 2009.

60. Candace Queen Rachel, "Gender in the Black Coptic Church," interview by Leonard C. McKinnis, Chicago, IL, June 7, 2018.
61. Empress Hatshepsut, "Gender in the Black Coptic Church," interview by Leonard C. McKinnis, Chicago, IL, June 7, 2018.
62. Queen Mary Magdalene, "Gender in the Black Coptic Church," interview by Leonard C. McKinnis, Chicago, IL, June 7, 2018.
63. Keri Day, *Unfinished Business: Black Women, the Black Church, and the Struggle to Thrive in America* (Maryknoll, NY: Orbis Books, 2012), 26.
64. Candace Queen Rachel Gardiner, "Women in the Black Coptic Church," interview by Leonard C. McKinnis, Chicago, IL, June 15, 2009.
65. Tamura Lomax, *Jezebel Unhinged: Loosing the Black Female Body in Religion and Culture* (Durham, NC: Duke University Press, 2018), ix.
66. Jacquelyn Grant, "Womanist Theology: Black Women's Experience as a Source for Doing Theology, with special attention to Christology," in James H. Cone and Gayraud S. Wilmore, *Black Theology: a documentary history, volume two: 1980–1992* (Maryknoll, NY: Orbis Books, 1993), 278.
67. Monica Coleman, *Making a Way out of No Way: A Womanist Theology* (Minneapolis: Fortress Press, 2008), 6.
68. Linda E. Thomas, "Womanist Theology, Epistemology, and a New Anthropological Paradigm," *Cross Currents* 48 (1998–99): 489.
69. Ibid., 209.
70. Ibid., 211.
71. Ibid. 211.
72. Kelly Brown Douglas, "Womanist Theology: What is its Relationship to Black Theology?" in James H. Cone and Gayraud Wilmore, *Black Theology: a documentary history, volume two: 1980–1992* (Maryknoll, NY: Orbis Books, 1993), 291.
73. Ibid.
74. James Cone, "Black Ecumenism and the Liberation Struggle," speech delivered at Yale University, February 16–17, 1978.
75. Ula Yvette Taylor, *The Promise of Patriarchy* (Chapel Hill: The University of North Carolina Press, 2017), 3.
76. Taylor, 5.
77. Empress Hatshepsut, "Gender in the Black Coptic Church," interview by Leonard C. McKinnis, Chicago, IL, June 7, 2018.
78. Delores Williams, *Sisters in the Wilderness: The Challenge of Womanist God-Talk* (Maryknoll, NY: Orbis Books, 1993), ix.
79. Coleman, 33.

5. DIVINE (PRIMORDIAL) BLACKNESS

1. Fred Moten, "Black Mysticism," *South Atlantic Quarterly* (2013): 738–739.
2. Amira Baraka, *Home: Social Essays* (New York: Akashic Books, 2009).
3. Field notes, Coptic Nation Temple, Chicago, IL, February 2017.

4. Here, Priest Meshach makes a reference to the Hebrew Bible, I Kings 8:10–12:10 "And when the priests came out of the holy place, a cloud filled the house of the Lord, 11 so that the priests could not stand to minister because of the cloud; for the glory of the Lord filled the house of the Lord. 12 Then Solomon said, 'The Lord has said that he would dwell in thick darkness.'" (NRSV).
5. Priest Meshach, "On Blackness and History," interview by Leonard C. McKinnis, Chicago, IL, July 10, 2019.
6. Student Handbook, Black Coptic Church, Coptic Nation Temple, Chicago, IL, 2008 (revised).
7. Priest Eli, "Theology of the Black Coptic Church," interview by Leonard C. McKinnis, Chicago, IL, June 15, 2017.
8. Empress Selah, "Christology of the Black Coptic Church," interview by Leonard C. McKinnis, Chicago, IL, January 20, 2009.
9. Ibid.
10. Alex Poinsett, "The Quest for the Black Christ: Radical clerics reject 'honky Christ' created by American culture-religion," *Ebony Magazine* (March 1969): 171.
11. James H. Cone, *A Black Theology of Liberation*, 2nd ed. (Maryknoll, NY: Orbis Books, 1986), 218.
12. West, 47.
13. Prophet Peter Banks, *Here Comes the Shadow of the Sun* (Chicago: True Temple of Solomon Black Coptic Church, 1972).
14. Queen Huldah, "Theology of the Black Coptic Church," interview by Leonard C. McKinnis, Chicago, IL, January 12, 2009.
15. Prophet Louis Cicero Patterson, *Black I Am That I Am God* (Chicago: Coptic Nation Temple archives, 1958).
16. Frantz Fanon, *Black Skin, White Masks*, revised edition (New York: Grove Press, 2008), 89–90.
17. Priest Meshach, "On Blackness and History," interview by Leonard C. McKinnis, Chicago, IL, July 2018.
18. Ibid.
19. Moten, "Blackness as Nothingness (Mysticism in the Flesh)," *The South Atlantic Quarterly* 112, no. 4 (Fall 2013).
20. Calvin Warren, "Black Mysticism: Fred Moten's Phenomenology of (Black) Spirit," *Zeitschrift für Anglistik und Amerikanistik* 65, no. 2 (2017): 226.
21. Fanon, 90.
22. Priest Gehazi, "Identity in the Black Coptic Church," interview by Leonard C. McKinnis, Chicago, IL, June 2017.
23. Prophet Hiram, "Identity in the Black Coptic Church," interview by Leonard C. McKinnis, Chicago, IL, June 2017.
24. Queen Maryann, "Black Coptic Church," interview by Leonard C. McKinnis, Chicago, IL, July 6, 2008.

25. Christina Sharpe, *In the Wake: On Blackness and Being* (Durham, NC: Duke University Press, 2016), 15.
26. Sharpe, 165.
27. Hartman, 6.
28. Sharpe, 22.
29. Warren, 5.
30. Ibid.
31. Warren, 7.
32. Warren, 30.
33. Warren, 2.
34. For Calvin Warren, the term "free black" presents an ontological and metaphysical problem, precisely because the "free black" cannot exist in an anti-Black world, or a world that requires the "free black" to exist as nothing or as a tool available for the production and maintenance of a world of terror. Argues Warren, "The term free black is a misnomer for describing a historical condition . . . of blackness, since the ontological relation is severed. [. . .] The struggles and challenges that free blacks experienced in antebellum society were really ontological problems. The free black presents or forces confrontation with the Negro Question. It is through the free black that the Negro Question emerges with ferocity. Can black 'things' become free?" (Warren, 16). For Warren, the tension that exists between "free" and "Black" intersects at the level impossibility; that is, in a world in which blacks navigate ontological terror, freedom is not within the realm of potentiality.
35. Warren, 16.
36. Warren, 37.
37. Warren, 2.
38. Priest Stephen, "Identity in the Black Coptic Church," interview by Leonard C. McKinnis, Chicago, IL, June 2017.
39. Priest Stephen, "Ritual in the Black Coptic Church," interview by Leonard C. McKinnis, Chicago, IL, June 2018.
40. Mother Queen Rebekah, "History of the Black Coptic Church," interview by Leonard C. McKinnis, Chicago, IL, June 2004.
41. Priest Meshach, "Identity in the Black Coptic Church," interview by Leonard C. McKinnis, Chicago, IL, June 2017.
42. Frank Wilderson, *Afropessimism* (New York: Liveright Publishing, 2020), 217.
43. Moten, "Blackness and Nothingness," 739.
44. Queen Huldah, "Identity in the Black Coptic Church," interview by Leonard C. McKinnis, Chicago, IL, June 2017.
45. Prophet Judah, "Identity in the Black Coptic Church," interview by Leonard C. McKinnis, Chicago, IL, June 2017.
46. Priest Meshach, "Identity in the Black Coptic Church," interview by Leonard C. McKinnis, Chicago, IL, June 2017.
47. Priest Meshach, "Identity in the Black Coptic Church," interview by Leonard C. McKinnis, Chicago, IL, June 2017.

48. Queen Huldah, "Identity in the Black Coptic Church," interview by Leonard C. McKinnis, Chicago, IL, June 2017.
49. Priest Stephen, "Theology in the Black Coptic Church," interview by Leonard C. McKinnis, Chicago, IL, June 9, 2017.
50. Queen Huldah, "On Blackness and History," interview by Leonard C. McKinnis, Chicago, IL, January 6, 2018.
51. Prophet Hiram, "Religious Practices in the Black Coptic Church," interview by Leonard C. McKinnis, Chicago, IL, June 7, 2017.
52. Queen Huldah, "On Blackness and History," interview by Leonard C. McKinnis, Chicago, IL, July 6, 2018.
53. Queen Magdalene, "On Blackness and History," interview by Leonard C. McKinnis, Chicago, IL, July 6, 2018.
54. Prophet Judah, "On Blackness and History," interview by Leonard C. McKinnis, Chicago, IL, July 6, 2018.
55. Mother Queen Rebekah, "History of the Black Coptic Church," interview by Leonard C. McKinnis, Chicago, IL, August 15, 2008.
56. Vincent Lloyd, *Religion of the Field Negro: On Black Secularism and Black Theology* (New York: Fordham University Press, 2018), 136.
57. Prophet Louis Cicero Patterson, *Black I Am That I Am God* (Chicago: New Covenant Coptic Temple archives, 1958).
58. Ibid.
59. Ibid.

BIBLIOGRAPHY

Anderson, Robert. *From Slavery to Affluence: Memories of Robert Anderson, Ex Slave.* Hemingford, NE: publisher unknown, 1927.

Anderson, Victor. *Beyond Ontological Blackness: An Essay on African American Religious and Cultural Criticism.* New York: The Continuum Publishing Company, 1995.

Andrews, Dale P. *Practical Theology for Black Churches: Bridging Black Theology and African American Religion.* Louisville: Westminster Knox Press, 2002.

Assmann, Jan. *Moses the Egyptian.* Cambridge, Harvard University Press, 1997.

Baer, Hans. *The Black Spiritual Movement: A Religious Response to Racism*, 2nd ed. Knoxville: University of Tennessee Press, 2011.

Baer, Hans A. and Merrill Singer. *African American Religion: Varieties of Protest and Accommodation.* Knoxville: University of Tennessee Press, 1992.

Banks, Peter. *Black I Am That I Am God.* Chicago: True Temple of Solomon Archives, 1977.

Barth, Karl. *Church Dogmatics, Vol. 1, part 1: The Doctrine of the Word of God.* Translated by G. T. Thomson. New York: Charles Scribner's Sons, 1936.

———. *Church Dogmatics, Vol. 1, part 2: The Doctrine of the Word of God.* Edited by G. W. Bromiley and T. F. Torrance. Translated by G. T. Thomson. New York: Charles Scribner's Sons, 1936.

Beaman, Jean. *Citizen Outsider: Children of North African Immigrants in France.* Berkeley: University of California Press, 2017.

Best, Wallace. *Passionately Human, No Less Divine: Religion and Culture in Black Chicago, 1915–1952.* Princeton: Princeton University Press, 2008.

Bethune-Baker, J. F., Introduction to *The Early History of Christian Doctrine to the Time of the Council of Chalcedon.* Reprint, London: Methune & Co. Ltd., 1954.

Boff, Leonardo. *Jesus Christ Liberator: A Critical Christology for our Time.* Maryknoll, NY: Orbis Books, 1978.

Boff, Leonardo and Clodovis Boff. *Introducing Liberation Theology.* Maryknoll, NY: Orbis Books, 1998.

Breasted, James H. *The Dawn of Conscience.* New York: Charles Scribner's Sons, 1933.

———. *Development of Religion and Thought in Ancient Egypt.* New York: Harper and Row, 1959.

Budge, E. A. Wallis. *Egyptian Ideas of the Afterlife.* Garden City, NY: Dover Publications, 1995.

———. *Osiris and the Egyptian Resurrection*, 2 vols. Garden City, NY: Dover Publications, 1973.

Bultmann, Rudolph. *History and Eschatology*. Edinburgh: The University Press, 1957.
Cannon, Katie G. *Black Womanist Ethics*. Atlanta: Scholars Press, 1988.
———. *Katie's Canon: Womanism and the Soul of the Black Community*. New York: The Continuum Publishing Company, 1995.
Chapman, Mark L. *Christianity on Trial: African-American Religious Thought Before and After Black Power*. Maryknoll, NY: Orbis Books, 1996.
Chavis, Benjamin F. "Liberation Theology and the Black Church." *CRJ Reporter* (Summer 1980): 36–40.
Chireau, Yvonne. *Black Magic: Religion and the African American Conjuring Tradition*. Berkeley: University of California Press, 2006.
Cleage, Albert J. *The Black Messiah*. New York: Sheed and Ward, 1969.
———. *Black Christian Nationalism: New Directions for the Black Church*. New York: William Morrow and Company, 1972.
Coleman, Monica. *Making a Way out of No Way: A Womanist Theology*. Minneapolis: Fortress Press, 2008.
Coleman, Will. *Tribal Talk: Black Theology, Hermeneutics, and African/American Ways of 'Telling the Story.'* University Park, PA: Pennsylvania State University Press, 2000.
Cone, Cecil. *The Identity Crisis in Black Theology*. Nashville: AMEC Press, 1975.
Cone, James H. *A Black Theology of Liberation*. Philadelphia: J. B. Lippincott Co., 1970.
———. *A Black Theology of Liberation*, 2nd ed. Maryknoll, NY: Orbis Books, 1986.
———. *The Spirituals and the Blues*. New York: Seabury Press, 1972.
———. *God of the Oppressed*. New York: Seabury Press, 1975.
———. *My Soul Looks Back*. Nashville: Abingdon Press, 1982.
———. *For My People*. Maryknoll, NY: Orbis Books, 1984.
———. *Speaking the Truth*. Grand Rapids, MI: Eerdmans Publishing Co., 1986.
———. *Martin & Malcolm & America: A Dream or a Nightmare*. Maryknoll, NY: Orbis Books, 1991.
———. *Risks of Faith: The Emergence of Black Theology of Liberation, 1968–1998*. Boston: Beacon Press, 1999.
Crawley, Ashton. *Blackpentecostal Breath: The Aesthetics of Possibility*. New York: Fordham University Press, 2016.
Cummings, George C. L. *A Common Journey: Black Theology and Latin American Liberation Theology*. Maryknoll, NY: Orbis Books, 1991.
Curtis Edward. *Black Muslim Religion in the Nation of Islam, 1960–1975*. New edition, Chapel Hill: The University of North Carolina Press, 2006.
Curtis, Edward E., IV and Danielle Brune Sigler, eds. *The New Black Gods: Arthur Huff Fauset and the Study of African American Religion*. Bloomington: Indiana University Press, 2009.
David, Rosalie. *The Ancient Egyptians: Religious Beliefs and Practices*. London: Routledge and Kegan Paul, 1982.
Day, Keri. *Unfinished Business: Black Women, the Black Church, and the Struggle to Thrive in America*. Maryknoll, NY: Orbis Books, 2012.

DeFrantz, Thomas F. and Anita Gonzalez, eds. *Black Performance Theory*. Durham, NC: Duke University Press, 2014.
Dorman, Jacob. *Chosen People: The Rise of American Black Israelite Religions*. Oxford: Oxford University Press, 2013.
Douglas, Kelly Brown. *The Black Christ*. Maryknoll, NY: Orbis Books, 1994.
———. *Sexuality and the Black Church: A Womanist Perspective*. Maryknoll, NY: Orbis Books, 1999.
Douglass, Frederick. *Narrative of the Life of Frederick Douglass, An American Slave*. Boston: Anti-Slavery Society, 1845. Scanned 1999. Documenting the American South, University of North Carolina at Chapel Hill, www.docsouth.unc.edu.
Dubois, W. E. B. *The Souls of Black Folk*. Classic edition, New York: Putnam Books, 1989.
Dunbar, P. L. *The Complete Poems of Paul Laurence Dunbar*. New York: Dodd, Mead, and Company, 1913.
Earl, Riggins R., Jr. *Dark Symbols, Obscure Signs: God, Self, and Community in the Slave Mind*. Maryknoll, NY: Orbis Books, 1993.
Erskine, Noel. *Plantation Church: How African American Religion was Born in Caribbean Slavery*. Oxford: Oxford University Press, 2014.
Evans, James H., Jr. *Black Theology: A Critical Assessment and Annotated Bibliography*. Westport, CT: Greenwood Press, 1987.
———. *We Have Been Believers: An African American Systematic Theology*. Minneapolis: Fortress Press, 1992.
Fauset, Arthur Huff. *Black Gods of the Metropolis: Negro Religious Cults of the Urban North*. Philadelphia: University of Pennsylvania Press, 1944.
Felder, Cain H., ed. *Stony the Road We Trod: African American Biblical Interpretation*. Minneapolis: Fortress Press, 1991.
Frazier, E. Franklin. *The Negro Church in America*. New York: Schocken Books, 1963.
Gabriel, Richard A. *Jesus the Egyptian: The Origins of Christianity and the Psychology of Christ*. New York: iUniverse, Inc, 2005.
Gardiner, James J. and J. Deotis Roberts. *Quest for a Black Theology*. Philadelphia: Pilgrim Press, 1970.
Gardiner, Meshach, Priest. *Coptic, After the Order of Melchizedek*. Chicago: Coptic Nation Temple Archives, 2006.
Genovese, Eugene D. *Roll, Jordan, Roll: The World the Slaves Made*. New York: Random House, 1972.
Gilkes, Cheryl Townsend. *If It Wasn't for the Women: Black Women's Experience and Womanist Culture in Church and Community*. Maryknoll, NY: Orbis Books, 2003.
Glaude, Eddie. *Exodus! Religion, Race, and Nation in Early Nineteenth-Century Black America*. Chicago: The University of Chicago Press, 2000.
———. *In a Shade of Blue: Pragmatism and the Politics of Black America*. Chicago: University of Chicago Press, 2007.
Goatey, David Emmanuel. *Were You There? Godforsakenness in Slave Religion*. Maryknoll, NY: Orbis Books, 1996.

———. *Black Religion, Black Theology: The Collected Essays of J. Deotis Roberts.* Harrisburg, Virginia: Trinity Press International, 2003.

Goba, Bonganjalo. "Toward a 'Black' Ecclesiology." *Missionalia* 9 (Aug. 1981): 47–59.

Grant, Jacquelyn. *White Women's Christ and Black Women's Jesus: Feminist Christology and Womanist Response.* Atlanta: Scholars Press, 1989.

Greenblatt, Stephen. *Renaissance Self-Fashioning: From More to Shakespeare.* Chicago: The University of Chicago Press, 1980.

Grimal, Nicolas. *A History of Ancient Egypt.* London: Basil Blackwell, 1992.

Gutierrez, Gustavo. *A Theology of Liberation: History, Politics, and Salvation.* Maryknoll, NY: Orbis Books, 1990.

Haight, Roger. *Jesus: Symbol of God.* Maryknoll, NY: Orbis Books, 2005.

Hardy, Edward Rochie. *Christology of the Later Fathers,* The Library of Christian Classics, Vol. III. Philadelphia: The Westminster Press, 1954.

Harris, James H. *Pastoral Theology: A Black Church Perspective.* Minneapolis: Fortress Press, 1991.

Hartman, Saidiya. *Lose Your Mother: A Journey Along the Atlantic Slave Route.* New York: Farrar, Straus, and Giroux, 2008.

———. *Wayward Lives, Beautiful Experiments: Intimate Histories of Riotous Black Girls, Troublesome Women, and Queer Radicals.* New York: W.W. Norton & Company, 2019.

Harvey, Stefano and Fred Moten. *The Undercommons: Fugitive Planning and Black Study.* Brooklyn, NY: Autonomedia, 2013.

Hayes, Diana L. *And Still We Rise: An Introduction to Black Liberation Theology.* New York and Mahwah, NJ: Paulist Press, 1996.

Higginbotham, Evelyn Brooks. *Righteous Discontent: The Women's Movement in the Black Baptist Church, 1880–1920.* Cambridge, MA: Harvard University Press, 1993.

Hood, Robert E. *Must God Remain Greek? Afro Cultures and God-Talk.* Minneapolis: Fortress Press, 1990.

———. *Begrimed and Black: Christian Traditions on Black and Blackness.* Minneapolis: Fortress Press, 1994.

Hopkins, Dwight N. *Black Theology U.S.A. and South Africa: Politics, Culture, and Liberation.* Maryknoll, NY: Orbis Books, 1989.

———. *Shoes That Fit Our Feet: Sources for a Constructive Black Theology.* Maryknoll, NY: Orbis Books, 1993.

———. ed., *Black Faith and Public Talk: Critical Essays on James H. Cone's Black Theology and Black Power.* Maryknoll, NY: Orbis Books, 1999.

———. *Introducing Black Theology of Liberation.* Maryknoll, NY: Orbis Books, 1999.

———. *Down, Up, and Over: Slave Religion and Black Theology.* Minneapolis: Fortress Press, 2000.

Hopkins, Dwight N., and George C. L. Cummings, eds. *Cut Loose Your Stammering Tongue: Black Theology in the Slave Narratives.* Maryknoll, NY: Orbis Books, 1991.

Hussein, Nadia. *Black Land: Imperial Ethiopianism and African America.* Princeton, NJ: Princeton University Press, 2019.

Isasi-Diaz, Ada Maria. *En la Lucha: A Hispanic Women's Liberation Theology*. Minneapolis: Fortress Press, 1993.
Jackson, Zakiyyah Imam. *Becoming Human: Matter and Meaning in Antiblack World*. New York: New York University Press, 2020.
Johnson, Sylvester. *African American Religions, 1500–2000: Colonialism, Democracy, and Freedom*. Cambridge: Cambridge University Press, 2015.
Jones, Major J. *Black Awareness: A Theology of Hope*. Nashville: Abingdon Press, 1971.
———. *Christian Ethics for Black Theology*. Nashville: Abingdon Press, 1974.
———. *The Color of God: The Concept of God in Afro-American Thought*. Macon, GA: Mercer University Press, 1987.
Kelley, Robin D. G. *Freedom Dreams: The Black Radical Imagination*. Boston: Beacon Books, 2003.
Khabeer, Su'ad Abdul. *Muslim Cool: Race, Religion, and Hip Hop in the United States*. New York: New York University Press, 2016.
King, Karen. *The Gospel of Mary of Magdala: Jesus and The First Woman Apostle*. Santa Rosa, CA: Polebridge Press, 2003.
Jackson, John: *Thin Description: Ethnography and the African Hebrew Israelites of Jerusalem*. Cambridge: Harvard University Press, 2013.
Jones, William R. *Is God a White Racist?* 1973. Reprint, Boston: Beacon Press, 1998.
Kelley, J. N. D. *Early Christian Doctrines*. New York: Harper & Row Publishers, 1958.
Landes, Ruth. "Negro Jews in Harlem," *Jewish Journal of Sociology* 9 (1967): 175–191.
Leitch, James W. *Theology of Hope: On the Ground and the Implications of a Christian Eschatology*, trans. Jurgen Moltmann. New York: Harper & Row Publishers, 1965.
Lincoln, C. Eric and Lawrence Mamyia. *The Black Church in the African American Experience*. Durham, NC: Duke University Press, 1990.
Lloyd, Vincent. *Religion of the Field Negro: On Black Secularism and Black Theology*. New York: Fordham University Press, 2018.
Lomax, Tamura. *Jezebel Unhinged: Loosing the Black Female Body in Religion and Culture*. Durham, NC: Duke University Press, 2018.
Long, Charles H. *Significations: Signs, Symbols, and Images in the Interpretation of Religion*. Philadelphia: Fortress Press, 1986.
McCormick, Stacie Selmon. *Staging Black Fugitivity*. Columbus: The Ohio State University Press, 2019.
McGuire, Meredith B. *Lived Religion: Faith and Practice in Everyday Life*. Oxford: Oxford University Press, 2008.
McKay, Claude. *Amiable with Big Teeth*. New York: Penguin Books, 2017.
Miller, Monica. *Slaves to Fashion: Black Dynamism and the Styling of Black Diasporic Identity*. Durham, NC: Duke University Press, 2009.
Mitchell, Henry H. *Black Belief*. New York: Harper & Row, 1975.
Mitchell, Henry H. and Nicholas C. Cooper-Lewter. *Soul Theology: The Heart of American Black Culture*. San Francisco: Harper and Row, 1986.
Morenz, Siegfried. *Egyptian Religion*. Ithaca, NY: Cornell University Press, 1992.

Morgan, Huldah, Queen. *Priests and Kings: Unveil the Name*. Chicago: Coptic Temple of Kemet Archives, 2007.

Moten, Fred. *In the Break: The Aesthetics of the Black Radical Tradition*. Minneapolis: University of Minnesota Press, 2003.

———. *Stolen Life: Consent not to be a Single Being*. Durham, NC: Duke University Press, 2018.

Moyd, Olin P. *Redemption in Black Theology*. Valley Forge, PA: Judson Press, 1979.

Mullen, Bill V. *Afro Orientalism*. Minneapolis: University of Minnesota Press, 2004.

Needleman, Jacob. *The New Religions*. Reprint, New York: TarcherPerigee, 2009.

Niebuhr, H. Richard. *Christ and Culture*. San Francisco: Harper & Row Publishers, 1951.

Ormiston, Gayle L. and Alan D. Schrift. *Transforming the Hermeneutic Context: From Nietzsche to Nancy*. Albany: State University of New York Press, 1990.

Paris, Peter J. *The Social Teachings of the Black Churches*. Philadelphia: Fortress Press, 1985.

———. *The Spirituality of African Peoples: The Search for a Common Moral Discourse*. Minneapolis: Fortress Press, 1995.

Patterson, Cicero, Prophet. *Here Comes the Shadow of the Sun*. Chicago: True Temple of Solomon Archives, 1959.

Patterson, Orlando. *Slavery and Social Death: A Comparative Study*. Cambridge: Harvard University Press, 1982.

Pinn, Anthony. *Varieties of African American Religious Experience*. Minnesota: Fortress Press, 1998.

Pinn, Anthony B. *Why Lord? Suffering and Evil in Black Theology*. New York: The Continuum Publishing Company, 1995.

———. *Varieties of African American Religious Experience*. Minneapolis: Fortress Press, 1998.

———. *Terror and Triumph: The Nature of Black Religion*. Minneapolis: Fortress Press, 2003.

Pinn, Anthony B. and Dwight H. Hopkins. *Loving the Body: Black Religious Studies and the Erotic*. New York: Palgrave Macmillan, 2004.

Plastras, James. *The God of Exodus: The Theology of the Exodus Narratives*. Milwaukee: Bruce Publishing, 1966.

Price, Charles Reavis. "Expressions of Ethiopianism in Jamaica." *New West Indian Guide* 77, no. 1/2 (2003): 31–64.

Price, Richard and Michael Gaddis, trans. *The Acts of the Council of Chalcedon*. Cambridge, England: Liverpool University Press, 2005.

Raboteau, Albert. *Slave Religion: The "Invisible Institution" in the Antebellum South*. Oxford: Oxford University Press, 2004 (Updated edition).

Raboteau, Emily. *Searching for Zion: The Quest for Home in the African Diaspora*. New York: Grove Press, 2013.

Rahner, Karl. *Foundations of Christian Faith: An Introduction to the Idea of Christianity*. Translated by William V. Dych. New York: The Seabury Press, 1978.

Reid, Ira D. *In a minor key; Negro youth in story and fact.* Westport, CT: Greenwood Press, 1940.

Richardson, Cyril C. ed. *Early Christian Fathers.* New York: Touchstone, 1996.

Roberts, J. Deotis. *Liberation and Reconciliation: A Black Theology.* Philadelphia: Westminster Press, 1971.

———. *A Black Political Theology.* Philadelphia: Westminster Press, 1974.

———. *The Roots of a Black Future: Family and Church.* Philadelphia: Westminster Press, 1980.

———. *Black Theology Today.* Lewiston, NY: Edwin Mellen Press, 1983.

———. *Black Theology in Dialogue.* Philadelphia: Westminster Press, 1987.

———. *The Prophethood of Black Believers.* Louisville: Westminster/John Knox Press, 1994.

Rukuni, Rugare and Erna Oliver. "Africanism, Apocalypticism, Jihad and Jesuitism: Prelude to Ethiopianism." *Hervormde Teologiese Studies* 75, no. 3 (2019): 127–137.

SchÜssler-Fiorenza, Elisabeth. *In Memory of Her: Feminist Theological Reconstruction of Christian Origins.* New York: The Crossroad Publishing Company, 1983.

———. *Rhetoric and Ethic: The Politics of Biblical Studies.* Minneapolis: Fortress Press, 1999.

———. *Wisdom Ways: Introducing Feminist Biblical Interpretation.* Maryknoll, NY: Orbis Books, 2001.

Sernett, Milton. *Bound for the Promised Land: African American Religion and the Great Migration.* Durham, NC: Duke University Press, 1997.

———. *African American Religious History: A Documentary Witness*, 2nd ed. Durham, NC: Duke University Press, 2000.

Sharpe, Christina. *In the Wake: On Blackness and Being.* Durham: Duke University Press, 2016.

Shepherd, Simon. *The Cambridge Introduction to Performance Theory.* Cambridge: Cambridge University Press, 2016.

Simmons, Martha. *Preaching with Sacred Fire: An Anthology of African American Sermons, 1750 to the Present.* New York: Norton, 2010.

Singleton, Harry H., III. *Black Theology and Ideology: Ideological Dimensions in the Theology of James H. Cone.* Collegeville, MN: Liturgical Press, 2002.

Smith, Theophus H. *Conjuring Culture: Biblical Formations of Black America.* New York: Oxford University Press, 1994.

Sobrino, Jon. *Christ the Liberator: A View From the Victims.* Maryknoll, NY: Orbis Books, 2001.

Sorett, Josef. *Spirit in the Dark: A Religious History of Racial Aesthetics.* Oxford: Oxford University Press, 2016.

Taylor, Ula Yvette. *The Promise of Patriarchy: Women and the Nation of Islam.* Chapel Hill: The University of North Carolina Press, 2017.

Thistlewaite, Susan Brooks and Mary Potter Engel, eds. *Lift Every Voice: Constructing Christian Theologies from the Underside.* New York: Harper and Row, 1989.

Thomas, Linda E., ed. *Living Stones in the Household of God: The Legacy and Future of Black Theology*. Minneapolis: Fortress Press, 2004.

Thurman, Howard. *Jesus and the Disinherited*. Nashville: Abingdon-Cokesbury Press, 1949.

———. *Deep River and The Negro Spiritual Speaks of Life and Death*. Richmond, IN: Friends United Press, 1983.

Tillich, Paul. *Systematic Theology, Vol. 1, Reason and Revelation, Being and God*. Chicago: University of Chicago Press, 1951.

Townes, Emilie M. *Womanist Hope/Womanist Justice*. Atlanta: Scholars Press, 1993.

———. *In a Blaze of Glory: Womanist Spirituality as Social Witness*. Nashville: Abingdon Press, 1995.

Trimie, Darryl M. *Voices of the Silenced: The Responsible Self in a Marginalized Community*. Cleveland, OH: The Pilgrim Press, 1993.

Turman, Eboni Marshall. *Toward a Womanist Ethic of Incarnation: Black Bodies and the Council of Chalcedon*. London: Palgrave Macmillan, 2013.

Walker, Theodore, Jr. *Empower the People: Social Ethics for the African American Church*. Maryknoll, NY: Orbis Books, 1991.

Ware, Frederick L. *Methodologies of Black Theology*. Cleveland: Pilgrim Press, 2002.

Warren, Calvin. *Ontological Terror: Blackness, Nihilism, and Emancipation*. Durham, NC: Duke University Press, 2018.

Washington, Joseph R. *Black Religion*. Boston: Beacon Press, 1964.

Webster, John, ed. *The Cambridge Companion to Karl Barth*. Oxford: Cambridge University Press, 2000.

Weisenfeld, Judith. *New World A-Coming: Black Religion and Racial Identity during the Great Migration*. New York: New York University Press, 2018.

West, Cornel. *Prophesy Deliverance! An Afro-American Revolutionary Christianity*. Philadelphia: Westminster Press, 1982.

———. *Race Matters*. Boston: Beacon Press, 1993.

———. *Keeping Faith*. New York: Routledge, 1993.

West, Cornel and Eddie S. Glaude, eds. *African American Religious Thought: An Anthology*. Louisville, KY: Westminster John Knox Press, 2003.

Wheatley, Phillis. "To the University of Cambridge, in New England," in Henry Louis Gates and Nellie McKay, eds., *The Norton Anthology of African American Literature*. New York: W. W. Norton & Co., 1997.

Wilderson, Frank. *Afropessimism*. New York: Liveright Publishing, 2021.

Williams, Delores S. *Sisters in the Wilderness: The Challenge of Womanist God-Talk*. Maryknoll, NY: Orbis Books, 1993.

Williams, Wendi S. *WE Matter! Intersectional Anti-Racist Feminist Interventions with Black Girls and Women*. New York: Taylor and Francis, 2022.

Wilmore, Gayraud S. *Last Things First*. Philadelphia: Westminster Press, 1982.

———. *Black Religion and Black Radicalism*. 2nd rev. ed. Maryknoll, NY: Orbis Books, 1983.

Wilmore, Gayraud S. and James H. Cone, ed. *Black Theology: A Documentary History*: 1966–1979. Maryknoll, NY: Orbis Books, 1979.

———. *Black Theology: a documentary history, volume two: 1980–1992*. Maryknoll, NY: Orbis Books, 1993.

Young, Henry J. *Hope in Process: A Theology of Social Pluralism*. Minneapolis: Fortress Press, 1990.

Young, Josiah Ulysses, III. *Black and African Theologies: Siblings or Distant Cousins?* Maryknoll, NY: Orbis Books, 1986.

———. *A Pan-African Theology: Providence and the Legacies of the Ancestors*. Trenton, NJ: Africa World Press, 1992.

Young, William. "The Shape of Reflexivity: A Pragmatist Analysis of Religious Ethnography." *American Journal of Theology and Philosophy* 35, no.1 (January 2014): 42–64.

INDEX

Page numbers in *italics* indicate Figures.

Africa: African diaspora, 19–20; African societies, 33; Afro-pessimism from, 20, 33; Battle of Adwa in, 12; to Black people, 55; Caribbean world and, 11; in collective identity, 57; culture of, 155; Great Migration and, 10–11; ideology of, 19–20; pan-Africanism, 54–55; slavery and, 98; West Africa, 1, 14

African Americans: Black identity and, 11–12; Black religions and, 185–87; Christianity to, 9; community of, 146; culture of, 47, 130–31; faith healing to, 5–6; racial identity for, 5; religion of, 51–54, 74; in religious studies, 33; stereotypes of, 11; West on, 197n26; white supremacy to, 15

African Methodist Episcopal (AME), 41, 142

Afrofuturism, 206n58

Afro-Pessimism, 20, 33, 90, 152, 170–72, 170–73, 175–76, 182

Alpha and Omega Spiritualist Church, Inc., 42

AME. *See* African Methodist Episcopal

The Ancient Order of Ethiopian Princes, 58–59

Anderson, Victor, 32–33, 176, 196n20

Andrew (prophet), 96

anthropology, 12, 14, 27, 43, 178–79

anti-Blackness: to Black autonomy, 20; Black identity and, 17; Blackness and, 30–31, 87; in culture, 171–72; narratives of, 158–59; personhood and, 180–81; in religion, 10, 83; violence and, 2; Warren on, 215n34

assimilation, 33

Atlanta, Georgia, 25, 35–36, 41–44, *42*

Baer, Hans, 43, 75, 77–78

Baldwin, James, 69–70

Banks, Peter. *See* Peter

baptisms, 119–24, *122*, *123*, 129, 185–86

Baraka, Amira, 152

Barth, Karl, 80

Battle of Adwa, 12

Bethel (queen), 86

Black autonomy, 12, 20, 53, 68, 185–86

Black bodies: Black identity and, 32–33; Black life and, 53, 166; Blackness and, 154–55, 183–84; Huldah (queen) on, 177; NOI and, 103–4; philosophy of, 178–79; Sunday's Best and, 101–2; in theology, 47

Black Catholics, 28

Black Christians, 56–57, 116

Black Church: baptisms in, 119–23, 119–24, *122*, *123*; Black Monarchy in, 148; Black women in, 134; community in, 100–103, *102*; culture of, 144–45; Gilkes on, 131–32; leadership in, 186–87; Meshach (priest) on, 207n1; mothers in, 131; music in, 112–13; rituals in, 130; in sociology, 127–28

The Black Church in the African American Experience (Lincoln and Mamiya), 127–28
Black Coptic Empress, 72
Black Coptic Empress and Students, 72
Black dignity: in BCC, 67; Blackness and, 118–19; Douglass on, 120–21; liberation and, 84–87; performative imagination and, 20–21, 73–74; rituals for, 100–106, *101–2, 104, 106–7, 108–10, 111, 112–14*; search for, 60; in slavery, 69
Black existence, 67, 170–71
Black folk. *See* Black people
Black futurism, 18
Black God, 73
Black Gods of the Metropolis (Fauset), 23
Black I Am That I Am God (Cicero), 183
Black identity: African Americans and, 11–12; African diaspora and, 19–20; anti-Blackness and, 17; Baldwin on, 69–70; at BCC, 73–78; Black bodies and, 32–33; Black life and, 84–85; with Black Monarchy, 68–70, *71–72, 72–73*; Blackness and, 15, 60; Black people and, 185–87; for Black women, 10, 134–40; in Chicago, 50–51; Christ and, 4; to Cicero (prophet), 97–98; colonialism in, 54; community and, 87–88; in earthquakes, 8, 10; with Ethiopia, 105–6, 183; Ethiopianism in, 10–14; Exodus and, 117–18; in Great Migration, 9, 51; Hatshepsut (empress) on, 126–27; to Hosea, 1–2; imagined communities and, 14–15; in NOI, 65; in North America, 1–2, 4, 8; ontology of, 175–76; with Passover, 115; performative imagination and, 17–23; philosophy of, 46–48; Queens of Ethiopia and, 73; race in, 128; racism in, 113–14; reconstructing, 63, 65; religion and, 38; Selah (empress) on, 93; slavery in, 69; social salvation and, 78; Stephen (priest) on, 93–94; as subaltern, 74–75

Black Jewish groups, 74–75
Black Jews, 5, 14–17, 117–18. *See also* Hebrew tradition
Black joy, 172
Black liberation, 142, 185–86
Black men, 7, 32, 128–29, 140–44
Black Messiah, 82, 119
Black metropolis, 49–51
Black Monarchy: in Black Church, 148; Black identity with, 68–70, *71–72, 72–73*; in COGIC, 132; at Coptic Nation Temple, 86–88, *88–89,* 90; faith, 128–29; Royal Empress and, *106*; as social salvation, 81–86; in TTS, 137
Black Muslim Religion in the Nation of Islam (Curtis), 78
Blackness: anti-Blackness and, 30–31, 87; Blackbeing and, 172, 180–82; Black bodies and, 154–55, 183–84; Black dignity and, 118–19; Black identity and, 15, 60; Black people and, 17–18, 163–64; in Christianity, 122; in colonialism, 12; in Ethiopianism, 56; Fugitive, 160; hope in, 180–82; Huldah (queen) on, 57; identity and, 29–30, 54; intersectionality and, 31; Meshach (priest) on, 32, 59, 154–55, 159, 162, 173–74; at MST, 65; in North America, 5; ontological blackness, 196n20; ontological dilemma of, 164–68; ontological terror and, 168–73; as *otherwise*, 68–70, *71–72, 72–73,* 100, 123–24, 176–77, 182; in performative imagination, 52–53; philosophy of, 32–33, 60; primordial, 159–64; as protest, 90–91; religion and, 2–3, 85; sexism and, 186; in TTS, 9; to white people, 92–93. *See also* divine Blackness
Black non-being, 162–63
Blackontology, 162–64, 173–81, 183–84
Black people: Africa to, 55; Afro-pessimism and, 170–72; Black identity and, 185–87; Blackness and, 17–18, 163–64; in Chicago, 51–52, 149–50;

Christianity to, 77–78; conversion by, 28; culture of, 11–12; to DuBois, 46–47; God and, 207n4; Grant on, 145; in Great Migration, 5–6; in Harlem Renaissance, 50–51; history of, 13, 30–31, 112; identity of, 175–76; imagined communities of, 116–17, 152; Meshach (priest) on, 87–88, 90; Mother Queen Rebekah on, 181; as nobodies, 100–101; in North America, 3, 20–21, 52, 57–58, 74, 79–81, 119; oppression of, 204n38; Peter (prophet) on, 159–60; police and, 44–45; racism against, 58–59; in religious cults, 16–17; scholarship from, 22; in slavery, 4, 8, 48; Sunday's Best for, 100–102, *101*–2; theology of, 25–26; TTS to, 84; UNIA for, 57; in United States, 44–46, 120–21, 165; violence against, 171; West on, 158–59; in white culture, 45–46; white people and, 126–27. *See also specific topics*
Black performance theory, 17–23
Black Performance Theory (DeFrantz and Gonzalez), 17
Black pride, 10, 57
Black religions: African Americans and, 185–87; in Atlanta, 41–44, *42*; Black theology, 144–48; in Chicago, 5–10, 6, 24, 28–29, 138–39; Cicero and, 73–74; in community, 7–8, 22; Curtis, 8–9; in diaspora, 23; divine Blackness and, 8, 152–56, *153*, 180–84; earthquakes and, 4–5; Ethiopia in, 53–54; Fauset on, 51–52; fugitives and, 199n4; in Great Migration, 4, 15–17, 49, 94–95; Hatshepsut (empress) on, 133–34; Head Queens in, 132–33; history of, 50–51; imagined communities in, 14–15; in journalism, 44–46; in North America, 30, 80, 195n4; oppression of, 48; phallic spirituality in, 140–44; politics of, 140–44, 149–51; rituals in, 94–99; scholarship on, 33–34; spiritual hierarchies in, 125; theology of, 76–77; white supremacy and, 20–21; wives in, 137–38
Black Spiritualists, 39–40, 42, 55–56
Black theology, 144, 145–46, 196n20
Black women: in BCC, 13–14, 90–91; in Black Church, 134; Black identity for, 10, 134–40; community for, 6–7; in Coptic National Temple, 125–34, *126*; diversity of, 147; gender to, 149–51; God and, 3–4, 150–51; in hats, *102*; Hatshepsut (empress) on, 150; in NOI, *104*; superwoman narrative and, 127–28, 143, 150; testimonies of, 109–10, 112; in TTS, 108; womanhood for, 32; womanist tradition, 144–49
Brown, Letitia Woods, 130–31
Brown, Michael, 171–72
Butts, Calvin O., 76–77

California, 46
Camus, Albert, 21
Candace Queen Rachel (Gardiner): on BCC, 65–67, 85, 96–97; on Cicero (prophet), 141–42; on faith, 139; Meshach (priest) and, 153–54; on Mother Rebekah, 136; on Queens of Ethiopia, 130–31; Shiphrah (queen) and, 133; on United States, 126–27; on women, 133
Candace Queens of Meroe, 135
Capernaum (queen), 95, 134–40
Caribbean, 11
Chandler, Nahum, 32–33, 152
Chicago, Illinois: Atlanta and, 25, 35–36; baptisms in, 121–22, *122*, *123*; Black identity in, 50–51; Black people in, 51–52, 149–50; Black religions in, 5–10, 6, 24, 28–29, 138–39; Chicago Commission on Race Relations, 58–59; culture of, 15; Ethiopianism in, 35; history of, 16; "Negro boys on Easter Morning, Southside Chicago," *101*, 102; Queens of Ethiopia in, *126*; religiosity in, 30; after World War I, 49. *See also* Coptic Nation Temple

Christ, Jesus: Black identity and, 4; Christology, 155, 161; God and, 147; Meshach (priest) on, 178; in New Testament, 45–46, 82; race of, 1, 29, 41, 60, 122, 147, 157–58, 174–75; representations of, 39; in TTS, 29

Christianity: to African Americans, 9; BCC and, 34; Black Christians, 56–57, 116; Blackness in, 122; to Black people, 77–78; Christian gospel, 21; Exodus in, 55, 114–20, 136, 152; faith in, 21; God in, 76, 179–80; in Haiti, 4; hegemony of, 49–50; Islam and, 54; MST and, 5; in New Testament, 45–46, 82; in North America, 144; philosophy of, 51; Protestantism, 2–3, 5, 23, 49; race and, 22; theology of, 199n54; to white people, 48

church mothers, 131–32

Church of God in Christ (COGIC), 28, 132

Cicero (prophet), 202n57; Black identity to, 97–98; Black religions and, 73–74; Candace queen Rachel on, 141–42; community of, 5–6, 19; death of, 134–35; on degrees, 77; Eli (priest) on, 132; Ethiopianism to, 13, 54–60, 185; Garvey and, 85–86; heroic identity to, 87; history of, 29–30, 35–36, 36–37, 38–41, 40, 46–48; Huldah (queen) on, 135, 160, 177; identity to, 78; imagined communities to, 105; Jacob (prophet) on, 7; legacy of, 44–46, 84, 94, 119–20, 143–44; Maryann (queen) on, 165–66; Meshach (priest) on, 8, 59–60; mission of, 1; Mother Queen Rebekah and, 135–36; ontology and, 174; Peter (prophet) and, 165, 186; philosophy of, 183; religion to, 49–54, 148; on salvation narratives, 83; Selah (empress) on, 85–86; spiritual teachings of, 14–15, 25, 41–44, 42, 72; theology of, 156–57; white supremacy to, 73, 75, 164–65

citizenship, 57–58

classism, 135

Clayton, Horace, 50–51

clothing. See Black dignity

COGIC. See Church of God in Christ

Coleman, Monica, 146, 150–51

collective identity, 57

colonialism, 2, 12, 14, 27–28, 47, 54, 167

community: of African Americans, 146; in Atlanta, 40; BCC Statement of the Faith in, 56; in Black Church, 100–103, 102; Black identity and, 87–88; Black religions in, 7–8, 22; for Black women, 6–7; of Cicero (prophet), 5–6, 19; Coptic communities, 52; divine Blackness in, 13–14; hierarchies in, 26; identity in, 18–19; imagined communities, 14–15, 86–88, 88–89, 90, 105, 116–17, 152; Meshach (priest) on, 92, 161; of Protestantism, 49; religion in, 23–24, 23–25; spiritual teachings in, 36, 38; women in, 31. See also imagined communities

Cone, James, 76, 92, 115, 148, 158

contradiction, in BCC, 80–81

conversion, 7–9, 28, 45, 73–74, 140–41

Coptic Nation Temple: Black Monarchy at, 86–88, 88–89, 90; Black women in, 125–29, 125–34, 126; Ethiopia and, 61, 61–63, 84–85; King Solomon's Temple and, 61–63, 64, 65; performing otherwise at, 63, 64, 65–68; rituals at, 90–92

Coptic Temple of Kemet, 10

culture: of Africa, 155; of African Americans, 47, 130–31; anti-Blackness in, 171–72; assimilation into, 33; of Black Church, 144–45; Black existence in, 67, 170–71; Black life and, 50–51, 146; of Black metropolis, 49–51; of Black people, 11–12; of California, 46; of Chicago, 15; citizenship and, 57–58; cultural norms, 100; of Egypt, 13; of Ethiopia, 75; of Harlem Renaissance,

50; military, *40*; of North America, 26, 31; Nurhussein on, 59; participation in, 67–68; power in, 28; race in, 126–27; religion and, 28; spiritual identity in, 29–30; of UHPTS, 41–44, *42*; of United States, 185–87; of UPHTS, 43–44; of white people, 45–46
Curtis, Edward, 8–9, 78

Daddy Grace, 16–17
Daniel, Gladys, 27
David (prophet), 114–15, 118
Day, Keri, 143
Day of Pentecost, 119–20, 129, 140–41, 143
Debra (Princess), 92, 98, 123–24
DeFrantz, Thomas, 17
degrees, 63, 77
Descartes, Réne, 166–67
diaspora, 23
diasporic spidering, 19–20
divine Blackness: Black life and, 168–69; Blackontology and, 173–80; Black religions and, 8, 152–56, *153*, 180–84; in community, 13–14; God and, 156–59; ontology and, 164–73; primordial Blackness and, 159–64
Dorman, Jacob, 14, 72–73, 117
double-consciousness, 46–47
Douglas, Kelly Brown, 147–48
Douglass, Frederick, 22, 120–21
Drake, Brenda, 3
Drake, Sinclair, 50–51
Du Bois, W. E. B., 46–47, 63, 166–67
Dunbar, Paul Laurence, 11
Durkheim, Émile, 27

earthquakes, 1–2, 4–5, 8, 10, 15–16, 18–19
Ebony Magazine, 157
Egypt, 5, 13–15, 30–31, 46–48, 54–55, 72–73
Elder Michaux (Solomon Lightfoot Michaux), 16–17
Eli (priest), 84–85, 90, *111*, 119–20, 130, 132
Ellison, Ralph, 57

eschatology, 59–60, 76, 82–83
Ethiopia: The Ancient Order of Ethiopian Princes, 58–59; to Black Christians, 56–57; Black identity with, 105–6, 183; in Black religions, 53–54; colonialism and, 14; Coptic Nation Temple and, *61*, 61–63, 84–85; culture of, 75; Egypt and, 30–31, 46–48, 54–55, 72–73; Ethiopian Hebrew, 105; flag of, 35, *36*, 54, 59–60, 119; history of, 10–13; homelessness and, 54–57; Huldah (queen) and, 52, 60; identity with, 58; rituals from, 155–56. *See also* Queens of Ethiopia
Ethiopianism: BCC and, 5; in Black identity, 10–14; Blackness in, 56; in Chicago, 35; to Cicero (prophet), 13, 54–60, 185; as fugitive, 57–60; gender and, 25; identity with, 54–57; ideology of, 54; in North America, 48
ethnographic studies, 23–28
Europe, 47
Exodus (book), 55, 114–20, 136, 152

faith: in BCC, 30–31, 139; BCC Statement of the Faith, 56; Black Monarchy, 128–29; in Christianity, 21; in God, 77; healing, 5–6, 43–45, 55, 57, 59, 61; of Mother Queen Rebekah, 45; performative imagination and, 26–27; in rituals, 142–43; in spiritual teachings, 23–24; theology and, 39–40
Fanon, Frantz, 161, 165, 171
Fard, Wallace D., 75
Father Divine's Peace Mission Movement, 4–5, 16–17, 97–98
Fauset, Arthur, 15–16, 22–23, 51–52
feminist theory, 145–46
Ford, Josiah, 75
Franklin, Maggie, 39–40
Frederick, Marla, 27
Freedom Dreams (Kelley), 54–55
fugitives, 57–60, 68, 160, 199n4

Gardiner, Rachel. *See* Candace Queen Rachel
Gardiner, Roderick. *See* Meshach
Garvey, Marcus Mosiah, 12–13, 56, 57, 85–86, 108, 143–44
Gehazi (priest), 57, 94–95, 165
gender: in BCC, 65–66; to Black women, 149–51; Ethiopianism and, 25; hierarchies, 63; oppression, 149; politics of, 125–29, *126*, 134–40, 144–49; Queens of Ethiopia and, 90–91; race and, 13–14, 31–32. *See also* Black men; Black women
George-Graves, Nadine, 19–20
Gilkes, Cheryl Townsend, 130–32, 134, 138
Glaude, Eddie, 48
God: Black, 73, 156–57, 174–75; Black autonomy and, 12, 53; Black God of the Metropolis, 23, 46; Black liberation and, 185–86; Black Messiah and, 119; Black people and, 207n4; in Black theology, 147–48; Black women and, 3–4, 150–51; Christ and, 147; in Christianity, 76, 179–80; divine Blackness and, 156–59; faith in, 77; in Hebrew Bible, 32; history of, 114–15; in hymns, 115–16; Meshach (priest) on, 7, 175; to Muhammad, 104; North America and, 5; ontology of, 161–62; Queens of Ethiopia and, 67–68; race and, 79, 161–62; slavery and, 30; theology of, 114; to white people, 77–78; women and, 140
Gonzalez, Anita, 17
Grant, Jacquelyn, 145
Great Migration: Africa and, 10–11; Black identity in, 9, 51; Black people in, 5–6; Black religions in, 4, 15–17, 49, 94–95; Father Divine's Peace Mission Movement in, 4–5, 16–17, 97–98; history of, 49–50; in journalism, 24; *otherwise* in, 63, 65; Protestantism and, 2–3; religion in, 23, 48; religiosity in, 33

Greenblatt, Stephen, 100
Gutierrez, Gustavo, 82, 204n38

Haile Selassie (emperor), 12, 105
Haiti, 1–2, 4
Harlem Renaissance, 50–51
Hartman, Saidiya V., 2, 168
Hatshepsut (empress), 36, 58–59, 96–97, 126–27, 133–34, 150
Head Queens, 132–33
Hebrew tradition: in BCC, 207n4; Black Jewish groups, 74–75; Black Jews, 5, 14–15, 14–17, 117–18; Ethiopian Hebrew, 105; Exodus in, 55, 114–20, 136, 152; Hebrew Bible, 32; to Meshach (priest), 214n4; in Old Testament, 56; Passover in, 114–24, 122–23; Protestantism and, 5; Royal Black Jews, 70
Here Comes the Shadow of the Sun (pamphlet), 159
heroic identity, 83–84, 87
hijabs, 103–4, *104*
Hiram (prophet), 135, 137, 165–66
holy garments, 61, 67, 103–6, *104*, 108–10, *111*, 112–14, 122–23. *See also specific topics*
homelessness, 18–19, 46–48, 54–57
Hosea (prophet), 1–2, 8
Huldah (queen): on BCC, 10, 70, 98, 106, *107*, 108–10, 112; on Black bodies, 177; on Blackness, 57; on Cicero (prophet), 135, 160, 177; on degrees, 63; Ethiopia and, 52, 60; on identity, 85–86, 93; Maryann (queen) and, 141; Mother Queen Rebekah and, 179–80; on white people, 69; on women, 129–30
Hurley, George (prophet), 55–56
hymns, 115–16

ideational attractiveness, 72–73
identity: Blackness and, 29–30, 54; of Black people, 175–76; to Cicero (prophet), 78; collective, 57;

in community, 18–19; in double-consciousness, 46–47; with Ethiopia, 58; with Ethiopianism, 54–57; formation, 150; heroic, 83–84, 87; history and, 46–48; holy garments and, *104*, 105–6, 108–9, 112–14; hope and, 90; Huldah (queen) on, 85–86, 93; imagination and, 55; to Jacob (prophet), 52; language and, 69–70; of Mother Queen Rebekah, 136–37; ontology and, 176–77; of Queens of Ethiopia, 86–87; race and, 25, 30; racial, 5, 56–57, 73; religion and, 35; religious, 31; salvation and, 78–81; self-positioning in, 28–29; spiritual, 15–16, 26, 29–30; with spiritual names, 94–99. *See also* Black identity
ideology, 11–13, 19–20, 46–48, 54
If It Wasn't for the Women (Gilkes), 130–31
Illinois Solidarity Party, 70
imagined communities, 14–15, 86–88, 88–89, 90, 105, 116–17, 152
intersectionality, 31, 65
Islam, 28, 54, 78, 103–4, *104*. *See also* Nation of Islam
Israel, 14, 30–31

Jackson, Jesse, 157
Jacob (prophet), 7, 52, 73–74, 114
Jamaica, 11, 39
Jesus Christ. *See* Christ
Jews. *See* Hebrew tradition
Jim Crow laws, 58
Johnson, Sylvester, 1
Jones, William, 79
journalism, 24, 43–46, 61–62, *64*
Judah (prophet), 75–76, 177, 181

Keller, R. C. (reverend), 61, *64*, 70
Kelley, Robin G., 54–55
Khabeer, Su'ad Abdul, 24
King, Martin Luther, Jr., 41, 85
King Solomon's Temple, 61–63, *64*, 65

language, 30, 69–70, 119, 165, 172, 204n38
Lee, Shaloma. *See* Hatshepsut
liberation, 78–82, 84–87, 142, 146–47, 149, 170–71, 185–86
Lincoln, C. Eric, 101, 127–28
Lockhart, Booker, 42
Lomax, Tamura, 144–45

Magdalene (queen), 46, 113–14, 142–43, 180–81
Malcolm X, 41
Mamiya, Lawrence H., 101, 127–28
Mariyah. *See* Debra
Martin, Maryann. *See* Maryann
Martin, Trayvon, 171
Maryann (queen), 38–39, 41, 52, 132, 141, 165–67, 207n4
Matthew, Arthur (Rabbi), 75
McBride, Renice, 171
Melchizedek. *See* Cicero
Meshach (priest), 214n4; on BCC, 132–33, 182–83; on Black Church, 207n1; on Black history, 13, 176; on Blackness, 32, 59, 154–55, 159, 162, 173–74; on Black people, 87–88, 90; Candace Queen Rachel and, 153–54; on Christ, 178; on Cicero (prophet), 8, 59–60; on community, 92, 161; on God, 7, 175; leadership of, 96, 98–99, 123–24, 152–53, *153*; Mother Queen Rebekah and, 175; on Passover, 115, 118; on Sunday's Best, 105–6; on women, 139–40
messianic typology, 45–46
Michal (queen), 141
Michaux, Lightfoot Solomon, 16–17
military culture, *40*
Miller, Pamela, 3–4
Mitchell, Claire, 27
modernity, 27–28, 47
Moltmann, Jürgen, 81–82
Moorish Science Temple of America (MST), 5, 38, 65, 94, 105, 173
Morgan, Huldah. *See* Huldah

Moses figures, 135–36, 135–37
Moten, Fred, 152, 163–64
Mother Queen Rebekah, 89; on Black history, 60; on Black people, 181; Capernaum (queen) and, 134–40; Cicero (prophet) and, 135–36; faith of, 45; Huldah (queen) and, 179–80; identity of, 136–37; legacy of, 119–20; Meshach (priest) and, 175; spiritual teachings of, 3–4
MST. *See* Moorish Science Temple of America
Muhammad, Elijah, 9, 38, 41, 75, 104, 108, 143–44. *See also* Nation of Islam
music, 112–13, 115–16, 121–22
Muslim Cool (Khabeer), 24

Narrative (Douglass), 22
narratives, of anti-Blackness, 158–59
National Committee of Black Churchmen, 157
Nation of Islam (NOI): BCC and, 77; Black bodies and, 103–4; Black identity in, 65; Black Jewish groups and, 74–75; Black women in, *104*; COGIC and, 28; conversion to, 8–9; MST and, 38, 94, 173; religion and, 183–84; scholarship on, 78; women in, 148–49
"Negro boys on Easter Morning, Southside Chicago," *101*, 102
The Negro in Chicago (Chicago Commission on Race Relations), 58–59
New Heaven Coptic Temple, 62
New Testament, 45–46, 82
New York City, 50–51
Noble Drew Ali, 38, 108
nobodiness, 85, 100–101
NOI. *See* Nation of Islam
North America: Black death in, 59–60; Black identity in, 1–2, 4, 8; Blackness in, 5; Black people in, 3, 20–21, 52, 57–58, 74, 79–81, 119; Black pride in, 57; Black religions in, 30, 80, 195n4; Christianity in, 144; culture of, 26, 31; Ethiopianism in, 48; God and, 5; history of, 148–49; rituals in, 33; slavery in, 22–23; writers in, 11. *See also specific regions*
Nurhussein, Nadia, 54, 59

"Ode to Ethiopia" (Dunbar), 11–12
Old Testament, 56
Ontological Terror (Warren), 168–72
ontology: Black, 162–64; of Black identity, 175–76; Blackontology, 162–64, 173–81, 183–84; Christology and, 155; of God, 161–62; ontological blackness, 196n20; ontological dilemma, 164–68; ontological terror, 168–73
oppression, 48, 149, 204n38. *See also specific topics*
ordination certificates, 42
Orthodox Coptic Church, 14
otherwise: BCC and, 164; Blackness as, 68–70, *71–72*, 72–73, 100, 123–24, 176–77, 182; in Great Migration, 63, 65; holy garments and, 108; hope for, 90; performing, 63, 64, 65–68, 95; philosophy of, 172; in religion, 173; rituals and, 93–94; salvation and, 98–99

Papas, Maria, 70
Passover, 114–24, *122–23*
patriarchy, 141–44. *See also* gender
Patterson, Claudia, 39
Patterson, Louis Cicero. *See* Cicero
Patterson, Orlando, 4
Patterson, Primus, 39
Pentecost practice, 31
performative imagination: Afro-Pessimism and, 172–73; in BCC, 31, 62–63, 76; Black dignity and, 20–21, 73–74; Black identity and, 17–23; Blackness in, 52–53; Black non-being and, 162–63; of devotees, 63; faith and, 26–27; heroic identity in, 83–84; with

Passover, 118–19; performing *otherwise*, 63, 64, 65–68, 95
personhood, 180–81
Peter (prophet), 71; for Black men, 7; on Black people, 159–60; Capernaum (queen) and, 95; Cicero (prophet) and, 165, 186; Judah (prophet) on, 181; leadership of, 6, 61, 70, 134–35, 137
phallic spirituality, 140–44
Poinsett, Alex, 157–58
police, 44–45
politics, 70; of Black religions, 140–44, 149–51; of gender, 125–29, 126, 134–40, 144–49
post-colonialism, 27–28
post-modernity, 27–28
Price, Charles Reavis, 12
primordial Blackness, 159–64
protest, 90–91
Protestantism, 2–3, 5, 23, 49

Queens of Ethiopia: Black Coptic Empress and Students, 88; Black identity and, 73; Candace queen Rachel on, 130–31; in Chicago, 126; God and, 67–68; identity of, 86–87; liberation and, 81–82; rituals with, 61–62, 65–66, 90–91
"The Quest for the Black Christ" (Poinsett), 157–58

Raboteau, Emily, 19, 21
race: in Black identity, 128; Chicago Commission on Race Relations, 58–59; of Christ, 1, 29, 41, 60, 122, 147, 157–58, 174–75; Christianity and, 22; in culture, 126–27; gender and, 13–14, 31–32; God and, 79, 161–62; humanity and, 158; identity and, 25, 30; philosophy of, 53; racial identity, 5, 56–57, 73; racial liberation, 149; racial redemption, 11; religion and, 49–51, 155–56; scholarship and, 33, 147–48; spiritual identity and, 15–16

racism, 58–59, 113–14, 128, 143–44, 182, 196n20
Ras Tafari (emperor), 13
Rastafarians, 11, 39
Rebekah. *See* Mother Queen Rebekah
Reid, Ira De Augustine, 16–17, 24
religion: of African Americans, 51–54, 74; anthropology of, 43; anti-Blackness in, 10, 83; in Atlanta, 40–41; Black identity and, 38; Blackness and, 2–3, 85; to Cicero (prophet), 49–54, 148; in community, 23–24, 23–25; culture and, 28; earthquakes and, 18; eschatology and, 59–60, 76, 82–83; gender in, 138; in Great Migration, 23, 48; history of, 24–25, 49–50; identity and, 35; ideology and, 11, 46–48; Israel and, 30–31; messianic typology in, 45–46; NOI and, 183–84; ordination certificates, 42; *otherwise* in, 173; philosophy of, 185–87; race and, 49–51, 155–56; religiosity, 30, 33; religious cults, 16–17; religious ethnography, 27; religious identity, 31; religious imagination, 52–53; slavery and, 21–22; spiritual teachings and, 42–43; symbolism in, 66–67; theology and, 69; United States, 15. *See also specific topics*
religio-racial, 22, 49, 94–95, 98, 105, 121–22, 173
religio-self-fashioning, 105, 164, 173, 177
religious studies, 1–2, 8–9, 33
rituals: in baptisms, 185–86; in Black Church, 130; for Black dignity, 100–106, 101–2, 104, 106–7, 108–10, 111, 112–14; in Black religions, 94–99; at Coptic Nation Temple, 90–92; from Ethiopia, 155–56; faith in, 142–43; of freedom, 92–93; fugitives and, 68; in North America, 33; *otherwise and*, 93–94; for Passover, 114–24, 122–23; with Queens of Ethiopia, 61–62, 65–67, 90–91; spiritual identity and, 26; theology and, 29, 156

Royal Black Jews, 70
Royal Black Monarchy. *See* Black Monarchy
royal titles. *See* spiritual names
Rubenstein, Mary Jane, 163
El-Rukns, 28

salvation, 78–81, 82–83, 98–99
Sarah (queen), 110
"School of Wisdom," 72
Searching for Zion (Raboteau), 19
Selah (empress), 74, 85–86, 93, 141, 157
self-positioning, in identity, 28–29
Sernett, Milton, 16, 49–50
sexism, 128, 186
Sharpe, Christina, 166
Shiphrah (queen), 86–87, 133, 138–39
Sisters in the Wilderness (Williams), 150–51
Slave Religion (Raboteau), 21
slavery: Africa and, 98; to African Americans, 54; Baer on, 77–78; Black dignity in, 69; in Black identity, 69; Black people in, 4, 8, 48; classifications in, 75; God and, 30; history of, 152–53; for humanity, 168; legacy of, 58; liberation from, 170–71; narratives from, 81; in North America, 22–23; Pentecost practice and, 31; religion and, 21–22; scholarship on, 2, 20–21
social earthquakes. *See* earthquakes
social salvation, 75–76, 78, 81–86, 185–86
sociology, 16–17, 101, 127–28
somebodiness, 85, 90–91
spiritual hierarchies, 125
spiritual identity, 15–16, 26, 29–30
spiritual names, 63, 77, 94–99, 122–23. *See also specific topics*
spiritual teachings: of Cicero (prophet), 14–15, 25, 41–44, 42, 72; in community, 36, 38; education for, 7; faith in, 23–24; of Garvey, 12–13, 56; holy garments in,

61, 67; men and, 33; of Mother Queen Rebekah, 3–4
Stephen (priest), 82, 93–94
Sunday's Best, 100–106, *101–2, 106*
Sun Ra, 35
superwoman narrative, 127–28, 143, 150
symbolism, in religion, 66–67

"Take Me to the Water to Be Baptized" (song), 121
Taylor, Ula Yvette, 148–49
theology: of AME, 41; anthropology and, 178–79; of BCC, 167; Black, 144–48, 196n20; Black bodies in, 47; of Black people, 25–26; of Black religions, 76–77; of Christianity, 199n54; of Cicero (prophet), 156–57; faith and, 39–40; of God, 114; of liberation, 78–82; religion and, 69; rituals and, 29, 156
A Theology of Liberation (Gutierrez), 82, 204n38
Thomas, Linda, 146
Tillich, Paul, 25–26, 67, 80
Townes, Emilie, 147
tradition. *See specific topics*
True Temple of Solomon (TTS): Black Coptic Empress at, 72; Black Monarchy in, 137; Blackness in, 9; to Black people, 84; Black pride at, 10; Black women in, 108; Christ in, 29; Coptic Temple of Kemet and, 10; history of, 6; politics of, 70
Turner, Henry McNeil, 41
Turner, Nat, 21

UHPTS. *See* Universal House of Prayer and Training School
UNIA. *See* Universal Negro Improvement Association
United States: Alpha and Omega Spiritualist Church, Inc., 42; Black people in, 44–46, 120–21, 165; Black Spiritualists

in, 39–40; Candace queen Rachel on, 126–27; census data, 202n57; culture of, 185–87; Europe and, 47; history, 21; Jim Crow laws in, 58; religion, 15; white supremacy in, 22, 58–59; in World War II, *40. See also specific regions*
Universal Hagar's Spiritual Church, 55–56
Universal House of Prayer and Training School (UHPTS), 41–44, *42*
Universal Negro Improvement Association (UNIA), 12–13, 57
Universal Prayer House and Training School (UPHTS), 56

violence, 2, 171–72
Vrdolyak, Edward R., 70

Walton, Veronia (prophet), 43
Warren, Calvin, 32–33, 167–72, 183, 215n34
Weisenfeld, Judith, 49, 56–57
West, Cornel, 158–59, 197n26
West Africa, 1, 14
Wheatley, Phillis, 11
white people: Blackness to, 92–93; Black people and, 126–27; Christianity to, 48; culture of, 45–46; God to, 77–78; Huldah (queen) on, 69; in Old Testament, 56; racism by, 196n20; white normativity, 179
white supremacy: to African Americans, 15; Black religions and, 20–21; to Cicero (prophet), 73, 75, 164–65; in Exodus, 117–18; history of, 54–55; in United States, 22, 58–59
Williams, Delores, 150–51
Willis, Steven (Priest Gehazi), 57, 94–95, 165
Wilmore, Gayraud, 20–21
Wilson, Darren, 171–72
women: in AME, 142; in BCC, 129–34; in community, 31; feminist theory, 145–46; God and, 140; Huldah (queen) on, 129–30; leadership by, 150–51; Meshach (priest) on, 139–40; in NOI, 148–49; sexism against, 128, 186; as teachers, 140–44; as wives, 137–38; womanhood, 32; womanist scholars, 33; womanist tradition, 144–49. *See also* Black women
World War I, 39, 49
World War II, *40*

Zion, 17–24

ABOUT THE AUTHOR

LEONARD CORNELL MCKINNIS II is Assistant Professor of Religion and Black Studies at the University of Illinois at Urbana-Champaign. His research sits at the intersection of Black religions, Black theology, new religious movements, and ethnographic approaches to the study of religion. His work has been supported by the Louisville Institute, the American Academy of Religion, and Mellon Funding. He is a Public Voices Fellow with the OpEd Project.

www.ingramcontent.com/pod-product-compliance
Lightning Source LLC
Chambersburg PA
CBHW020250030426
42336CB00010B/699